BTEC Tech Award

CHILD DEVELOPMENT

Student Book

Hayley Marshall-Gowen

Claire Sayce

Diane Walker-Cairns

Published by Pearson Education Limited, 80 Strand, London, WC2R 0RL.

www.pearsonschoolsandfecolleges.co.uk

Copies of official specifications for all Pearson qualifications may be found on the website: qualifications.pearson.com

Text © Pearson Education Limited 2019
Typeset by PDQ Digital Media Solutions
Original illustrations © Pearson Education Limited 2019
Cover illustration by Jo Goodberry, NB Illustration

First published 2019

22 21 20 19
10 9 8 7 6 5 4 3 2 1

British Library Cataloguing in Publication Data
A catalogue record for this book is available from the British Library

ISBN 978 1 292 23102 0

Acknowledgements
The publisher would like to thank the following for their kind permission to reproduce their photographs:

(Key: b-bottom; c-centre; l-left; r-right; t-top)

(Key: t-top; b-bottom; c-centre; l-left; r-right; m-middle)

Front cover: 123RF: Trendsetter Images

Component 1: 123RF: Mario Ondris 4, Khatawut Chaemchamras 13, Anna Bulashenko 15tr, 15tc, 15ml, 15tl, 15mr, Andrei Afanasiev 25tl, Jperagine 29, Zven0 35mr, Feverpitched 41, Zurijeta 53; **Alamy Stock Photo**: Chuck Franklin 25br, Steve Prezant/Image Source 25bl, Sanjeevi v25tr; **Getty Images**: Westend61 42; **Imagestate**: John Foxx Collection 37; **Pearson Education Ltd**: Lord and Leverett 6mr, Jules Selmes 6tr, 19, Roddy Paine 11; **Shutterstock**: 2xSamara.com 3, Zulufoto 6tl, Marlon Lopez MMG1 Design 6ml, Wavebreakmedia 6mr, 39, Kurhan 18, Zynatis 24, Alex Staroseltsev 27, Eleonora_os 35tr, Nikodash 38, Yuliya Evstratenko 44, ArtOfPhotos 46, Olga Enger 49, Monkey Business Images 51.

Component 2: 123RF: Oksun70 57, Szeyuen 104; **Pearson Education Ltd**: Jules Selmes 59, 61, 64ml, 67, 69, 70, 74, 86, 90, 93, 94, 102, Rob Judges 64b, Lord and Leverett 76ml, Carla Mestas 92, Roddy Paine 58; **Shutterstock**: Riopatuca 60, Emese 62, Karen H. Ilagan 72, Kelly MacDonald 75, Cristina Annibali 76bl, Yulya Shilova 84, Artem Efimov 89, Zurijeta 96, Chonrawit boonprakob 99, George Filyagin 98, Eric Broder Van Dyke 100; **SOZAIJITEN**: 82.

Component 3: 123RF: Alona Stepaniuk 139tc, Klavdiia Berezkina 139tr, Roman Stetsyk 168mr; **Agefoto Stock Photos**: SuperStock/Brand X Pictures 181; **Alamy Stock Photo**: Carolyn Jenkins 139ml, CBsigns 139mr, MediaWorldImages 153, Ingram Publishing 164, ZUMA Press, Inc. 175; **British Toy and Hobby Association**: Lion Mark, used with permission from British Toy and Hobby Association 139tl; **Digitalvision**: RobvanPetten135; **Pearson Education Ltd**: Jules Selmes 121, 128ml, 140, 150, 165, 166, 171, Studio 8 134, 151; **Getty Images**: Maria Desantis/EyeEm 128mr, Jasmin Merdan/Moment 172; **Shutterstock**: Jaren Jai Wicklund 111, Maria Uspenskaya 112, Jaimie Duplass 113, Thomas M Perkins 115, Melpomene 117, Wavebreakmedia 118, Firma V 122, Unguryanu 123, Stockyimages124, Ann in the uk 127, Steve Heap 128mc, Serhiy Kobyakov 131, GUNDAM_Ai 132, Oleg Mikhaylov 142, Vladvm 143, Champion studio 144, EdBockStock 147, Venus Angel 149, Stephen Denness 168ml, Lori Martin 168mc, Andrey_Kuzmin 170, Photka 176, Thomas M Perkins 179.

All other images © Pearson Education

The author and publisher would like to thank the following individuals and organisations for permission to reproduce the following materials:

p5: UK Department of Health & Social Care: GIRLSUK–WHO Neonatal and Infant Close Monitoring Growth Chart, 2009. Retrieved from www.rcpch.ac.uk/sites/default/files/Girls_neonatal_and_infant_close_monitoring_growth_chart.pdf; BOYSUK–WHO Neonatal and Infant Close Monitoring Growth Chart, 2009. Retrieved from www.rcpch.ac.uk/sites/default/files/Boys_neonatal_and_infant_close_monitoring_growth_chart.pdf; UK Department of Health & Social Care. Contains public sector information licensed under the Open Government Licence v3.0.

Contents

CONTENTS

About this book

This book is designed to support you when you are taking a BTEC Tech Award in Child Development.

About your BTEC Tech Award

Congratulations on choosing a BTEC Tech Award in Child Development. This exciting and challenging course will introduce you to the early years sector. The early years sector focuses on the learning, development and care of children from birth to 5 years. In the UK, there are approximately 2 million childcare places for children aged under 5 and many different types of early years settings, ranging from childminders and nannies, to nurseries, crèches and pre-schools. Knowledge of child development is also important in a variety of healthcare roles such as paediatricians, psychologists, occupational therapists, and speech and language therapists.

How you will be assessed

You will be assessed in two different ways. Components 1 and 2 are assessed through internal assessment. This means that your teacher will give you an assignment brief and indicate to you the deadline for completing it. The assignment will cover what you have been learning about and will be an opportunity to apply your knowledge and skills. You teacher will mark your assignment and award you with a grade. Your third assessment (for Component 3) will be an external assessment. This will be a task that is set and marked by Pearson. You will have a set time in which to complete this task. The task will be an opportunity to bring together what you have learnt in components 1 and 2.

About the authors

Hayley Marshall-Gowen worked in the early years sector before becoming a lecturer in further education. She went on to become Head of Childcare at a secondary school and has also been an examiner for childcare qualifications. She now works in regulation and inspection. Hayley has written several books and teaching resources, and enjoys seeing students develop into confident practitioners.

Claire Sayce started her career in childcare and education by studying a BTEC National Diploma in Nursery Nursing. She worked in the early years sector for a number of years and was Officer in Charge at a private day nursery before becoming a lecturer in Child Care and Education in a further education college. Claire went on to work in a number of roles such as Lead Trainer for Caring Services (covering Children's Play, Learning and Development/ Child Development, Health and Social Care and Applied Psychology). She has developed a range of training materials that have been used by teachers across the UK and still works in further education.

Diane Walker-Cairns has been working with young people for over 15 years. She began volunteering with young offenders, offering support and guidance with a view to getting them back into education to improve their outcomes. She qualified as a teacher 10 years ago and has since taught health and social care, child development, psychology and sociology. Diane currently works in an academy where she is Head of Health, Social and Child Studies for students aged 14–19 years. She is passionate about teaching and motivating students to follow their ideal career path. Many of her students go on to study child nursing, midwifery or teaching.

How to use this book

The book has been designed in a way that will help you to easily navigate through your course. Each component from the course is covered in a separate chapter that makes clear what you are learning and how this will contribute to your assessment. There are opportunities for you to test your understanding of key areas, as well as activities that will challenge and extend your knowledge and skills. You will get the most from this book if you use each feature as part of your study. The different features will also help you develop the skills that will be important in completing your assignments as well as preparing you for your external assessment.

Features of the book

This book is designed in spreads, which means that each pair of facing pages represents a topic of learning. Each spread is about 1 hour of lesson time. Your teacher may ask you to work through a spread during a lesson or in your own time. Each spread contains a number of features that will help you to check what you are learning and offer opportunities to practise new skills.

Getting started A short activity or discussion that will introduce you to what you will be covering in the lesson.

Activity These will help you learn about the topic. You may be asked to work in pairs, groups or on your own.

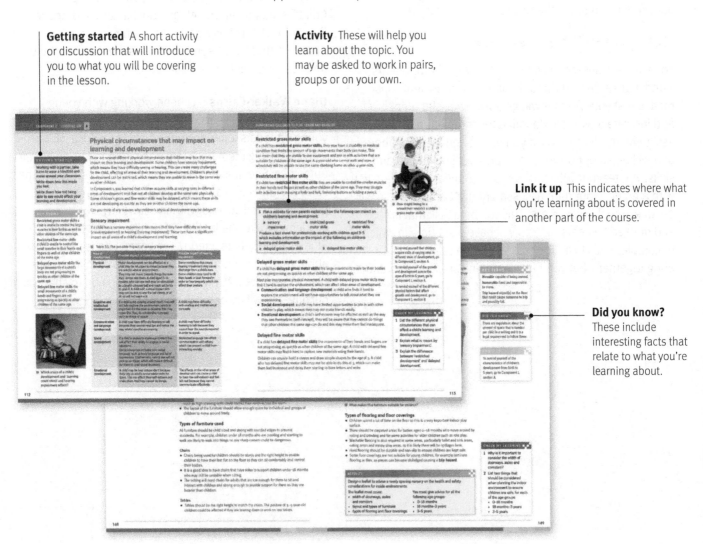

Link it up This indicates where what you're learning about is covered in another part of the course.

Did you know? These include interesting facts that relate to what you're learning about.

At the end of each learning aim there is a section that outlines how you will be assessed and provides opportunities for you to build skills for assessment.

Assessment Activity This is a practice assessment that reflects the style and approach of an assignment brief. In Component 3, tasks in the assessment activity features will be similar to those you should expect in your external assessment.

Tip A hint or tip that will help you with your assessment.

Checkpoint This feature is designed to allow you to assess your learning. The 'strengthen' question helps you to check your knowledge and understanding of what you have been studying, while the 'challenge' questions are an opportunity to extend your learning.

Take it further This provides suggestions for what you can do to further the work you've done in the practice assessment.

01 Children's Growth and Development

Introduction

Have you ever wondered why most children learn to walk before they learn to talk? In this component you will learn about the characteristics of children's development between birth and 5 years of age. You will start with learning the difference between growth and development and go on to find out about children's physical, cognitive and intellectual, communication and language, and social and emotional development.

You will also explore the factors that can influence a child's rate of growth and development. You will examine how physical influences, such as ill health and diet, can affect children. You will learn about how environment, such as poor housing and abuse, can have long-term effects on children's growth and development. Lastly, you will investigate how socio-economic factors, such as early education, can affect children.

LEARNING AIMS

In this component you will:

A	Understand the characteristics of children's development from birth to 5 years old.
B	Explore factors that affect growth and development.

Growth

There is a wide range of 'normal' when it comes to growth. A person's size, shape and weight depend on multiple factors.

You might be the same age as your classmates, but have you noticed that your heights vary greatly?

Changes to physical size

Growth is an increase in size. It is something that can be measured. The body of a newborn is very different to that of an adult. The head is disproportionately large in size compared to the rest of its body. This is because it contains a brain that by the age of 9 months old is already half the size of a full-grown adult. Newborns have just enough strength and control over their muscles to move their head from side to side. However, they are unable to hold up their own head so an adult must support their head when holding them.

Bone changes

Babies have more bones than adults. They are born with approximately 300 bones, whereas adults have just 206. Their bodies need to be soft and flexible to withstand being squeezed down the birth canal during birth. As they grow, their bones harden and some small segments of bone fuse together to make larger bones.

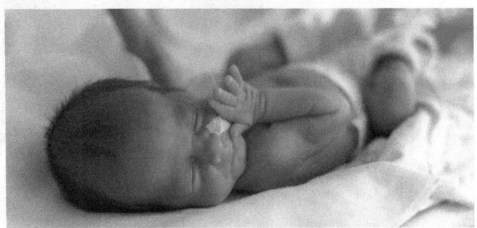

◘ **The newborn skull has two small areas where the bones have not fused, called fontanelles. These gaps usually close at around 6 months of age.**

Children grow rapidly from birth to the age of 5. The areas of the body that grow quickly in young children are the skeleton, the muscles and the brain. Children increase in weight and height and the circumference of their head gets bigger.

Look at these comparisons of growth between a newborn and a 5-year-old.

◘ **Table 1.1: Comparisons of growth between a newborn and a 5-year-old.**

Newborn	5-year-old
Large head in comparison to body	Head more in **proportion** to body
Weak muscles unable to lift own head	Able to coordinate movements and use muscles
Length around 50 cm	Height around 113 cm
Weight around 3.4 kg	Weight around 20.4 kg

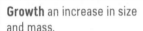

How growth is measured and plotted

It is essential for doctors and health care professionals, such as health visitors, to measure a child's growth. This helps them to make sure that the child is developing well. This will help to identify any possible signs of ill health or disability. It will also show whether the child's growth is **consistent** with the expected patterns.

Growth is measured in several ways:
- weighing the child
- measuring length and then height (as children can stand up)
- measuring head **circumference**.

These measurements are carried out as soon as babies are born, and repeated at regular intervals until the health professionals are satisfied that the child is growing well. They can assess this by using a developmental chart (or centile chart), such as Figure 1.1. This is a graph where health professionals can mark children's development on a line that plots the growth that the child is expected to make. If the marks they make over time do not follow the line, the child's growth is not following an expected pattern. For example, this might be because they are not gaining weight.

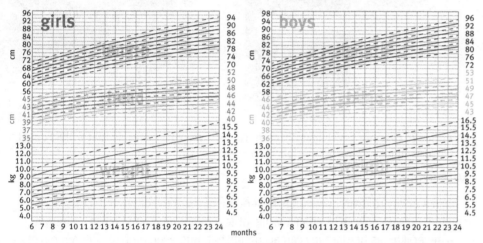

▣ Figure 1.1: Development charts (girl left, boy right) enable health professionals to see whether children's development is meeting expected patterns. If they are not, it could suggest the child has a medical condition, a disability or they are not having their needs met, such as not getting enough food and nourishment.

ACTIVITY

Look at the following case study.

The health visitor has just weighed 5-month-old Arun on the baby scales. She notices that he is not following the expected line for his birth weight and he now weighs less than at his 4-month-old health check.

1 What might the health visitor expect to see when she plots Arun's growth on a development chart?

2 How might the health visitor check Arun's growth when he is 4 years old?

CHECK MY LEARNING

Now you understand what growth is and how it is measured in children, draw a mind map of reasons for measuring children's growth.

Development

How do you know everything you know today?

You have seen, heard, watched and understood. Over time, you have mastered new skills and learnt new things. This is how you have developed.

Although everyone develops at a different rate, generally, **development** follows a pattern or a consistent sequence as shown in the following pictures.

■ Although children develop at different rates, it would be unlikely that a child could write their name before they learnt to walk.

Milestones

A child's ability to learn new things is dependent on many different factors. Some children pick up new skills quickly while others might need to practise something new several times before they can accomplish it. But, even though children develop at different rates, the stages they go through usually follow the same sequence or pattern. For ease, professionals tend to separate children's development into different areas so it can be identified and assessed more easily. These are often placed in stages at the age where they are most likely to happen. These are called **milestones**.

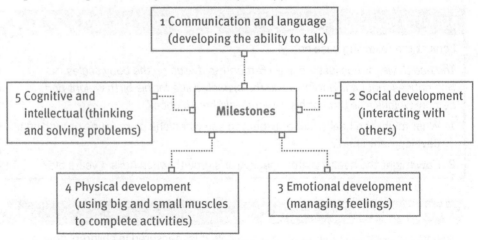

■ Figure 1.2: The skills shown in the pictures at the start of this section can be separated into different areas.

■ Table 1.2: The skills learnt illustrate learning across the different areas.

Skill	Area of learning
Smiling at a familiar face	**Communication and language**: the smile is a form of non-verbal communication that means 'hello'. **Social development**: the child is making a connection with someone they want to engage with. **Emotional development**: the smile says 'I am happy to see you'.
Banging a drum	**Physical development**: the child needs to move their hands to bang on the drum, so there is purpose in their movement. **Cognitive and intellectual development**: the child understands cause and effect: banging on the drum makes a noise.
Walking	**Physical development**: it takes balance, control and coordination to be able to walk. **Cognitive and intellectual development**: the child will walk when they want to go somewhere, or reach something. They work out that walking will achieve this.
Writing name	**Physical development**: children need to use hand–eye coordination and be able to hold a pencil before they can write. **Cognitive and intellectual development**: children need to understand letters, formation of letters and their name before they can write it.

Holistic development

Children's development is **holistic** in the sense that it rarely occurs in one area alone. By looking at Table 1.2, we can see that even something that appears straightforward, such as walking, still requires development in other areas. Children will not walk unless they have the desire to. If a child is encouraged to walk and praised for trying, they may persevere in order to please their parent or carer. This is a good example of where physical and emotional development are linked.

KEY TERM

Holistic parts that are interconnected.

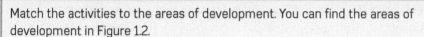

ACTIVITY

Match the activities to the areas of development. You can find the areas of development in Figure 1.2.

1 Baby starts to say 'mamamama'.
2 A 3-year-old can hop on one foot.
3 A 2-year-old plays alongside a child the same age as herself.
4 A 5-year-old completes a simple jigsaw puzzle.
5 A 1-year-old hides their face when they are scared by a puppet.

When you have completed this task, you could make up another example for each area of development.

Choose a way to present your answers, such as a chart or diagram.

CHECK MY LEARNING

Working with a partner, name the five different areas of development and give an explanation for each one.

Developmental milestones

As with growth, there is a wide range of what is considered to be 'normal' development. Developmental milestones (also called developmental norms) are worked out by studying groups of children. The study will take into account all children's significant development and then find an **average** (usually the **mean**). Why do you think some children might have a slower rate of development than others?

 Table 1.3: An example of how developmental milestones could be worked out.

How developmental milestones are worked out
Twenty children are studied to see when they take their first steps. • One child takes their first steps at the age of 9 months. • Three children take their first steps at 11 months. • Six children take their first steps at 12 months. • Six children take their first steps at 14 months. • Three children take their first steps at 18 months. • One child takes their first steps at 20 months. By calculating the mean, we learn that the average age for children to take their first steps in this study is 12.6 months. However, anywhere between 9 months and 20 months would be considered 'normal'.

DID YOU KNOW?

How the **mean** is worked out.

If you have three numbers (2, 6, 10) and you want to know what the mean number is, you add the numbers together: 2 + 6 + 10 = 18.

Then you divide the number 18 by 3, because there are three numbers in the list.

This makes the mean 6.

Who uses developmental milestones?

Young children's development is generally formally measured by early years professionals (such as nursery staff and childminders). This is because they are responsible for supporting children's learning and need to see whether children are making good progress. They might review children's development by observing them. They will then use developmental milestones, such as the Department for Education's version, which is called Early Years Outcomes. This enables them to see whether children's development is progressing as they would expect.

◨ Table 1.4: People who might use developmental milestones.

People who use developmental milestones	Reason for using developmental milestones
Nursery staff and child minders	To assess whether their teaching is effective and to see if children are making good progress.
Parents and carers	To see if their children are making good progress and to know what to expect next.
Doctors	If a parent or early years professional raises a concern, a doctor might assess a child's physical development. For example, check a child's hips, legs and feet if they are not walking.
Speech and language therapists	If a parent or early years professional raises a concern, the speech and language therapist might review their development against expected patterns of communication and language.
Health visitors	If a child is not making expected progress, a health visitor might review their progress to help identify possible learning difficulties or disabilities.

ACTIVITY

Look at the following case studies.

Eila

Eila is 36 months old. She doesn't use any words or language at all when she plays. She doesn't seem interested in music or songs and doesn't join in with singing groups. The staff at her nursery have also noticed that she doesn't respond when they call her name and wonder if there is a problem with her hearing.

1 What area of Eila's development do you think is most affected?

2 What other areas of development do you think might also be affected by Eila's hearing difficulty?

Jeeven

Jeeven is 2 years old. He broke his leg badly in a car accident and has spent three months in hospital.

3 Jeeven's physical development is likely to be affected because he has a badly broken leg.

Discuss, and give reasons to explain, the impact it may have on other areas of his development.

You could present this as a report or in a table.

Summary of growth and development

- There is a wide range of what is considered to be normal growth and development.
- Development is holistic; developing in one area supports progress in other areas of development.
- Growth and development are measured to ensure that children make good progress.
- A child's growth and development does not usually follow a rigid pattern, but, by having expected patterns, professionals can quickly identify any potential issues.

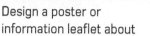

CHECK MY LEARNING

Design a poster or information leaflet about development milestones.

You need to include the following information.

1 How development milestones can be used to help measure children's progress.

2 Why one person might use development milestones.

Growth and development from 0–18 months: physical development (1)

Have you ever thought about what a newborn baby can do?

Newborn humans appear pretty helpless. They need someone to meet all of their basic needs in order for them to survive. However, despite this apparent vulnerability, newborn babies are born with an impressive set of skills.

Infant reflexes

Infant or primitive reflexes

Babies born on or around **full-term** have **primitive** reflexes. These reflexes are apparent immediately after they are born. Midwives or doctors check the reflexes to confirm that the baby is well and their central nervous system is working. It is thought that these reflexes originate from a time when humans were much less evolved and so these reflexes helped the baby to survive in the early stages of life. Primative reflexes generally disappear around the ages of 2 to 6 months, when babies make more deliberate actions and movements.

Table 1.5 shows what amazing reflexes a newborn baby is born with.

▣ **Table 1.5: Newborn babies' amazing reflexes and the reasons these reflexes exist.**

Reflex	Description	Possible reason for reflex
Sucking reflex	The newborn will automatically suck on anything that touches the roof of their mouth, such as a nipple or teat of a bottle.	This is a survival instinct so that the baby can feed as soon as they are born.
Startle reflex (also known as Moro reflex)	If the baby's head is suddenly moved or they hear a loud noise, they fling their arms and legs in the air and make a grasping movement. Often, they will cry straight afterwards.	Mothers often carry their newborns around. If the baby is slipping from their grasp, this response might alert the new mother that she is about to drop the baby.
Walking or stepping reflex	If babies' feet come into contact with a flat surface, they will make stepping motions as if walking.	It could be that, when being carried around by their mothers, the baby would be able to hold on and move its body as the mother moved across the ground, helping it to stay clinging on to her.
Rooting reflex	When a finger, breast or teat is brushed across the baby's cheek, they will turn their head towards it.	This is another survival instinct. It means that the baby can find the nipple or teat to attach for feeding.
Grasp reflex (also known as palmar grasp)	If a finger is placed in the palm of a baby's hand, they will close their fingers tightly around it. So strong is their grasp that they can support their own body weight for a few seconds if gently lifted while over a soft surface.	It is likely that this is again a reflex that enabled babies to tightly grip onto their mothers while being carried.

Development of the senses

Sensory development

A newborn's senses are still developing. It will startle at loud noises. It may recognise its mother's voice from hearing it in the womb. A newborn's eyesight is fuzzy and out of focus. It can taste the sweetness of milk and enjoy the comforting sensation of sucking. Around 6 months of age babies will put everything they encounter into their mouths. This is an important stage of development as they begin to feel and taste things around them. Parents and carers must be extra careful to make sure they do not put anything dangerous into their mouths.

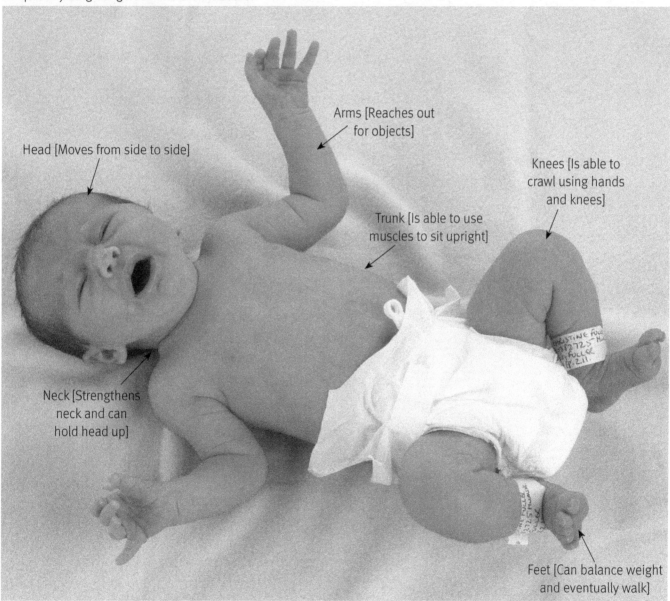

Head [Moves from side to side]

Arms [Reaches out for objects]

Knees [Is able to crawl using hands and knees]

Trunk [Is able to use muscles to sit upright]

Neck [Strengthens neck and can hold head up]

Feet [Can balance weight and eventually walk]

◪ It is helpful to think about young children's physical development as top to toe. Physical development generally starts with gaining control of the head and moves down the body to the toes and walking.

LINK IT UP

For more about development milestones, go to 'Developmental milestones'.

Growth and development from 0–18 months: physical development (2)

Control over the body

Physical development usually happens in a sequence.

Gross motor skills

Head control

Baby's head falls backwards and adult must support it.

Baby can hold their head upright for a few moments.

Baby has full control and can turn and move their head with control.

Sitting up

If put in a seated position, baby falls forward.

Baby can sit upright with support.

Baby can sit upright without support.

Baby can pull themselves to sit upright.

Prone position (lying on stomach)

Baby lies on tummy with hands and feet drawn in towards body.

Baby raises their chest off the floor by pushing up on their hands.

Baby might roll or turn over.

Baby can bear weight on their knees and hands.

Baby can crawl.

Walking

Baby has sagging knees and cannot bear weight on feet.

Baby will bear weight on feet when held.

Baby can stand for a moment holding on to furniture or someone's hands.

Baby can walk a few steps.

Baby can walk confidently and is able to run.

Fine motor skills

Using hands

Baby reaches for objects but often misses them.

Baby can reach and hold objects.

Baby uses whole hand to grasp objects.

Baby uses finger and thumb to pick up small objects.

■ Walking takes a great deal of balance and coordination. What is different between the way this baby is walking and the way that an adult walks?

Freedom to move

It is essential that babies and young children have the opportunity to move and stretch their muscles. If babies spend too much time restricted in seats or chairs, they are not able to practice kicking and stretching their arms and legs, which is essential for the healthy development of their muscles.

ACTIVITY

Create a presentation to share with your class.

You need to demonstrate your knowledge of physical development.

Physical development involves the big muscles in the body (gross motor skills) and the smaller muscles in the hands (fine motor skills).

1 Suggest one suitable activity or toy that will support the fine motor skills of a baby aged 0–18 months.

2 Suggest one suitable activity or toy that will support the gross motor skills of a baby aged 0–18 months.

When you have decided upon your activities or toys, suggest how they might help to promote the baby's physical development.

CHECK MY LEARNING

Write a sequence of physical development for a newborn baby up to the age of 18 months.

You could choose to divide this into gross motor skills and fine motor skills.

Growth and development from 0–18 months: cognitive and intellectual development

GETTING STARTED

Solve this simple problem. Unscramble these letters to spell a word.

tompenvedel

What skills did you use? How did you go about it? How long did it take?

Babies very quickly learn new skills and make sense of the world. They learn through watching and copying. Did you know that babies develop more quickly when they get a response? A baby will smile more often if someone smiles back at them. They learn to talk when someone talks back to them.

Memory and information processing

Babies have a great memory. They need this to help them to learn and remember all the new information they encounter. They also need to work out what to do with the information they learn. One way that babies demonstrate this is by looking for a toy they have dropped over the side of a high chair. They remember the toy exists and look for it. They will often take delight in doing this over and over again.

Problem-solving skills

KEY TERM

Perseverance continued effort and determination, despite difficulty.

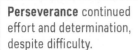

Intellectual or cognitive development has nothing to do with being a genius or how many questions you can answer. It is about how you approach a problem and try to solve it, and what you do if you cannot solve the problem. Concentration and **perseverance** are all part of intellectual and cognitive development. Young children need to have a desire to try, try and try again. They need to face problems they cannot solve and be challenged. If, after trying to walk for the first time, a baby fell over and gave up, they would never learn to walk.

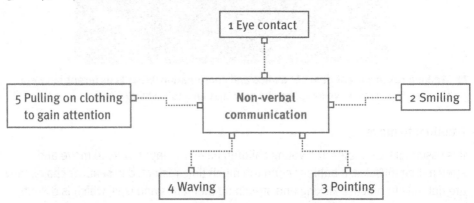

Figure 1.3: Ways that babies communicate before they talk.

Recognition of self

One of the most sophisticated and complicated ideas that a child has to discover is that they exist and are a separate, individual person. They must learn this before they can start to understand about how they impact on the world, such as how they can cause others to feel by their actions. They need to know they have a name and understand that, when someone uses that name, they are talking to them.

1 The child tries to fit a shape into a space, it doesn't fit

2 The child tries to put the shape in to another space and it fits.

3 The child realises each shape must have its own space.

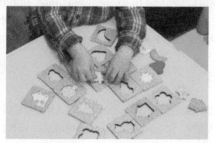

4 The child tries to fit the shape into a space and will try another space until successful.

5 The child recognises the shape and matches it to the correct space.

■ The shape sorter activity requires the child to use their physical and cognitive skills. Why do you think babies like this simple activity?

The mirror test

One way that **psychologists** have explored this aspect of development is through 'The Mirror Test'. This is also sometimes known as the 'Rouge Test'.

The child is placed in front of a mirror. Without the child realising, a small red dot or lipstick mark is placed on their forehead.

- The 6–12 month-old baby will gaze for a few seconds at themselves in the mirror and then smile in a friendly way as though they are meeting another baby.
- The 13–24 month-old baby will see themselves and see the dot on their head, they will point at the dot in the mirror, seeming to not recognise the other child is themselves.
- The 20–24 month-old baby will approach the mirror, see the dot and rub their head to remove it.

Therefore, psychologists believe that, until the child tries to rub the dot off their own head, they are not aware of the concept that the image in the mirror is themselves.

KEY TERM

Psychologist a professional who studies the human mind and why people do things.

ACTIVITY

Look at the following case study.

Maisie is 7 months old. She lies on her back and reaches for her mobile. Maisie tries over and over again to reach the mobile. Finally, she touches the mobile and it makes a noise.

1 What do you think made Maisie want to reach for the mobile? Discuss with a partner.

2 Together, describe two ways that parents or carers could encourage Maisie to reach for other toys. You could write this as a plan or find some images on the computer and make notes.

CHECK MY LEARNING

Look at the 'shape sorter' activity. For each of the five steps, explain what the child is learning at each step. You could do this by imagining what the child is thinking.

Growth and development from 0–18 months: communication, language and emotional development

The main way that babies communicate with others is by crying. This tells those around them that they need something and expect to have their needs met. They might cry because they are hungry, cold or even uncomfortable. Young children need to hear lots of language in order to learn how to talk. Until they learn to talk, babies become experts at using body language to make themselves understood and for social interaction. At around 6 months old babies will start early talking or **babbling**, which is the beginning of talking and eventually holding a conversation.

Social development

Babies love to be around other people. They learn about them and from them and it stimulates them to talk and think. Socialisation is essential to their learning. The first social experiences babies will have are with their parents, carers and siblings. They might also spend time with grandparents and other family or friends. Later, they will have secondary socialisation with people outside of their families.

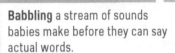

KEY TERMS

Babbling a stream of sounds babies make before they can say actual words.

Psychiatrist a medical professional who specialises in mental health.

◨ **Table 1.6: Ways that parents and carers can help young children to socialise.**

Places where babies can socialise	How it helps their social development
Toddler groups	This is a great way for children to learn about sharing, turn taking and watching what others can do.
Supermarkets	Babies will smile at strangers and enjoy the response they receive back.
Playgrounds	Babies enjoy watching others and will show excitement at others' enjoyment.
Libraries	Hearing stories and other people's voices will intrigue babies, who will be fascinated by them.

Emotional development

Newborn babies cry to communicate. As they develop, they are able to find other ways of expressing themselves. They will smile and later giggle as they show their emotions. At around 1 year old, they will show distress in being away from their main carer. This is called separation anxiety. By 18 months old, babies will start to be wary of strangers and unfamiliar situations.

Ways that children attract attention of caregivers

Around the age of 6 to 8 weeks, babies start to smile. This is a clever way that they build bonds with those around them. Their crying might turn more into single sounds, such as a shout or a squeal. Babies sometimes surprise themselves with the noises that they can make.

Development of bonds and trust

Babies need to have close attachments with the people who care for them in order to develop well emotionally.

- It is important for babies to form attachments to a small number of adults.
- The attachments that babies make are not just because they need feeding; it is to make them feel safe and secure.
- Attachment is a two-way process between the adult and baby. The adult needs to bond with the baby too.
- Physical closeness is important in helping the attachment process.
- Poor experiences of attachment can have a damaging effect on a child's ability to form relationships for the rest of their life.

Emotional resilience

Children that have developed strong attachments are more likely to be emotionally resilient. This means that they can control their emotions and are confident. They can recover quickly from upsets.

ACTIVITY

The **key person** is the named practitioner in an early years setting with responsibility for a child. Create a table that lists what you think their responsibilities might be and how they would benefit a child's emotional and social development.

Security and self-esteem

Children's emotional development has a big impact on their social development. It shapes how they get on with others.

Emotionally secure children might display the following characteristics:

- confidence
- willingness to try new things
- affection for others
- contentment.

Children that are emotionally insecure might display the following characteristics:

- spitefulness
- aggression
- extreme shyness
- fearfulness.

Increase in independence

Babies start to crave independence from a young age. They will want to start to do things for themselves, such as getting dressed and feeding themselves. This is an important part of growing up and becoming able to do things for themselves.

CHECK MY LEARNING

Discuss with a partner possible reasons why children who are emotionally insecure might find it difficult to make friends.

DID YOU KNOW?

The key person approach used in nurseries and pre-schools was developed in response to John Bowlby's theory that children need few adult carers. The key person is usually a member of staff who forms an attachment to the child, helping them to settle at the nursery or pre-school.

KEY TERMS

Key person the named practitioner in an early years setting with responsibility for a child.

Self-esteem confidence in own abilities and worth.

Growth and development from 18 months to 3 years: physical development

GETTING STARTED

Write a brief explanation of gross motor skills and fine motor skills to refresh your learning.

Physical development

Now the child is a toddler who is mobile, more independent and starting to understand more about the world around them. They are like sponges that will soak up every experience on offer.

Who do you think children learn most from at this age?

Development of the senses

From the age of around 18 months, children are eager to find out about and discover the world. They do this by using all of their senses. At around 18 months children will start to explore more of the world using their hands instead of their mouths. They can now hold and grasp things much better. They will still be putting things into their mouths, but beginning to recognise when these do not taste good.

◘ This child is investigating the toy using their hands to hold it. What safety measures do you think parents will still need to take when choosing toys for children around 18 months old?

Overstimulation

During this period of development, children continue to learn through all of their senses. They experience the world through different sights, smells, sounds and tastes. Toys designed for children this age are generally brightly coloured and musical to gain their attention. However, it is easy to see how young children can quickly become overstimulated and distressed if presented by lots of new experiences all at once. This might be why young children often enjoy playing with wrapping paper and empty boxes on their birthday or at Christmas as these do not overload their senses.

Gross motor skills

Children need to develop the big muscles in their legs and arms, sometimes called gross motor skills, and the smaller muscles in their hands, sometimes called fine motor skills.

◪ Table 1.7: Examples of gross motor skills and fine motor skills.

Gross motor skills	Fine motor skills
Running	Holding a crayon or paint brush
Catching a ball	Using a spoon or fork
Climbing stairs	Doing up buttons and zips
Throwing a beanbag	
Climbing	

Fine motor skills

Developing hand–eye coordination

An essential part of children successfully gaining control over their physical skills is developing their hand–eye coordination. It is difficult to catch a ball or write your name with your eyes closed. This is because your eye follows the ball or the pencil and tells your hands where they need to be. Young children take some time to develop their hand–eye coordination. This means their actions are not always coordinated.

◪ If an adult throws a ball towards a child, they will often grasp too late as their brain is not yet sending quick enough messages from their eyes to their hands.

ACTIVITY

Young children need to have plenty of opportunities to practice their physical skills.

Create a mind map to explain how the following activities help to increase children's physical skills:
- playing at soft play areas
- dressing a doll
- chalking on a board.

When you have finished, you could suggest an outdoor activity that might help children to develop their physical skills.

CHECK MY LEARNING

List five physical skills that you would expect a 3-year-old to be able to do without help.

Growth and development from 18 months to 3 years: cognitive and communication development

Cognitive and intellectual development

Children between 18 months and 3 years old are beginning to increase their interest and attention span. At around 2 years old, children start to develop their own fascinations and will respond enthusiastically to familiar items or characters. One way for parents and carers to develop children's intellectual learning is through books.

Development of information processing

Developing a love of books

Reading to children and helping them to develop an interest in and enjoyment of books helps to boost their intellectual and cognitive development. Listening to someone read not only helps to promote children's speech and language, it unlocks their imagination and helps them to experience different emotions.

Memory

Young children will often be able to retell a story from memory. This can make it appear that they can read much earlier than they actually can. This is because children can become so excited and interested in characters that they will know a story off by heart. Repetition is important for children's learning and they show delight in repeating songs and rhymes they know.

The little mouse felt sad, where was his mummy?

'Hooray', said the little mouse. His Mummy wasn't missing after all and he felt happy.

▣ Stories help children to think and develop empathy. What emotions do you think the book here might provoke in children?

Responding to pitch and tone of voices

Story times are a great way for children to hear different pitches and tones of voices. They need to be able to understand that the way words are said can affect their meaning.

Look at these two sentences.

1 Put the toys in the box, please.

2 Do you want to go to bed?

These sentences can have a very different meaning depending on how they are said. The first sentence could be said sternly as a command or softly with a long tone to plead. The second sentence could be said as a warning or a gentle question to a tired child. Young children need to know the difference to understand what is expected from them.

Problem-solving skills

Understanding pitch and tone in someone's voice and retelling stories uses complicated problem solving. Look at the following steps that children might take to solve the problem of completing a jigsaw puzzle.

1 The child needs to understand what a jigsaw puzzle is.
2 The child needs to know that pieces fit together to create a picture.
3 The child needs to try the pieces until they fit together.
4 The child needs to know when the jigsaw is complete.

Communication and language development

Development of speech sounds and language skills

At around 18 months, parents and carers will notice words amongst the babbling. At first, this is likely to be naming people and things. At this early stage, children have no concept of the uniqueness of words. This can lead them into thinking that all ladies are called 'Mummy'. They might recognise the noise a dog makes and call all dogs 'woof'. The way that adults respond to these early uses of language determines how quickly children use and repeat language. As they begin to understand the power and purpose of language, children copy everything they hear and their vocabulary rapidly develops.

Listening and attention skills

Communicating successfully requires children to listen and pay attention. Young children find this difficult and it is a skill they need to learn.

Formation of sentences

At around 2 years old, children know around 50 words and might put two or three words together to make a sentence, such as 'Daddy car gone'. These sentences do not always make sense but, as children develop and the more words they learn, the longer the sentences they use. By the age of 3 years, children have increased the number of words that they know and will want to use talking to connect with others.

The rules of conversation and using social skills

Children's enthusiasm to talk and their impatience might mean that they talk over others, butt into conversations or simply ignore you if they lose interest. It is important that adults help children to understand the rules of conversation, e.g. speaking, stopping and listening before speaking again. This is a skill that many children will not fully understand until they are around 6 or 7 years old.

DID YOU KNOW?

It is not uncommon for young children to develop a stammer. This is thought to be because they are learning so quickly that their brains are working faster than their ability to talk, meaning they stumble over words. This is usually a temporary phase.

ACTIVITY

Look at the following case study and respond to the questions. Make notes and discuss with a partner.

Amira is almost 2 years old. She is just starting to copy what she hears. She will say familiar words, such as 'daddy' and 'more'. Amira loves music and playing with toy animals.

1 What do you think Amira's next milestones in talking will be?
2 Give two ways that her carers might be able to encourage her development.

CHECK MY LEARNING

With a partner, identify three stages of children's communication and language development between 18 months and 3 years.

Growth and development from 18 months to 3 years: social and emotional development

Social development

Between the ages of 18 months to 3 years, children make important steps in their social development. This is because it is often around this age that children start to spend more time away from their parents and carers.

Secondary socialisation

Children might start nursery, pre-school or attend a childminder's care at around the age of 2 years old. For the first time, they might need to meet people and work out relationships by themselves.

Development of friendships

When children start pre-school or nursery they will meet other children. Developing friendships is difficult for young children. This is because, at this age, young children think of themselves more than others. They might not want to share or take turns. However, children quickly enjoy playing with others and they learn important social skills that help them to become well-adjusted adults.

Development of secure, positive relationships with others

Exploring a new environment

When children start a nursery, pre-school or childminder's care for the first time, they need to learn about the new environment, the new people and the new rules they need to follow. For some children, it might be the first time they have needed to follow routines and rules. This can be an anxious time for young children. Recognising the importance of having a regular main carer, most early years settings have a key person system to help children to settle in.

Building confidence and self-esteem

Young children need adults to help them to feel confident. Their key person can help with this. Children need praise to know when they are doing well and to raise their self-esteem. Rules are important to help children to know what is expected from them, but too many rules can stop them from developing well and make them lose their confidence.

ACTIVITY

Write a set of rules or a list of rights for young children to learn about and follow in an early years setting.

Remember, you need to keep it simple so that children can understand what is expected of them.

You can explain why each rule is needed.

Emotional development

Development of bonds and trust

Children have to learn to get along with others. By nature, young children think the world revolves around them and have not yet learnt to think about others and their feelings. As they start to play and learn as part of a group they might display a wide range of behaviours.

Increase in independence

Self-soothing

Even from a young age children learn to soothe themselves when their primary carer is not present. This is a mechanism that they use to help comfort themselves and make them feel better. Some children have dummies or special objects, sometimes called security blankets or comforters. Look at the following case study.

Kristof didn't settle well at pre-school. He missed his mum terribly when she dropped him off and would cry and sit by the door. His key person Monika spent time comforting him. She noticed that he would carry a blanket to the pre-school and his mum would take it home with her. Monika spoke to Kristof's mum about the blanket. Kristof's mum felt embarrassed to leave the blanket at pre-school because it is quite grubby as he doesn't like it being washed. The next day, Kristof's mum left the blanket for him to have at pre-school and he settled much more quickly.

It is possible that Kristof had become attached to the blanket and felt secure when he had it with him. The blanket seemed to be grubby and his mum mentioned he did not like it being washed. This could be because the blanket smelt familiar and reminded Kristof of his home and his family.

Children do not necessarily need items for comfort and can often find ways of comforting themselves. This is a normal and healthy stage of social and emotional development for children at times when they feel anxious. However, if children display lots of signs of self-comforting and it continues as they grow older, it could be a sign that they are traumatised or distressed and need some professional help.

Developing emotional resilience

Tantrums

Young children do not have the vocabulary or experience to describe how they are feeling. Sometimes their emotions can become so strong that they do not know how to deal with them. At around the age of 2, some children can have what is sometimes called 'temper tantrums'. They feel cross and angry, often without really knowing why. This can lead to them displaying the way they feel by laying on the floor, shouting, crying or refusing to cooperate. Although it is often exhausting for parents and children, it is a normal stage of development that will decrease as children's ability to recognise and understand their feelings increases.

◘ Table 1.8: Behaviour displayed by young children as they start to play and learn as part of a group.

Type of behaviour	Reason for behaviour
Hoarding toys	If children are used to having all their toys to themselves, sharing them can be difficult. Also, some children might feel that the toys are far better than the ones they have at home and want to play with everything at once.
Snatching	Children might assume that all the toys and equipment belong to them, just like the ones at home.
Hitting	If children do not have good communication skills they might be unable to resolve arguments by talking about it and so they lash out.
Biting	This could be because children are still exploring the world using their mouths and do not appreciate it causes others pain.

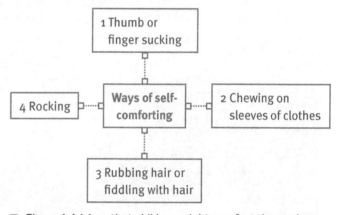

◘ Figure 1.4: Ways that children might comfort themselves. Did you have a way of comforting yourself as a child?

CHECK MY LEARNING ■■

Write five points for nursery assistants to consider when welcoming a new child.

Growth and development from 3 to 5 years: physical development

Children are becoming increasingly confident, sociable and capable as they leave babyhood behind and start to prepare for going to school. What skills do you think are most important for young children to learn before they start school?

Development of the senses

Between the ages of 3 and 5 years, children are growing into confident, independent young people. They are increasingly becoming interested in the world around them and find it impossible to resist touching and exploring the things they encounter. As they become ready for starting school, children need to learn that there are times when they need to follow some rules about what they can and cannot touch.

Gross motor skills

By the age of 4 to 5 years, children are refining their gross motor skills. They no longer need to walk with their arms outstretched to balance and their movements are deliberate and purposeful. They are able to run, climb and balance skilfully. However, children around this age lack spatial awareness. Their coordination is not fully developed so children might have frequent trips, bumps and falls as they play.

■ As children grow they need further ways to test out their abilities and challenge what they can do. Playgrounds offer opportunities for developing gross motor skills.

◻ Table 1.9: How play area equipment can strengthen children's gross motor skills.

Item of equipment	Which muscles are being strengthened
Swings	As children use their legs to work themselves on the swing, they use their stomach, back and neck muscles as well as the muscles in their legs and arms.
Monkey rings	As children hang from the monkey rings they strengthen their grip and small muscles in their hands. They strengthen their arm and shoulder muscles.
Slide	Climbing to the slide relies on grip and leg strength. Sliding down requires strong stomach and back muscles. This is why young children will often fall to a laying down position when going down a slide, because their muscles are not very strong.
Balance beam	Balancing helps children to develop their core muscles.
Climbing frame	Climbing develops leg strength, grip and strength in arms and shoulders.

Encouraging children to be active

Parents, carers and childcare professionals all have a role to play in encouraging children to be fit and physically active. In July 2011, the government published information about physical activity for young children. This sets out how important it is for children to walk, run and enjoy freedom to strengthen their gross motor skills.

ACTIVITY

Investigate what play provision is available for children locally. Is there a range of play equipment for young children to be able to develop their physical skills?

1 Complete a study into the benefits of your local park for developing children's physical skills.

2 Recommend some changes that might improve the play provision.

Fine motor skills

Children are in control of their fine motor skills. They can use tools and have greater control over the movement of their fingers. It is essential that children practice their fine motor skills as they are needed for writing, cutting and typing on computers.

Writing

Children cannot just pick up a pencil and write. There are various stages they go through before they learn to hold a pencil and have full control over it. Pencil grip is important because it affects the fluency of writing and legibility of the child's handwriting.

1 Fisted grip

2 Digital grip

3 Tripod grip

4 Dynamic tripod

◻ Tripod grip means that only small movements of the wrist are needed when writing. This means that children can write sentences without getting aching wrists.

CHECK MY LEARNING ◼◻◻

Review the types of physical development below and give an explanation of each:
- fine motor skills
- gross motor skills
- hand–eye coordination
- dynamic tripod grip.

Growth and development from 3 to 5 years: cognitive and communication development

Cognitive and intellectual development

Between the ages of 3 and 5 years, children have a wide range of knowledge. They have begun to understand words and their meaning and have become aware of numbers.

Development of information processing

Promoting early reading and writing

By now, children can hold a pencil and make marks, although they might not grip it correctly. They know that print carries meaning because they enjoy having books read to them and they might be starting to recognise their own written name. There are many ways that adults can help to increase children's interest in reading and writing.

▣ Table 1.10: Ways that adults can encourage early reading and writing.

Activities to encourage early reading	Activities to encourage early writing
• Singing songs and rhymes • Reading stories together • Looking at pictures and photographs • Role playing stories and characters • Having name cards or placemats • Displaying pictures with words • Practising sounds of letters, such as 'ssssssnake' • Having a range of different types of books to look at	• Having lots of different materials to draw and write with • Threading beads onto a string, playing with dough and using scissors to strengthen finger muscles • Finger painting

Memory

From 3 years old children develop long-term memories so are able to recall information to apply later. For example, they remember sounds that letters make to help them to read or recall a past event to solve a problem.

Children have a superb memory and are now learning so much so quickly that at times their memory becomes jumbled. They might, for example, not quite remember what is real and what is not. Children might retell parts of a story or television programme they have heard but think that it happened to them. Some children develop an incredible ability to remember things that interest them, such as the names of dinosaurs, types of trains or makes of cars.

Learning by rote

Many years ago, children were taught to learn by reciting information over and over again until they knew it. This was a popular way to teach mathematics. However, it was not always a successful method for all children.

Young children can often count up to ten. However, this does not mean that they know about numbers or mathematics. Learning about even basic mathematics is a complicated process.

Step 1: Children need to know that numbers exist and what their purpose is.

Step 2: Children need to know that a numeral represents a number.

Step 3: Children need to understand how many make up that numeral.

Step 4: Children need to understand that numbers come in order, starting at zero.

Step 5: Children need to understand that combining numbers together or removing them creates new numbers.

Children do not need to necessarily follow this order, but they need to understand each step.

Problem-solving skills

Matching and sorting

During children's play they will start to sort, match and order items. They do this with exceptional skill when they have a particular interest. For example, children that are interested in dinosaurs will be able to quickly identify toy dinosaurs and will instantly recognise that toy farm animals are not dinosaurs. This process involves:

Recognition: Acknowledge that it is a similar type, not a human figure or toy car.

Identification: Look for familiar features, shape, size or colour (e.g. scales, teeth, familiarity).

Matching: Accept or dismiss items, e.g. this is not a dinosaur because I know it is a pig.

Communication and language development

By 3 years old, children are generally able to speak in sentences that make sense, but might not be quite accurate. For example:

'Go zoo now'

The meaning is clear, although there are no **connective words** used and the sentence is not correct. By 5 years old, the child will be able to fill in the gaps and the sentence feels more accurate. For example:

'Please can we go to the zoo now?'

Children will also ask many questions as they seek to understand things around them. They can follow quite complex instructions as they are able to understand, order and act.

For example:

'We can go to the zoo, but you need to put the toys away, find your shoes and get your coat on.'

At 4 to 5 years old, most children would understand and be able to follow this instruction.

Children are now confident communicators who can hold a conversation and use talking to share their ideas and thoughts. However, they might still need reminding about the rules of conversation, such as waiting to have their turn to talk.

As children develop a concept of self, they start to identify themselves differently as they speak.

Initially children might use their name, e.g. 'Lucy do it'.

They then understand that they are 'me' and might say 'me do it'.

Eventually this becomes 'I will do it'.

■ Children need to know that numbers represent a group of objects. What are the early experiences you think children have with numbers?

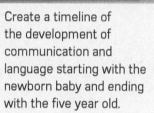

ACTIVITY

Create a timeline of the development of communication and language starting with the newborn baby and ending with the five year old.

You might choose to do this using a computer or present your work in a table or as a collage.

KEY TERMS

Connective words connect other words or phrases.

CHECK MY LEARNING

Choose an activity from Table 1.10 that encourages early reading.

Expand on this, such as making up a new children's song or rhyme or creating a display using pictures with words.

Growth and development from 3 to 5 years: social and emotional development

Social development

When children play they are starting to understand the world around them, solve problems and learn about how to get along with others. Children's play happens in stages and this helps friendships to form.

Development of secure, positive relationships with others

Children are now starting to feel confident and secure enough to separate from their parents and spend periods of time away from them. Around this time other people, such as teachers, start to influence the way that they think. Young children will often enjoy playing at being teachers. This helps them to work out these new relationships.

Primary and secondary socialisation

Developing new relationships with more people is not always easy for young children. They can find this quite overwhelming as they begin to learn that other children think, look and sound differently to themselves. Children might start to deal with arguments for the first time and learn how to resolve them.

Building confidence and self-esteem

Bounce back ability

Children need to be confident and able to get along with their peers. They need to share resources and ideas to become effective learners at school and for the rest of their lives. Young children will not always be able to agree and there will be disputes, but by developing emotionally, they will be able to resolve conflict themselves and bounce back quickly from disappointments and move forward feeling positive.

Development of friendships

Stages of play

In the 1930s Mildred Parten identified five stages of children's play.

Stage one: **Solitary play** – children play by themselves.

Stage two: **Spectator play** – children watch others while they play.

Stage three: **Parallel play** – children play alongside, but do not interact with each other.

Stage four: **Associative play** – children play the same thing, such as role play, but do not play together.

Stage five: **Cooperative play** – children play together, negotiate plans and share ideas.

ACTIVITY

1 Create a table divided into two headings of 'social development' and 'emotional development'.

2 Under each heading, write a list of expectations for development in each area from 0–18 months, 18 months to 3 years, and 3 years to 5 years.

Emotional development

Development of bonds and trust

As children become able to talk and express themselves more easily, they start to be able to express their close bonds with people who are important to them.

Here are some ways that they might show this:

- drawing pictures for their family
- holding hands
- telling family members that they love them
- wanting to copy them.

These behaviours show that children are happy, confident, and trust the people who care for them.

Increase in independence

There are some activities that children should be able to do for themselves between the ages of 3 and 5 years. These are show in Figure 1.5.

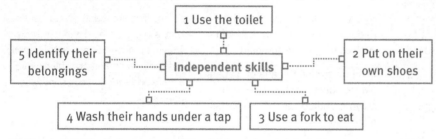

1 Use the toilet

5 Identify their belongings

Independent skills

2 Put on their own shoes

4 Wash their hands under a tap

3 Use a fork to eat

◨ Figure 1.5: The independent skills children develop help them to get ready for starting school. Can you think of any other skills that are important?

Developing emotional resilience

Young children need positive relationships, praise and encouragement in order to build their self-esteem.

◨ Table 1.11: How to tell if a young child has low or high self-esteem.

Evidence of high self-esteem	Evidence of low self-esteem
• Willingness to take part • Ability to make friends • Ability to recover quickly after failure • Stable emotions • Pride in achievements and efforts	• Unable to play • Poor concentration • Emotional outbursts • Disappointment in effort and work • Inability to get along with others

This is how adults can promote children's self-esteem:

- having realistic expectations
- praising children when they achieve something
- encouraging and not criticising
- joining in with children's play
- listening to what children say
- being respectful of children's ideas, views and efforts.

◨ Disputes are inevitable when young children play together. How might adults help to minimise arguments amongst young children?

CHECK MY LEARNING

Look at the stages of play.

1 Identify when you think children are most likely to form friendships.

2 Why might this also be a time when children are likely to come into conflict with each other?

Summary of growth and development

	0–18 months	18 months–3 years	3–5 years
Physical development	The newborn baby has only primitive reflexes, such as rooting, sucking, startling, grasping and walking/stepping. Their senses are fuzzy as their ears and eyes begin to adapt to the world outside the womb. They recognise the smell of their main carer. At around 6 months old children gain control of their neck muscles and are able to sit and roll over. They might learn to crawl. They reach for objects and start to put their hands to their mouths. At around 1 year old babies might be able to stand without support. By 18 months, most are able to walk without support. They will enjoy exploring the world by putting everything they encounter into their mouths.	At 2 years old children can squat, stand, run and stop. They are able to balance better, although they might need to stretch out their arms for balance at times. They can feed themselves quite well using a spoon as they have better hand–eye coordination. They cannot resist touching and tasting everything they encounter even if it is not meant to be eaten. By 3 years old children can start to build on their large movements, such as hopping or jumping. Children around the age of 3 years old are able to make marks with crayons and pencils, although this might look like scribbles.	At around 4 years old children's balance and coordination has improved so much they can now climb and start to pedal bicycles. They can probably throw and catch a ball quite well and will be able to walk up and down stairs. They are developing into eager learners using all of their senses so they might enjoy dancing and copying by watching others. As children approach 5 years of age they are able to hold and use tools. They can form the letters that spell out their name and are able to use a knife and fork and scissors with good skill.
Cognitive and intellectual development	Newborn babies are watching, listening and making sense of what they see, hear, feel and touch. At around 6 months old babies will start to recognise their name and turn their head when called. At around 1 year old babies will understand that things exist even when they are out of sight. They will look for objects they have dropped. They are fascinated by their own image. At 18 months old babies will explore how things feel using their mouths and might enjoy particular materials that feel nice when they are chewed.	At around 2 years old children will start to respond to the pitch and tone of voices. They will look at things that interest them but are quickly distracted. At around 2½ years old children start to have an amazing memory. They can recognise animals and toys and follow action songs and rhymes. Being able to say a few words they can now communicate. Around 3 years old children are starting to demonstrate how much they know. They can sort items by shape and perhaps count up to ten.	At 4 years old children are becoming such confident talkers that they know around 5,000 words. By the time they are 5 years old, many children recognise letters and are able to read and write basic words. Children at 4 years old have a better attention span and will spend time concentrating on things that interest them. They can probably recognise different colours and shapes and be able to put their counting into use, such as counting out how many pieces of fruit they have to eat.

	0–18 months	18 months–3 years	3–5 years
Communication and language development	Newborn babies can only communicate through crying. Soon, this will turn to cooing and at around 6 weeks old babies will smile at familiar faces. They will turn their heads to look for sounds they hear and will enjoy hearing people talking to them. At around 6 months some babies will start to babble. At around 18 months babies will start to use the odd word such as 'mummy' or 'daddy'.	Children are starting to quickly develop speech. At around 2 years old children can copy many words and will start to quickly pick up new words every week. By 2½ years old children will start to combine words together such as 'cat gone now'. Around 2½ years old they know what is said to them and will be able to follow some simple instructions.	By 3, children are able to use words in a sentence (that might not sound quite right) but miss out some connective words. Children's enthusiasm to talk can mean they interrupt. By 5, children understand more about listening and can wait their turn. At 5, children can follow instructions, understand what is said to them and use around nine words in a sentence. They might not always use words in the right context, but their conversations are much more adult.
Social development	Newborns quickly develop a strong attachment to their main carers. They cry to get their attention and will stop when the carer meets their needs. By 6 weeks, the baby will smile and make eye contact. At around 1 year, children will become anxious if they are separated from their main carer. Children around 18 months will enjoy watching others and spending time with children around the same age.	At around 2 years old some children will start nursery, pre-school or a childminder's care. They might be upset at first but this secondary socialisation helps them to become fond of people outside their immediate family. At 2½ years old children do not think about the thoughts and feelings of others. They might take toys they want from others. They will start to play alongside others and will enjoy being praised by their parents and carers, which helps to raise their self-esteem.	At 3, children will feel more confident when their main carer leaves them in the care of other familiar people. At 4 years old, children are getting ready to spend time at school. They will be able to mix with other children and can take turns and share (with encouragement). At 5, children are confident and the views of their classmates are important to them. They will gain a sense of pride in showing their work. As children settle into school they start to form closer friendships.
Emotional development	A newborn baby cries for attention. As they hear sounds and familiar voices they will turn their head. At around 6 weeks, babies will smile at any smiling face and by 3 months they will start to giggle loudly at things. At around 6 months, babies will be quite happy to be in the company of new people. By 1 year, they are wary of strangers and will cry if separated from their main carer. By 18 months old, babies will want to explore the environment and are more resilient, although they need to know their main carer is nearby.	At around 2 years old children know who they are, for example saying 'I'm a big boy'. They will still be wary of people they do not know, but will be more confident when meeting new people. At around 2 years old children might have 'temper tantrums' where they have strong feelings and are not sure how to deal with them. They will test the boundaries to see what will happen. By 3 years old children might be able to comfort themselves and might use methods such as sucking their thumb or twiddling their hair.	By 4 years old, children show their affection for others, (e.g. by talking about them and drawing pictures). At 4 years old children are becoming more independent and will want to do things for themselves, which is important for when they start school. By 5 years of age, with the right support, children will be willing to part with their parents and play and able to make friends. By 5, children can generally manage their feelings well and understand the feelings of others. They know how to behave and want to please adults rather than testing boundaries.

Learning aim A: assessment practice

How you will be assessed

You have looked at the difference between growth and development and how children develop between birth and the age of 5. Now you will need to demonstrate your understanding of how growth and development are measured. You will be expected to show that you can identify the different areas of development and the usual stages of development in each area between the ages of birth and 5 years. You will also need to be able to show you understand how the different areas of development are linked for each of the age groups.

The questions, activities and tips in this section are designed to help you prepare for your assessment. Working through these pages will give you the opportunity to revise your knowledge of the topics you have been studying and to gather together notes and information that will be useful when you complete your assignment.

TIPS

The grading criteria for Learning Aim A use different verbs such as **identify**, **outline**, **describe**, **discuss** and **evaluate** and it is important to understand the difference.

It helps to know what the words **identify**, **outline**, **describe**, **discuss** and **evaluate** mean.

Imagine you are being asked the same questions about something very simple, such as the pen with which you are writing.

Identify what it is. *It is a pen.*

Outline what the pen is. *It is a plastic pen for making marks on paper.*

Describe the pen. You could say: *The pen has black ink and is a ballpoint pen with a lid.*

Discuss what the pen is. *It is an ink pen that is used by people to write information on paper.*

Evaluate the pen. *The pen is not very good because it leaks and leaves marks on the paper. It is uncomfortable to hold because it is quite narrow. However, it was affordable and it has not run out of ink yet. It does the job I need it to.*

CHECKPOINT

Strengthen

- **Describe** how children's growth and development are measured using growth charts and developmental milestones.
- **Identify** the five different areas of development.
- Give examples of children's growth and development in each of the five areas from birth to 5 years.

Challenge

- **Describe** how growth is measured in individual children.
- **Describe** how milestones in development are determined.
- **Discuss** why children who are behind in communication and language skills are often also behind in their cognitive and intellectual development.
- **Describe** how children need to develop emotionally to be able to successfully develop their social skills.
- **Evaluate** how children's physical skills, such as fine motor skills, are closely linked to their cognitive and intellectual development.

ASSESSMENT ACTIVITY   LEARNING AIM   A

Produce a guide for parents of a new baby.

The guide needs to **outline** how their child's growth will be measured and how their growth will be compared against expectations.

Discuss why growth and development should be measured.

In your guide, provide a timeline of expectations for children's development from birth to 5 years old in:

- physical development
- cognitive and intellectual development
- communication and language
- social development
- emotional development.

Evaluate how each aspect of development impacts upon the other.

TAKE IT FURTHER

Evaluate how having a weakness in one area of learning and development can impact upon another.

Explore how being particularly advanced in one area can be beneficial for other areas of development.

For example, *children who quickly develop speech and language are often more advanced in their emotional development. This could be because they are more able to express themselves and talk about how they are feeling.*

TIPS

Remember how different aspects of development affect each other. If children are not encouraged they are unlikely to persevere and complete tasks.

Consider the different type of development that happens within each area. For example:

- Physical development involves the gross and fine motor skills as well as hand–eye coordination.
- Emotional development involves building self-esteem and understanding emotions and behaviours.
- Social development generally happens in stages during play and involves children forming attachments to others.
- Communication and language starts as babbling, then moves to using individual words and then sentences.
- Cognitive and intellectual development involves children using all of their senses, recognising their sense of self and their ability to problem solve.

Physical factors that affect growth and development: prenatal (1)

KEY TERMS

Genes are inherited from both parents and are made up from DNA that give instructions for making up a human, animal or plant.

Chromosome part of a cell that carries the information that determines traits a person will inherit.

Foetus unborn baby growing in the womb.

Spina bifida a birth defect where bones in the spine do not form properly around the spinal cord.

How well a child will grow and develop can be determined early on, even before they are born. This is because some health factors begin during pregnancy. You might know of some life choices that can harm an unborn child and so should be avoided in pregnancy. How well a child grows and develops depends on different factors. Physical factors, such as the parents' genetics, what a child eats and their state of health; environmental factors, such as where a child lives and what they are exposed to and socio-economic factors, such as their experiences, social group, relationships and their education can all affect a child's growth and development.

Genetics and how genetic abnormalities occur

Genes are information cells passed from our parents. Who we are is determined by our **genes**. They decide our sex, our eye colour, our hair colour and our immediate and future health. Sometimes, there are abnormalities or differences in genes that can cause ill health or disabilities.

Some disabilities are present at birth, while some genetic abnormalities become apparent later. Down's syndrome commonly occurs because each cell in the body has three copies of chromosome 21 instead of the usual two. This is sometimes called trisomy 21. Less commonly, Down's syndrome can occur when part of chromosome 21 becomes attached to another chromosome during the formation of the reproductive cells.

There are physical signs of Down's syndrome that affect the way the person looks, such as a flat facial profile and nose and upward-slanting eyes. People with Down's syndrome might also have poor muscle tone, meaning they are slower to develop physically. People with Down's syndrome generally develop speech later and have delays in their learning.

◘ **Table 1.12: When do abnormalities occur and what do they cause?**

Type of genetic abnormality	Explanation of when the abnormality might occur	Genetic illness
Autosomal dominant	Autosomal dominant abnormalities occur when one mutated copy is passed down from one parent. This gives a 50% chance that a baby will inherit such a condition.	**Huntingdon's disease** affects around one in every 15,000 births and is due to an autosomal dominant gene. Huntingdon's disease can cause jerky movements and muscle problems. It can affect balance and cause difficulty with speech. People with Huntingdon's disease might find it more difficult to learn new things.
Autosomal recessive	Autosomal recessive abnormalities occur when two copies of the gene are passed on (one from each parent). This gives a 25% chance that a baby will inherit such a condition.	**Cystic fibrosis** is a condition that affects around one in every 2,000 births and is due to an autosomal recessive gene. Cystic fibrosis affects the lungs, pancreas, liver, kidneys and intestine. People with cystic fibrosis suffer frequent lung infections and may be underweight due to not being able to absorb enough calories.
X-linked dominant	When a mother is affected by an x-linked abnormality her children have a 50% chance of being affected. All fathers affected by an x-linked dominant abnormality will have affected daughters but not sons. However, if the mother also has the x-linked dominant abnormality, sons might also be affected.	**Haemophilia** is a condition that affects around one in 10,000 births and is an x-linked dominant gene. This affects mainly males. It affects the body's ability to make blood clot. As a result, injuries can be very serious as heavy bleeding can occur. People with haemophilia might avoid some sports that could cause injury. Good dental hygiene is important as gum disease can cause bleeding. Children with haemophilia might not be able to join in with the same physical activities as others.

Maternal nutrition and exercise

Parents cannot change their genes or prevent genetic abnormalities. However, parents can take action to make sure that they are healthy during pregnancy.

Healthy eating

During pregnancy, a healthy diet helps to provide a **foetus** with all the nutrients that it needs to grow and develop. Lacking in vitamins and minerals can lead to the foetus not developing correctly. It is recommended that foods high in folic acid are eaten in pregnancy to reduce the risk of **spina bifida**. Some foods are best avoided during pregnancy, such as soft unpasteurised cheeses and pâté. This is because they are thought to link to an increased risk of miscarriage or premature birth. Babies that are born prematurely are at a higher risk of some health conditions, such as cerebral palsy, vision problems and learning disabilities.

Exercise

It is not a good idea to suddenly take up strenuous exercise while pregnant. However, regular, gentle exercise, such as swimming and walking, can help with fitness in pregnancy. Being physically fit and active can help to maintain a healthy weight gain and prepare the mother for labour. Being overweight in pregnancy increases the risk of miscarriage, gestational diabetes and high blood pressure. Having high blood pressure in pregnancy can lead to the baby needing to be born early.

Effects of parental drug or substance abuse

Harmful substances

Taking drugs and other harmful substances during pregnancy, such as alcohol, is never good for health. It also poses a risk to the unborn baby. Babies that are exposed to toxic substances can be born with deformities. This is because drugs and alcohol are toxic and affect the foetus at the early stages of development. Later on in pregnancy, the unborn baby is exposed to harmful substances as they cross the **placenta**. This can lead to premature birth, death, being born suffering from withdrawal to drugs and learning disabilities.

Drinking too much alcohol in pregnancy can lead to foetal alcohol syndrome. This is where alcohol passes through the placenta and can damage cells in the brain, spinal cord and other parts of the baby's body. This causes the child to be born with physical and mental disabilities.

◧ Down's syndrome commonly occurs because each cell in the body has three copies of **chromosome** 21 instead of two

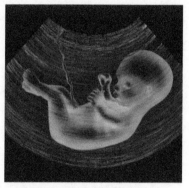

◧ Before birth the baby's future is being determined by its genes. There have been advances in detecting abnormalities early on in pregnancy. Why do you think some people are unhappy about this?

Physical factors that affect growth and development: prenatal (2)

GETTING STARTED

Take a few moments to practise being 'mindful'; this means clearing your mind, breathing deeply and becoming aware of your body relaxing.

Do this for a few moments. How do you feel afterwards?

Development begins from the moment of conception. Understandably, children's growth and development can be affected by their experiences before their birth. This is why it is important for mothers to look after themselves in pregnancy to help babies have the best possible start in life.

Why do you think that medical professionals are keen for mothers-to-be to attend regular antenatal appointments?

Mother's mental health

Pregnancy involves lots of changes to hormones and can affect the mother's mood and emotions. This is sometimes called 'baby blues' and is perfectly normal after the baby is born. The mother's hormones will soon return to normal after a few days. However, just like ill health involving any other part of the body, some people experience poor mental health. Some women are already living with mental health problems when they become pregnant and others may experience problems because of hormonal changes during pregnancy.

Having mental health problems may result in the mother not seeking care during pregnancy and making poor lifestyle choices. Post-natal depression is common after giving birth. A new mother can feel overwhelmed and anxious about being responsible for caring for a new life. Without good support, this can lead to poor attachment between mother and baby or the mother having negative thoughts and feeling desperate. Ultimately, this can mean she isn't able to care for herself and her baby well.

Mental health problems can be linked to other behaviours that could have a negative effect on the mother or the growth and development of the unborn child. Examples include poor diet, poor hygiene, substance abuse, failure to seek medical help for illness, or difficulty in forming relationships leading to isolation and depression.

Sometimes, a person's emotional state means they are not able to think clearly and make good decisions. If someone has significant mental health issues they might feel exhausted and unable to cope, meaning that they neglect the needs of their baby. More rarely, some people feel such a sense of desperation that they might harm themselves or their baby. If a professional is concerned about this, they will need to give the mother lots of help and support.

ACTIVITY

Look at the case study. What do you think the risks are for Belinda and her unborn baby?

Belinda has a long history of depression and self-harm. She is now 34 weeks pregnant. Initially, she seemed positive about the pregnancy and attended all of her appointments with her midwife. In the last few weeks Belinda has missed all of her appointments and does not respond to phone calls or letters from the hospital. At her last appointment, she was underweight and looked dishevelled. The midwife was concerned as she had some deep cuts on her arms.

Why do you think that medical professionals might be concerned about Belinda's baby after it is born?

Imagine you are the medical professional. Write a report about why you are worried about Belinda and her unborn baby's growth and development.

Premature birth

The average length of pregnancy is 40 weeks. Not all babies will arrive on time. Some will arrive later or be 'overdue' and some will arrive a couple of weeks early. Babies that are born before 37 weeks are considered to be **premature**.

This can have an effect on a baby's development.

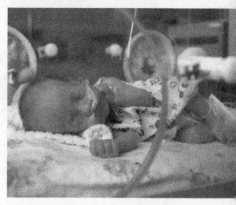

● Table 1.13: Growth of premature babies between 24 and 36 weeks

Number of weeks of pregnancy	Growth of the premature baby
24 weeks	• The baby is covered in fine hair called lanugo. • They have not developed fat so cannot keep warm. • Their eyes are still fused shut and eyebrows and eyelashes haven't developed. • Skin is delicate and thin. • All internal organs are under-developed.
26 weeks	• Lungs are under-developed and babies cannot breathe for themselves. • At this age, their skin has become slightly thicker and they have fingerprints.
30 weeks	• Vital organs are developed, but babies at 30 weeks will usually still require help with breathing. • Babies at this age have a weak sucking reflex, but can digest milk. • They might be physically small and have a large head and small body.
34 weeks	• The bones are now fully formed, but the lungs are not yet fully developed. • Babies can now suck, but get tired very easily so they cannot take in enough nourishment.
36 weeks	• Babies still do not have enough fat to keep themselves warm and their lungs are still not fully formed, but babies born at 36 weeks look more like full-term babies.

● At 24 weeks gestation, 40% of babies will survive. Just two weeks later at 26 weeks, around 77% of babies will survive.

KEY TERMS

Premature a baby born before their expected date of arrival. Medically, this is before 37 weeks of pregnancy.

How prematurity affects development

Being born prematurely can sometimes have an effect on children's development; this might include:

● Poor muscle tone: can mean that the child takes slightly longer to crawl or walk.

● Smaller in height and weight than peers: can mean children are 'babied' by other children the same age or adults have lower expectations because they perceive them as being younger.

● Delay in meeting developmental milestones: can mean that children need extra help to catch up with their peers.

● Hearing difficulty: can delay speech and can mean that children are less able to make relationships with others.

● Sight problems: can delay development and can mean that children need extra care to keep them safe.

● Cerebral palsy: can cause muscle weakness or, in more serious cases, can mean that children need lifelong special care.

● Learning difficulties: can lead to children not being able to develop at the same rate as their peers.

● More likely to have attention deficit hyperactivity disorder (ADHD): can lead to social difficulties.

DID YOU KNOW?

Albert Einstein, Isaac Newton and Charles Darwin were all born prematurely.

CHECK MY LEARNING

Have a discussion on your table about possible reasons why a foetus's growth may be delayed in the womb.

Physical factors that affect growth and development: health status

As children grow older, different factors affect their ability to grow and develop well. It is important for parents and carers to focus on promoting children's good health through diet and exercise. Can you think why young children might need a different diet compared to adults?

Health

Young children are more prone to ill health because their immune systems are not fully developed. Young children are also less able to prevent ill health, such as through washing their hands regularly, and helping to prevent the spread of infections through covering their mouths when they sneeze and cough.

There are different types of ill health. All can have a serious impact on children's growth and development. Some types of ill health can be life limiting, meaning that the child is not expected to live an average life span.

Examples of different conditions that affect children's health

Asthma

This is a common chronic disease of the airways in the lungs. It causes wheezing, tightness of chest and coughing. It can, in serious cases, result in death. Most children are able to take medication to keep their asthma under control. Although there is no cure, it can improve with age. Children with asthma might be less able to take part in physical activities due to being out of breath. If asthma is difficult to control, children might spend long periods in hospital and so miss out on mixing with others at nursery or pre-school.

Epilepsy

This is a common **chronic condition** where electrical bursts of activity in the brain cause seizures. These might be experienced in different ways by different people. Medication and sometimes surgery on the brain can help to control the condition. Children with epilepsy might be exhausted after having a fit. They may become very tired and as a result be too tired to concentrate and learn.

Cancer

This is a common illness that can affect any part of the body. It is where abnormal cells invade or spread in the body, causing damage to healthy tissue and organs. Cancer can be a chronic or **acute condition**. This is because it can cause long-term health issues. However, in some cases, it can be treated quickly.

There is a range of different treatments for cancer and advances are happening constantly in improving the lives of people with cancer. Treatment for cancer usually takes some time. It can affect children's physical appearance, for example they may lose weight or their hair. This can mean that other young children are confused by their appearance and do not play with them. This can be upsetting. Along with missing out on playing and mixing with others, children with cancer can feel lonely and isolated.

■ Asthma is a common condition that can be very serious

Sepsis

This is a very serious acute condition that can lead to multiple organ failure and death. It is a rare complication of an infection. Treatment is only effective in the early stages and includes antibiotics, fluids and oxygen. Sepsis can also lead to the need for amputation of limbs. Children who have experienced a serious acute illness, such as sepsis, will need a great deal of support to recover. They may need to learn to walk again and will often have memory loss and a delay in their learning. They might have a new physical appearance and this will affect their confidence and willingness to join in with others.

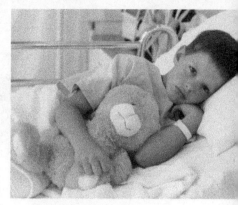

ACTIVITY

Choose a health condition to focus upon.

Design a poster that alerts others about how the condition can impact on children's growth and development.

For example:

Children who develop cancer will need to spend lots of time in hospital receiving treatment. The medication that they need to take can make them very vulnerable to infections. As a result, they cannot attend pre-school, nursery or school. This means they miss out on interacting with other children their age, which affects their social development. Being unable to eat because they are unwell can mean children become underweight.

■ Children with chronic ill health often spend time in hospital. How do you think professionals support children to reduce the impact of illness on development?

KEY TERM

Congenital disorder a condition that a child is born with.

■ Table 1.14: The effects of ill health on children's growth and development

Age	How ill health affects children's growth and development
0–18 months	Young babies are at greater risk from ill health. Chronic ill health affects babies' ability to grow and put on weight. Some conditions, such as asthma, make it difficult for babies to breathe while feeding. Weight loss in young children is serious and can be life threatening. Babies with chronic or life-limiting conditions are likely to spend a lot of time in hospital and so they might have difficulty forming attachments and become 'clingy' with their main carer.
18 months–3 years	As children get bigger and their bodies grow stronger, their ability to cope with serious illness increases. Chronic conditions can mean that, at this age, children are smaller than average. This can affect their ability to use play equipment and join in with their peers. Children might have lots of adult attention because of their ill health. This can mean that they are more comfortable around adults than children their own age meaning they can find it difficult to join in with other children's games, making it harder to make friends. It can also mean they have good communication skills and a wider vocabulary.
3–5 years	By this age, children might start to realise that they are different. Some ill health affects the way children look and act. This can mean that other children treat them differently. They might find this frustrating and it can affect their self-image. If children spend long periods in hospital they might miss out on attending pre-school, nursery or school. This can impact on their learning. For example, they might not have had experience of playing in large groups before and find the noise and crowded spaces overwhelming. Spending time in hospital can mean that children lack opportunities to use their physical skills, meaning some aspects such as balance and coordination are delayed.

CHECK MY LEARNING

Identify one chronic condition and its effects.

Identify one life-limiting illness and its effects.

Suggest ways that professionals and parents might help with the child's development in each case.

Physical factors that affect growth and development: diet and exercise

A healthy diet

What we eat affects our health positively or negatively. From birth, parents have to make choices about how to feed their children. Research tells us that breastfeeding is best for babies. It helps babies to build an emotional bond with their mother, protects from illness, and reduces the likelihood of obesity later, which could impact on physical development and health. Breast milk is packed full of antibodies that can help boost a baby's immune system. However, not all women are able to breastfeed. Babies who are not breastfed are given specially formulated powdered milk.

Everyone needs to eat a balanced diet. This is a mixture of carbohydrates, proteins, fats, vitamins and minerals, milk and dairy. Not eating a good diet can lead to deficiencies that can affect health. Young children need to have a portion size equivalent to the size of the palm of their hand.

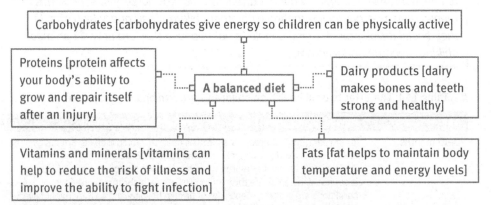

Figure 1.6: Young children need to eat little and often to help their bodies to grow

Table 1.15: The effects of diet on children's growth and development

Age	How diet affects children's growth and development
0–18 months	Up until around 6–9 months, babies only need milk to keep them healthy. As they grow older milk is not enough. A balanced diet is essential to help a child to grow. Lack of essential vitamins and minerals can make babies irritable and less likely to sleep well. Sleep is important for babies because this is when their bodies grow.
18 months–3 years	Children are now much more mobile so they need the right foods to give them energy. Young children need to eat little and often to help power their bodies. Without suitable foods children will become lethargic (sluggish and tired) and less likely to want to be active and learn.
3–5 years	As children get older they need to have enough food to help them to concentrate and learn. Some food additives and colourings have been found to affect children's concentration and behaviour. Food that is high in sugar leads to children gaining weight and having high energy followed by very low energy. This can make them disruptive and behave badly.

Too much or too little of an individual food group can make children unwell. Not enough vitamins and minerals in their diet can lead to the child's body being slow to heal. Hair and nails might become brittle and they might become constipated. In serious cases, being deficient in vitamin B12 can lead to anaemia. If left untreated, this can cause permanent damage to the body. Eating a balanced diet helps to prevent dietary deficiencies.

Exercise

It is not just what you eat that affects your health. Exercise is another component of being healthy. It is advised that children under the age of 5 are active for at least three hours a day spread out through the day. Children could ride bicycles, play on trampolines, crawl through tunnels or go swimming. Any activity that involves children moving their bodies is exercise. Young children who can walk should be encouraged to walk instead of being strapped into a buggy. This encourages their locomotion, coordination and balance. Being an overweight child usually leads to being an overweight adult and that has risks for health, such as diabetes and heart disease.

Children should maintain a healthy weight and take part in as much activity as possible. Being overweight can affect children's self-esteem and confidence. It can lead them to not feeling confident to join in with social activities and this can affect their well-being.

Exercise is fun for children and should be part of their daily routine. How else can parents and carers encourage children to be active?

■ Table 1.16: The effects of exercise on children's growth and development

Age	How exercise affects children's growth and development
0–18 months	Babies need to have space to move and stretch their muscles. They need to flex and strengthen the muscles in readiness for crawling and walking. Children at this age have bursts of energy and get tired quickly, so they need to rest and sleep often.
18 months–3 years	As children get older they need to sleep less and can be active for longer. Children need to build up stamina. Without the opportunity to run and enjoy freedom in their movements, they might be delayed in walking and developing their gross motor skills. This can lead to them having more frequent accidents.
3–5 years	Children should be physically active for three hours a day. This is to help reduce the risk of obesity and to make sure that children are healthy and growing well. As children get older a daily routine of exercise and fresh air helps them to concentrate and learn.

CHECK MY LEARNING

Plan one hour of activities for a 3-year-old child. It should include a suitable snack halfway through.

Your plan needs to suggest different ways that the child will be physically active and how this might promote their intellectual, emotional and social development.

Environmental factors that affect growth and development: housing

Where a child grows up and those around them can affect their lives. There has been lots of research that suggests that where you grow up and what experiences you have shape your future life. Experiencing **housing needs**, such as not having suitable housing or having to move to temporary accommodation, can be very distressing for children and their families. This can mean some families live in **areas of deprivation**. These might be areas where there is poor quality housing, overcrowding and high rates of crime.

Why do you think some families might not have a permanent home?

Living in a house that is safe and secure is taken for granted by many people. However, not everyone has the luxury of having a roof over their head. There are many reasons why families find themselves living in poor quality or temporary housing. Losing your home or living in poor quality housing is incredibly stressful and can lead to long-term difficulties, such as debt, depression and poor health. This can affect a person's capacity to parent and affect children's well-being.

◻ Many people take living in a house that is safe and secure for granted

Families that live in poverty often face social deprivation; this means not having normal interactions with the rest of society. They are also likely to be deprived of the essentials in life, such as food, clothing, warmth and amenities.

■ Table 1.17: The effects of housing on children's growth and development

Age	How housing can affect children's growth and development
0–18 months	Babies who live in cramped housing might not have a peaceful place to sleep. Noise and light disrupt sleep, leaving babies restless, tearful and unhappy. A quiet space can help babies to sleep well. The family might not have room to store suitable equipment for babies meaning that they might be more at risk of accidents. Having more space can allow babies to move around, especially as they practise learning to crawl and walk.
18 months–3 years	Children that have to move house often might find it difficult to settle. Parental stress at moving frequently might lead to family arguments and children not having attention from parents to help them to learn. A stable family home can help parents to develop relationships within the community that can be good for young children's social development, too. Overcrowded accommodation can mean that there is little space for children's toys to help them to learn. Having their own space can help children to understand about their own belongings and help them to gain a sense of identity.
3–5 years	Children who move house often might miss out on attending pre-school, nursery or school. This means that they do not start to form friendships with others and this can affect their learning. Living in a flat might mean that children do not have access to an outdoor space to play, so they cannot develop their large muscles as well as those with an outdoor space. Having a quiet place to rest and sleep helps children to wake up refreshed and ready to learn.

ACTIVITY

Look at the three case studies below.

Draw up a table identifying how you think each might affect children's growth and development.

Case study 1
Inka is 3 years old and lives with her mum. They are currently living in a hostel which is miles away from family. They hope to be re-homed soon. Inka is frightened as she is often woken up at night by other residents in the hostel.

Case study 2
David is 5 years old. His father has lost his job. His mother does not work. His parents cannot afford to pay their mortgage and their house is being repossessed. This will mean that the family will be homeless. David's mother suffers from depression and his father is under a lot of stress.

Case study 3
Tomas is 8 months old and his family live on the 18th floor of a block of flats. There is a high level of crime on the estate and Tomas's mother is too frightened to go out without her partner, who works long hours.

CHECK MY LEARNING

Give examples of the effects on aspects of a child's growth and development of living in poor housing conditions.

Assess the impact on growth and development of living in poor housing conditions.

Environmental factors that affect growth and development: the home

Where a child lives and their home situation will affect their growth and development. Unfortunately, not all children live in a home where they are safe. The NSPCC identified that there were over 51,000 children identified as needing protection from abuse in 2017.

Do you know what work the NSPCC does?

Abuse and neglect

There are four main types of **abuse**.

Physical

This is where children are deliberately hurt and can result in injuries, such as broken bones, cuts, bruises or burns.

Sexual abuse

This is where children are forced or coerced into sexual activity or exposed to sexual activity.

Neglect

This is a failure to meet children's basic needs, which causes ongoing harm.

Emotional

This is where actions or words are used to affect children's self-esteem and well-being.

These are not the only types of abuse. Children might also be exposed to online abuse even at a young age before they are able to use a computer themselves, domestic violence, aggression, child trafficking (where children are moved, often between countries, for **exploitation**, such as to obtain state benefits or to be abused by adults), female genital **mutilation** (which is a form of illegal surgery on females).

Child abuse has an immediate and sometimes long-term effect on children. Help is available for anyone who is concerned that they are the victim of abuse or they know someone who is being abused. Do you know who you could call if you had a concern about child abuse?

How abuse affects children's growth and development

Abuse always harms children. It can have an effect on every aspect of their development.

■ Table 1.18: The effects of abuse on children's growth and development

Area of development	How abuse can affect this
Physical	Children who suffer from neglect might be underweight and lack energy. Children might have injuries, such as broken bones, that affect their ability to grow properly.
Intellectual/cognitive	Children might have difficulty in concentrating. Children who are emotionally abused might fear failure and lack self-esteem so could be reluctant to try new things.
Language and communication	Children suffering from abuse might be reluctant to talk and appear quiet and withdrawn. They might develop a speech difficulty because of their anxiety.
Social	Children who have experienced violence might be aggressive themselves and find it difficult to make friends with others. They might be mistrustful. Children who experience neglect might hoard toys and find it difficult to share.
Emotional	Children might be very nervous, anxious and wary of adults, meaning that they cannot build trusting relationships with them. They might use self-comforting or self-harming, such as excessive chewing on clothes or head banging. Children might, in contrast, demand attention and have emotional outbursts.

Parental conflict

Children who grow up in households where there is constant **conflict**, such as arguing, shouting or physical aggression between adults, are victims of abuse. In the early years, children learn everything they know from the people around them. Therefore, if they see aggression, violence and verbal abuse, they will think that this is a normal way to act. Young children might be woken by arguments at night so their sleep is disrupted. They might also become anxious and fearful and find it difficult to want to play and learn.

■ Table 1.19: The effects of the home on children's growth and development

Age	How the home environment affects growth and development
0–18 months	Babies who suffer abuse will be slow in developing. They might have poor attachments to adults. Babies might cry often.
18 months–3 years	At this age, children might appear withdrawn and unable to play. Suffering abuse and parental conflict might mean that children are nervous and scared. They might show signs of distress, such as rocking or head banging. They might show little interest in playing.
3–5 years	Children that have spent time growing up around violence and abuse often do not know that this behaviour is wrong. This might mean that they act in an aggressive way and find it difficult to get along with other children. Children who have suffered neglect might be behind in their development, might speak less and might appear to have a lack of interest in playing and learning.

Environmental factors that affect growth and development: drugs, alcohol and smoking

Alcohol is often portrayed on television and in films as being glamorous and exciting. While drinking alcohol in moderation is not a concern for adults, heavy misuse of alcohol can have a devastating impact on a person's health and well-being.

Use of illegal drugs has different potential consequences. Not only will they make the user unwell and unpredictable in their behaviour, they can also lead to criminal activity and possibly imprisonment. Unpredictable and criminal behaviour poses a risk to children. If a parent is imprisoned, this can have financial, social and emotional implications for the family.

Smoking, though legal, has serious risks to health. Children who inhale second-hand smoke are at risk of developing cancer and breathing difficulties. Breathing conditions, such as asthma, are made worse by cigarette smoke.

Mothers are often asked about their alcohol and drug use and whether they smoke during pregnancy. Why do you think doctors might need to know this?

The effects of alcohol on children's development

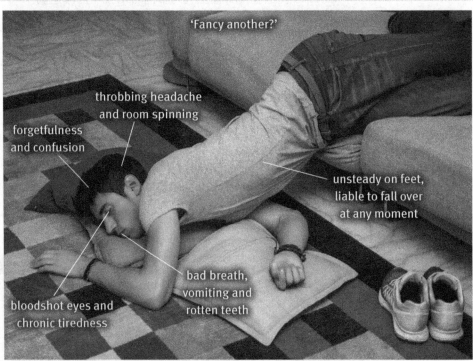

'Fancy another?'

throbbing headache and room spinning

forgetfulness and confusion

unsteady on feet, liable to fall over at any moment

bad breath, vomiting and rotten teeth

bloodshot eyes and chronic tiredness

◾ Do you think this person would be able to parent well?

If a parent or carer consumes alcohol there can be a harmful effect on children.

Drugs

There are two types of drugs; prescription medication and illegal drugs. **Prescription drugs** are drugs that have been given to a person by a medical professional. However, if these drugs are not used in the way the medical professional has prescribed, this can be detrimental to health. **Illegal drugs** do not have a medicinal purpose and have not been prescribed by a medical professional.

Consuming alcohol and drugs can have a negative effect on the individual such as:

- impaired judgement – can lead to parents missing feeds for babies, allowing young children to engage in dangerous behaviours or leaving children with people who are unsuitable to care for them
- more frequent accidents – the parent could fall on the child or while carrying them. They might break furniture or equipment, making it dangerous. If the parent drives, children are at serious risk of being in an accident
- poor physical and mental health – parents might neglect children's basic needs, fail to support their learning and disrupt their ability to make good attachments with other people
- confusion and forgetfulness – serious accidents, such as fires, can occur as parents might forget to switch off cookers and equipment. The parent might forget to collect children from nursery or school, meaning the child becomes distressed
- erratic and dangerous behaviours – erratic behaviour is frightening for children and leaves them with low self-esteem. They might also start to copy behaviour, leaving them liable to have accidents
- drugs and alcohol are poisonous to young children and, if they are able to get hold of them and consume them, it can be fatal.

Smoking

Smoking cigarettes damages health. Secondary smoke or passive smoking is also damaging to health. Children who breathe in smoke are more at risk of:

- respiratory difficulties
- ear infections
- eye infections
- worsening asthma
- some cancers.

It is illegal to smoke in public places and in 2015 it became illegal in England to smoke in a car with children inside. Smoking increases the risk of sudden infant death syndrome, where babies can die without any identifiable cause, and can also contribute towards the likelihood of children developing glue ear. Glue ear can affect children's hearing and lead to a delay in developing language and communication skills. Children who live in households where parents smoke might be more prone to breathing problems and this can restrict their physical development.

Parental health

There is lots of help and support for parents and carers who have difficulty with alcohol use, drug use and smoking. Doctors can provide support to help stop smoking, such as nicotine patches, chewing gum and nicotine replacements. Midwives and the National Health Service provide programmes that can help with reducing alcohol consumption. Those who are addicted to drugs can have drug replacement medication and attend programmes to help them to quit drug use.

Effects of exposure to smoking, alcohol and drugs on children's growth and development

There is very little difference across the age groups we are focusing on to exposure to substances. Parents who abuse alcohol and drugs have a poor ability to parent and this often leads to children being neglected.

ACTIVITY

Write a report about how a parent's alcoholism or drug taking can make them less able to parent children under 18 months and under 5 years old.

Consider the following areas:

1 Meeting children's physical needs

2 Meeting children's emotional needs.

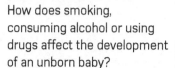

CHECK MY LEARNING

How does smoking, consuming alcohol or using drugs affect the development of an unborn baby?

What long-term effects might there be on the child?

Socio-economic factors that affect growth and development: discrimination

When looking at **socio-economic** factors we look at the relationship between social and financial factors.

Why do you think that income or lack of it has an impact on children's growth and development?

Discrimination

Discrimination occurs when assumptions are made about a person or group of people and they are treated less favourably as a result. Discrimination can take place for a variety of reasons, such as gender, race, age, social background or ability.

Social exclusion

Where someone lives and a low income can lead to them suffering a lack of opportunities compared with other people. The introduction of early years funding has meant that more children are able to go to a childcare provider. However, this can pose problems and dilemmas for families on a low income.

ACTIVITY

Look at the two scenarios regarding social exclusion.

1 *At Bluebell Nursery, children are only allowed to play in the outdoor woodland area if they have wellington boots and a waterproof suit.*

2 *Children must wear a full uniform when they start at Hatters Green Nursery School.*

1 How do you think children at Bluebell Nursery might feel if they are not able to play in the woodland?

2 Explain how children might feel if their parents could not afford the nursery uniform.

3 Write a short description of how feeling excluded may affect other areas of children's development.

Race and culture

Racial and cultural discrimination can have a negative impact on even the youngest children's well-being. Even very young children can be the victims of discrimination. For example, babies born of mixed ethnicity might be not quite fully accepted by either ethnic group and this can lead to poor attachments. Some cultural practices, such as dietary requirements, are not well understood by others, leaving children with limited choices of things to eat. This can mean that they miss out on having a balanced diet to support their growth and development.

Children who are in the minority within a childcare setting might feel self-conscious and unable to join in. If staff at the childcare setting do not consider the toys and resources they provide for children, children might not see any representation of themselves. This can affect their self-image and emotional well-being.

Look at the scenario below.

Jessi is 4 years old. He attends a nursery every day. Jessi is interested in fire engines and fire fighters. The nursery wanted to support Jessi and have bought a book about fire fighters, a toy fire engine and firefighter figures. However, all the figures and pictures in the book have the same colour skin and this is different to Jessi's.

If Jessi doesn't see a likeness of himself in the books and figures he might start to believe that he can never be a fire fighter. This might make him feel disappointed and could impact his self-esteem.

How discrimination affects children

- Children might become shy and withdrawn.
- Children might feel isolated from the people and the community where they live.
- Children might find it difficult to form relationships.
- Children could develop a lack of identity and confusion over who they are, affecting their self-esteem.
- Children could be less likely to want to join in with activities and mix with others.

 Children who are discriminated against could become less likely to join in with activities and mix with others. How do you think that might affect their development?

Impacts of discrimination on growth and development

The impacts of discrimination are generally the same for all ages of children. Discrimination leads to significant disadvantage. This can affect children's life chances and their future self-esteem and self-image.

CHECK MY LEARNING

Explain what is meant by discrimination and how it affects children's emotional development. Suggest how early years settings can help to make sure that young children are included and learn about others.

Socio-economic factors that affect growth and development: income and poverty

GETTING STARTED

How do you think the government tries to help families living in poverty?

Conduct some research to find out.

Living in poverty can lead to groups of people being isolated from others. Why do you think this is not a good thing for families with young children?

Poverty

You will have heard of the term 'poverty' but might not know what this actually means. There are different types of poverty and professionals use measures to identify those who are affected by poverty.

- Relative poverty. This is where there is not enough income to afford an ordinary living pattern. Those in relative poverty cannot afford the activities that the average person enjoys.
- Absolute poverty. This is when there is not enough income to afford the basics – food, clothing and shelter.

Why do some families live in poverty?

There are endless reasons why some people find themselves without enough money to meet their personal needs, including:

- parents lose their job
- relationship breakdown
- borrowing more money than they can pay back
- death of a partner
- injury and inability to work
- mental health issues
- being a victim of crime
- disability or illness
- disasters, such as floods or fire.

Mental health problems are more common in people who are living in poverty. Why do you think this might be?

Unemployed and workless households

Some children grow up in homes where their main carer or carers do not work. There might be many reasons for this, such as those listed. Those who are not able to work will usually be reliant on state benefits. People living on state benefits are more likely to live in poverty.

Access to good early education experiences

One strategy that the government has used to help families to get into work is providing free early education for children. This means that all 4-year-olds and some 2-year-olds can go to nursery or pre-school for a set number of hours and their parents do not have to pay. This helps parents to be able to work. Good quality childcare provides children with opportunities for learning that they might not have at home. This improves their chances of doing well in the future.

◼ Research shows children who grow up in households where parents work are more likely to go on to further education and less likely to live in poverty when they grow up. Why do you think this is?

◼ Table 1.20: The effects of poverty on children's growth and development

Age	How poverty affects children's growth and development
0–18 months	Parents might find buying essentials, such as nappies, difficult. The children might have ill-fitting clothing that restricts their movements. Lack of space might mean that children spend long periods in baby seats or small spaces meaning they cannot develop their physical skills, such as crawling and walking.
18 months–3 years	As children get older they need more stimulation. Having little money to afford toys and equipment might mean that children do not have the chance to learn through playing to boost their problem-solving skills. Children who grow up in poverty might have delayed development in all areas. This could be because parents are under stress and cannot give their children time and attention to support their learning.
3–5 years	Good quality early education can help to transform children's lives when they live in poverty. It can provide them with experiences that they cannot have at home. Without good quality early education, children might not develop communication and language skills that they need to be ready for starting school. As children become more aware of their identity and self-image, they may feel isolated from others. This can impact on children's ability to build relationships with others. This is because they might not have clothing or resources that meet their needs.

Although poverty has a negative impact on children, it is important to remember that many people go on to escape poverty and become very successful. Some families experience periods of poverty and go on to improve their situation.

ACTIVITY

Carry out some research about childcare in your local area.

Look for information on one type of childcare.

You might find information on your local authority website or nursery websites.

You could look for opening hours, the ages of children who can attend, how much it costs and what learning activities it offers.

Write a short review about the childcare you have found and explain how you think it might benefit children's physical, intellectual, social and emotional development as well as their communication and language.

CHECK MY LEARNING

Suggest two reasons why people might find themselves living in poverty and explain how living in poverty can affect children's physical development.

Socio-economic factors that affect growth and development: relationships with adults

GETTING STARTED

Identify why a child might be cared for by more than one carer and discuss this in small groups.

Relationships with significant adults

It is important that children form close attachments to their main carers. This helps them to feel secure and loved.

There are ways that parents and carers can help their baby to develop close relationships with them and their main carers, such as:

- holding them soon after birth
- sharing feeding when possible
- holding and cuddling them
- talking to them
- meeting their need for food, warmth, affection and cleanliness quickly
- spending time with them.

Some things can deter the baby from forming close relationships, such as:

- having multiple carers
- not being held regularly
- being left to cry
- rough handling
- lack of eye contact and not being spoken to.

Warmth and affection

Babies love and want to be cuddled. A Canadian study has shown that babies that are cuddled close to their mothers' bare skin after birth develop a more regular heart beat and are able to maintain a stable body temperature. This is especially important for premature babies who cannot easily regulate their own temperature.

Early years practitioners are aware of the need to cuddle babies and young children and show them affection. Young children are naturally trusting and will show affection to others. It is important that they feel a positive and genuine response back to their acts of affection in order to feel validated and secure. As children get older, practitioners teach them about boundaries and children become more sparing with their affection, saving it for those people closest to them.

ACTIVITY

Look at the daily routine below of an 18-month-old baby.

Write a suggestion for ways that the childminder can be affectionate and warm with the child to boost their sense of well-being at each time during the day.

7.30am	child arrives
9am	child shares story with childminder
9.30am	nappy change
10am	childminder takes child to shops and park
11.30am	child helps childminder to make lunch
12pm	child eats lunch
1pm	child gets ready for afternoon nap
2.30pm	child wakes up and has nappy changed
3pm	child plays with wooden bricks with childminder
4pm	child gets ready to go home.

Giving children attention

Parents and carers need to be 'available' for children. Parents and carers who spend their whole time looking at their mobile phones are unlikely to develop good relationships with their children. This is because eye contact and attention is important if children are going to thrive and develop strong attachments and good language and communication skills. Children who receive plenty of attention do not need to seek attention in negative ways, such as behaving badly. When adults take interest and play with children, they make better progress in their learning and development. It also raises their self-esteem and confidence.

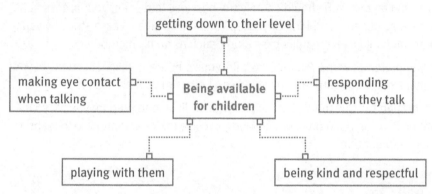

■ Figure 1.7: Ways that parents and carers can show children they are 'available'

■ Table 1.21: The effects of relationships on children's growth and development

Age	How relationships affect children's growth and development
0–18 months	Children who have not had affection and attention might not develop bonds with their parent or primary carer. Poor attachments can affect children's ability to form relationships with other people.
18 months–3 years	Children at this age might be starting to mix with other children. Children learn by copying others. Poor relationships might lead children to act aggressively as they have not learnt how to get along and play with others. This can mean they are not able to play and make friends.
3–5 years	Children who have poor relationships might not be able to express themselves well. They might have emotional outbursts and demand attention. This can be difficult when children are in a group, such as a nursery, pre-school or school. It can affect their ability to learn and make friends.

■ Children learn by copying others. How might an aggressive parent impact on a child's behaviour and development?

CHECK MY LEARNING

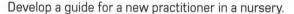

Develop a guide for a new practitioner in a nursery.

Outline how important it is to show children care and affection.

You might want to produce a 'good practice guide' explaining how good practice can promote children's emotional, social, communication and language skills.

Learning aim B: assessment practice

How you will be assessed

You have looked at a wide range of different factors that can affect children's growth and development. Now you need to show your understanding; this will be done through an assignment set by your teacher.

You are expected to explain how physical, environmental and socio-economic factors have an effect and impact on the growth and development of a child from birth to 18 months, 18 months–3 years and 3 years–5 years. You need to include information about prenatal factors. You should choose the best way to present your assessment, such as a study, observation, blog or poster. You may be given a case study by your teacher or you could use a real-life case study, such as family members.

How do you prefer to learn? You might want to make notes, highlight sections of your work or make cue cards with important facts to help with your assessment.

Working through the questions, tips and activities will help to prepare you for your assessment. You can build on your knowledge, revise topics and prepare to respond to your assessment brief.

TIPS

There are three new command words used in Learning Aim B that you might not be familiar with. In Learning Aim A you looked at a simple object, such as a pen, to help understand what the command word was asking you to do.

Using the same approach **explain** what a pen is.

A pen is an ink-filled tube with a nib that is held in the hand to write.

Compare a pen to something else, such as a pencil.

A pen is more effective than a pencil because it doesn't need sharpening. Pens have dark ink so the writing is clearer. Pens do not break as often as pencils. However, pencils are usually cheaper to buy and they can write upside down, pens cannot because the ink runs out.

Assess the pen.

The pen is smooth and easy to write with. It has a thin tube meaning it fits comfortably in the hand. It cost £1 and so was good value for money. The downside of the pen is that the ink takes a moment to dry so can be smudged, making the writing difficult to read.

CHECKPOINT

Strengthen
- Identify one environmental, physical and socio-economic factor that affects children's growth and development.
- Explain how each factor affects children's growth and development for children aged 0–18 months, 18 months–3 years and 3–5 years. You could choose one specific age from each band.

Challenge
- Compare two physical factors that impact on a baby during pregnancy.
- Compare the impact of two factors from each physical, environmental and socio-economic category and state how it impacts on the growth and development of children aged 0–18 months, 18 months–3 years and 3–5 years. You could choose one specific age from each age band.

ASSESSMENT ACTIVITY | **LEARNING AIM** | **B**

Read the following case studies.

Case study A

Oliver was born at 28 weeks of pregnancy. He suffers from foetal alcohol syndrome. His mother and father are both alcoholics. Oliver went to live with his grandmother and then his uncle because his parents did not always ensure that he had sufficient food. He was often left in a soiled nappy. Later he went to live with a foster family. His mother is currently not drinking alcohol so, at the age of 2, Oliver is now back living with her. He has just learned to say mama and dada. When his mother tries to cuddle him he often pulls away. He is smaller than other boys of his age and has just started to walk.

Case study B

Romana is 4 years old and has cystic fibrosis. Due to the stress of caring for a seriously ill child, Romana's parents argued constantly and have recently separated. Romana is living with her mother. Her mother has lost her job and is suffering from depression. She loves Romana and makes sure that she attends nursery every day. At nursery Romana loves to build models and story time. She has made a friend. However, Romana's mother cannot afford the mortgage for the house on her own and is worried about the future.

Case study C

Sanjeet is 8 months old. He lives with his parents on the second floor of a block of flats. This is his third home this year. The flat is cramped and damp and only has one small bedroom. His parents hope to move to a better area soon. There is a problem with vandalism and crime in the area and Sanjeet's parents have been racially abused on more than one occasion. Sanjeet's father works hard and spends long periods of time working away. His mother speaks little English and doesn't generally mix with other local parents as she is afraid to go out alone. Sanjeet cries a lot and his mother tends to spend all day sat watching the television with him trying to entertain him.

- You should identify each factor that will have an effect on the child's growth and development in each case study.

- Using each of the case studies, write or create a study about how the child's growth and development have been affected by physical, environmental and socio-economic factors.

- Explain the ways that each factor might affect the child and the impact this will have upon them.

- You could present your findings as a video report, a wall display or a written study.

- Identify what factors might have an impact on each child's development.

- Explain the reason why this might affect children's growth and development.

TAKE IT FURTHER

Remember to consider how early relationships and attachments are important to children's emotional and social development. When there is indication that families are moving around or children are changing carers, consider how this affects their attachments and ability to form relationships.

- For each case study, check that you have identified two different factors from each of the categories, physical, environmental and socio-economic, and included a pre-natal factor from the three case studies.

- Compare the impact that each factor has had on the growth and development of each child in the case studies.

- Consider the relevance of the different ages of the children.

- Come to a conclusion on the level of impact that each factor has had on the children's growth and development.

- In case study A, assess the impact that pre-natal factors may have on Oliver when he reaches 5 years of age.

- Using the case studies, assess the extent to which factors impact on each child's growth and development.

COMPONENT

02 Learning Through Play

Introduction

Play is both fun and motivating for young children. It helps to promote areas of development and allows children to gain new skills. Can you remember what toys and games you played with when you were 3 years old? What about the activities that you joined in with when you were 5 years old? Play can be different depending on the age of the child. This component details the different stages of play between birth and 5 years old.

You will learn that it is important for adults to provide play opportunities in different settings, such as community settings, early years settings and the home. In what way do you think they would be different?

Singing nursery rhymes can help a child with their communication development; what other activities could help? Have you ever played with a doll or used puppets? Have you thought about how using them has improved your emotional development? Using your knowledge and understanding from this component you will be able to plan suitable activities that will promote learning and development of young children.

LEARNING AIMS

In this component you will:

A	Understand how children play
B	Demonstrate how children's learning can be supported through play.

Stages of children's play: birth–2 years

Play is often seen simply as a fun activity for a child to keep them occupied. However, it is more than just fun; it is a vital tool that children use to gain a better understanding of the world around them. They are able to interact with others and learn mental, physical and **social skills** that are necessary in later life.

Children don't have to be taught how to play; they are born knowing how to do it. Play can be structured or unstructured and at times children may need an adult to support them. As children grow up they can use play as a way to express themselves and develop as an individual. Whatever form play takes, it is a very important part of growing up and learning.

How do you think play helped you to develop your social skills?

Unoccupied play

Unoccupied play usually occurs between birth and 3 months old. It is one way that babies learn about their body and begin to understand how to control their movements. Have you ever watched a baby kicking their legs around and moving their arms? To us, it doesn't seem like play, but this is unoccupied play. Babies will make seemingly random movements with their body, kicking, stretching, grabbing and moving their faces. This is their attempt at learning about their environment and how their muscles move.

Movements of arms and legs help to develop a baby's gross motor skills. Their muscles become stronger which helps when they learn to hold their head up or begin to crawl. Without the development of gross motor skills, a child would find it difficult to perform basic everyday tasks such as walking or climbing. This could prevent them from being able to play with other children.

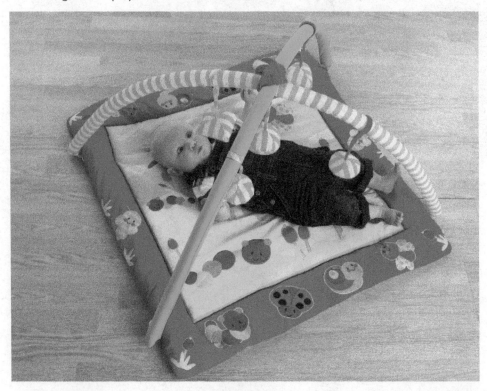

▪ The bright colours are attractive for this baby as he moves his arms and legs around.

Solitary play

Playing alone is a natural step in the process of play. **Solitary play** occurs from birth to 2 years of age. Children are not curious about what others are doing and don't show an interest in playing with their peers. Children will often sit and play with a toy and repeat actions, such as banging a spoon on a pan or moving parts on an activity cube. At times older children may choose to play alone even when they have the skills to play with others.

A small child playing with a treasure basket, taking objects out and exploring them, will be improving their confidence and imagination.

 Although there are other children in the room, this child is happy playing by herself. Why might the child not be ready to play with others?

ACTIVITY

Deborah is concerned about Harrison who is 20 months old. She is worried that he is not joining in play with other children in the same way as his brother who is 3½ years old.

Make notes on what you could say to Deborah to reassure her that his stage of play is expected at this age.

CHECK MY LEARNING

1 Identify the age group for unoccupied and solitary play. Give an example for each stage that identifies the characteristic of that play.

2 Describe how solitary play can give children the chance to:
* use their imaginative skills
* be able to explore.

Stages of children's play: 2–3 years

After the age of 2, children are keen to explore their environment and try to understand what is going on around them. Play allows them to do this. They need to touch each toy or object to work out how it moves, how it makes noises or how to use it. Their imagination is used more and more when playing. As well as trying to understand their environment they are also trying to understand other children.

How do you think 2–3-year-olds differ in play in comparison to younger children?

Spectator/onlooker play

Spectator/onlooker play takes place at around 2 years of age. Watching other children is central to this stage of play. Children are beginning to explore the world around them but still lack the skills to join in with others. This stage is important as children learn through personal interaction with others and the objects in their environment. Children will often notice other children around them and may sit and watch them without talking to them. They are using this time to think about what others are doing and how they are doing it. A child may take part in social interaction, starting to speak to other children and ask questions such as "What's that?" and "Can I have?" However, they do not take part in play.

During an arts and crafts activity in this stage of play, children will watch others play but not play with items, such as the paints or coloured markers, themselves. They may go over to the children playing and ask questions about what they are doing with the paint or offer support by giving suggestions. They may ask the children what they are drawing or tell them what colour they should use.

Limited social skills means that a child could find it difficult to join in play with others.

Parallel play

Around the age of 2–3 years, play has moved from simply observing others to sitting near them and playing at the side of them. This is referred to as **parallel play**. A child will play in close proximity to another child/children but will not join in play with them.

Playing at the side of another child is one way of beginning to build trust around others and to help with social interaction. While playing at the side of others, children are learning what their peers are doing and are starting the process of forming an understanding of others.

Parallel play can lead to new ways of playing and learning new skills. A child playing with blocks may watch another child stack them; this can lead to them mimicking that behaviour and learning the skills associated with construction play.

KEY TERMS

Spectator/onlooker play watching others play but not playing with them.

Parallel play playing at the side of others but not playing with them.

When taking part in creative activities such as playing with playdough, children will concentrate on their own model but will be able to see other children's creations, which will inspire them.

ACTIVITY

1 In small groups, create a role play that shows spectator/onlooker play. You should think about the activity the children will take part in and what other children around them will do at the same time. Carefully plan the questions the children may ask of each other. You should then present your role play to the rest of the class.

2 In your groups, give an example of how a 2-year-old might be playing and the skills a child may develop from parallel play.

CHECK MY LEARNING

1 Identify some examples of parallel play and spectator play.

2 What social skills might a child use when in the parallel play stage?

3 Describe how parallel play can help a child to learn new skills.

Stages of children's play: 3–5 years

By the time a child reaches 3 years old they have developed a sense of what being social is. At this point in their lives they have started developing friendships and have a clear preference for who they want to play with. Children are now more cooperative; they are more able to wait for their turn and share resources and toys. As their communication is now more developed, others around them find it easier to understand them. Vocabulary has increased and children will try to find the words they need to have a conversation with others, they particularly like to ask questions. They are moving away from playing on their own and are now gaining an interest in playing with others. However, playing with other children does not happen straight away. Why do you think this is?

Associative play

 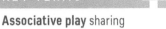
Between the ages of 3–4 years old children start to interact with others, becoming more interested in other children than the toys that are around them. However, there is not a large amount of interaction. This is called **associative play**. This type of play is different from parallel play as children are becoming more involved in what others are doing around them. Children may play the same game/activity or even share toys, but they will be playing in their own way. Social skills are being developed when children start to take turns using resources/equipment and share their ideas and thoughts about what they are doing.

A group of children using the sand pit may look like they are enjoying play together; however, they are acting independently from one another and playing on their own. Children playing in the sand pit will share buckets, spades and other equipment and will talk to each other about what they are creating. But they will be playing on their own. Children are curious and at this age, as they play and watch others, they want to learn more. For example, watching others play with sand can lead children to ask questions such as "Why is the sand soft?" and "How do I make a sandcastle?"

This is an important time for children as they are beginning to develop skills including:
- problem solving
- asking questions such as *How?*, *What?* and *Why?*
- improving socialisation skills
- improving communication.

◧ These children are sharing the blocks but building something of their own. How can this activity develop skills such as problem solving or communication?

Cooperative play

Cooperative play occurs from 4 years onwards. By this time children have acquired the necessary skills to be able to interact with each other for the purpose of play. They will have interest in both the activity and the other children involved. Children will begin to participate and work together towards a common goal.

Key features of cooperative play include the following:

- sharing
- following rules
- turn taking
- negotiating.

At this age, the equipment or toys given to children will often require them to share and take turns, especially if the activity has limited resources. Children will begin to try to follow the rules of the game or activity and learn to understand that winning isn't the most important factor.

▣ **Table 2.1: A summary of the different stages of play**

Stage	Description
Unoccupied	Physical movement of arms and legs by small babies.
Solitary	Children play alone.
Spectator	Children watch others play but may ask questions about what other children are doing.
Parallel	Children will play near others, often sitting next to them.
Associative	Children interact with others and share resources but will play on their own.
Cooperative	Children will interact with others and work towards a common goal.

ACTIVITY

It is important for parents/carers to know the different stages of play their child will go through.

Design a leaflet for parents/carers that explains the different stages and gives examples of how children are playing at each stage.

Show your leaflet to the rest of the class. Have you missed anything?

CHECK MY LEARNING

1 Describe the difference between associative and cooperative play, giving an example of each.

2 Why are language skills important to support children in associative play?

3 Describe the social skills children need to take part in cooperative play.

How play can be organised to promote learning: adult-led play

GETTING STARTED

In small groups, write down what you think 'adult-led play' means. Write a list of the ways you think an adult could lead an activity and why they would do it.

Because it is fun, play is a useful way of helping children to learn and develop new skills. To make sure that children are learning appropriately, adults can organise play. There are three types of play structure that promote learning. Can you think back to when you played games? Was there any structure to them?

Adult-led play

This type of play requires an adult to plan, organise and lead children in an activity. The adult tells the child what to do and how to play. As the activities are focused, children often don't see them as play. **Adult-led** activities are planned with an awareness of the child in a particular setting. They build upon what the child already knows and can do and considers their interests. The adult should carefully plan the activity based on the particular needs of the child and the milestones that they need to meet. The activity will follow a sequence of steps or tasks that children need to complete.

DID YOU KNOW?

Having experiences of play helps to make new connections between neurons in children's brains. These connections can make children smarter!

Did you ever do 'The Wheels on the Bus'? Both of these action activities need an adult to lead. Other examples of adult-led play can include:

- cutting fruit for a fruit salad
- a writing activity to develop pencil grip
- making cards
- cutting shapes
- bat and ball games.

Potential benefits

High-risk activities

Some activities would be high-risk for children if they were to carry them out on their own, as they could be putting themselves or others in danger. This is especially true if they are using high-risk equipment such as scissors, knives or cookers. Having an adult plan and lead the activity means that children are able to participate without the risk of hurting themselves. Children are able to learn specific skills and how to use the resources and equipment safely.

Taking children on a trip to the local park can also be high risk, especially if children need to cross roads. Having an adult lead this activity means that they can help children to climb down from equipment safely.

▣ An adult is needed when children cook to make sure that they know how to use equipment safely.

▣ Adults can give children the confidence and skills to use play equipment safely.

New vocabulary

Communication is important and adult-led play can support language development in children. When taking part in role play, children take on new characters and adults can prompt them to express their feelings and thoughts about a particular topic. This will help children to increase their vocabulary.

Discussions with older children can lead them to share their ideas, their likes and their dislikes. For example, having a discussion about food can encourage children to describe their favourite foods or their most hated foods. They can learn new vocabulary such as 'tasty', 'scrummy', 'slimy' or 'salty'.

Potential disadvantages

Learning is limited by the adult's choice of activity

As the adult chooses the activity or task for children, there will be a main learning focus. Although this may be beneficial in terms of meeting milestones or a particular target, it means that children's overall learning is limited to a particular learning outcome.

When a child becomes distracted adults are likely to bring the focus back to the task. This means that children do not have the opportunity to explore new concepts or skills.

Learning is limited by the time given to the activity

Learning can also be limited if an adult has planned for an activity to take a specific length of time. This can mean they stick to their plan and do not allow children the time to develop their own thoughts and ideas about a topic.

Limited repetition

Repetition allows children to practice the skills they have learned. It can increase confidence and **enhances** learning of new skills. When planning an activity, adults often have a set duration in mind. This can mean that children do not have enough time to repeat the actions/skills they have learned. Without repetition and practice, children will struggle to master skills.

For example, learning to write requires children to hold a pencil in a tripod grasp; this can take time to learn. Without repetition, a child may struggle to hold the pencil in the correct way, as they have not been able to practice, which can affect how they learn to write.

KEY TERMS

Adult-led adults make and lead an activity for children to complete.

Repetition repeating something.

Enhance increase or improve something.

ACTIVITY

At ABC Nursery, Mark is planning activities for a group of 3-year-olds. He has decided to get the children to create a 'shape' display. All the children will cut out different shapes and paint them, then stick them to the wall. When they have completed this activity, Mark will talk about the activity and ask questions.

1 Describe the benefits of Mark leading this activity.

2 In pairs, discuss, and then write down, the potential disadvantages of Mark leading this activity.

CHECK MY LEARNING

1 What is 'adult-led play'?

2 Describe two potential benefits and two potential disadvantages of adult-led play.

How play can be organised to promote learning: adult-initiated play

GETTING STARTED

What types of resources could be left out that would encourage mark-making?

Do you think children would play with them in the way you wanted? Explain your answer.

It is not always necessary for an adult to lead an activity. Adults may want children to learn at their own pace with the security of having resources/equipment chosen for them. Why do you think adults might want children to learn at their own pace?

Adult-initiated play

In this style of play an adult sets up a play scenario for children but does not lead it. The childcare worker or parent/carer will leave tasks and resources out for children but will allow them to complete the activities in their own way and in their own time.

KEY TERMS

Adult-initiated adults provide resources for an activity but let children play with them in a way they choose.

Independent learning skills being able to think, problem solve and act without an adult helping.

Providing resources encourages children to play with them in a certain way, leading them to develop new skills. For example, play money could be placed on a table with empty dishes. This would encourage children to sort the money. Smaller children could be given buckets and spades in the sand pit. Other examples of **adult-initiated** play can include:

- potato printing (leaving potatoes and paint out on tables)
- small world play (farmyard, city block, etc)
- beads and string set out.

Potential benefits

Children will play in new ways

Adult-initiated play allows children to explore the resources they have been given which helps them to learn new skills and concepts. This is because children can choose their own resources and play in their own way. By doing this they are more likely to become engaged and concentrate on the activity.

In the arts and crafts corner a nursery worker could leave out different sized brushes, sponges, cut potatoes and apples, and a selection of different coloured paints. Children will begin to explore the objects. They could stamp apples and potatoes onto paper, squeeze paint from the sponges and mix up paint colours.

Promotes independent learning skills

When an early years setting uses adult-initiated play, adults step back and allow the children to discover things for themselves. Children are able to learn new skills and concepts independently through problem solving and using resources/equipment in new ways.

◫ Leaving a child with a jigsaw they have never seen before will encourage them to problem solve on their own.

Potential disadvantages

Children may not learn the expected skill or concept

Adult-initiated play relies on children understanding the activity that the resources have been laid out for. Unfortunately, children may not always understand what the aim of the activity is and may not play in the way that is expected. This will mean that they do not learn the skills or concepts that adults expect them to learn. For example:

- A child may not use the bucket and spade in the sand but use their hands.
- Children may choose to use only one colour when painting and not learn how to mix a range of colours.

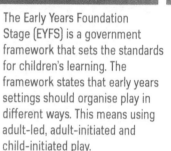

DID YOU KNOW?

The Early Years Foundation Stage (EYFS) is a government framework that sets the standards for children's learning. The framework states that early years settings should organise play in different ways. This means using adult-led, adult-initiated and child-initiated play.

ACTIVITY

Taryn is 3 and has just started nursery. Taryn's mother is unsure how adults at the nursery will provide adult-initiated play and how it will benefit Taryn.

Create a leaflet for Taryn's mum and other parents that:

1 describes adult-initiated play
2 has a range of play activity examples
3 describes the benefits of those activities.

CHECK MY LEARNING

1 In what ways can adult-initiated play encourage new skills/concepts?
2 Explain the potential disadvantages of adult-initiated play.
3 Describe the difference between adult-led and adult-initiated play.

How play can be organised to promote learning: child-initiated play

Play should not always be about what adults want a child to do or what they want them to learn. To make sure play stays fun for children, they should have their own time for discovery so they can play and learn how they want to. When a teacher gives you an activity to do, are you always happy to do it? Could you learn in a better way if you thought of your own activity?

Child-initiated play

Child-initiated play is sometimes called 'free play'. Adults provide a safe environment for the child to explore and try out their own ideas. Children are free to choose their own activity. They are in control of how they play, how long they play for and who to play with.

This type of play is usually more creative and imaginative as children are deciding what they would like to do rather than following instructions.

Adults are able to join in with the children but they must follow the instructions of the child.

Potential benefits

Develop social skills

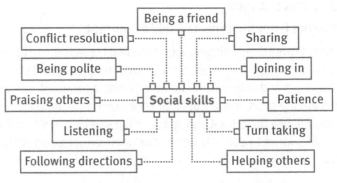

🔲 Figure 2.1: Skills children may develop from child-initiated play.

Child-initiated play provides an opportunity for the development of social skills. As children have chosen the game or activity, they are more likely to play for longer and want to interact with others. As children use the resources and activities around them and begin to interact with the others, they are increasing their development of social skills such as turn taking and sharing.

At times, during this type of play, children will make up games with their own rules. Children may not always agree but this is no bad thing as it encourages negotiation skills and helps children to find ways to work things out themselves.

Develop ideas freely

When children choose an activity or game they often do not see the activity as a learning experience and are more likely to spend time on it and focus. Children often see the environment differently and will play with activities/games in their own way. Child-initiated play allows a child to develop their own ideas more freely.

Potential disadvantages

Children focus on one area of learning or development

During child-initiated play, children may have a strong preference for a particular activity. This can lead to children excluding other play opportunities in favour of their preference. By choosing the same play activity over and over again children are limiting the skills they are learning and so could be limiting their development.

For example, a child that chooses to stack blocks each time may improve fine motor skills and could learn to sort by colour, but they are not developing gross motor skills or skills in expressing themselves.

Children may ignore others

Play is an opportunity to learn, develop and interact with others. However, child-initiated play can lead some children to isolate themselves. Children who prefer to be alone or those who are focused on a particular form of play may not socialise with others. This can lead to a lack of development in social skills.

Learning may be limited

- Children may not learn new concepts or vocabulary as there is often limited contact with adults.
- Without adults encouraging and supporting play, children may find it difficult to expand their knowledge.
- Children with learning difficulties may also find it challenging to participate in some of the activities and could miss out on opportunities to learn/develop new skills because they do not receive sufficient adult support.

☐ Children may move quickly between resources without fully exploring them.

ACTIVITY

Draw a table on A4 paper with three columns and three rows. List the three learning styles and outline advantages and disadvantages of each.

Learning style	Advantages	Disadvantages
Adult-led play		
Adult-initiated play		
Child-initiated play		

CHECK MY LEARNING

1 Define the term child-initiated play.
2 Why might some children not achieve learning goals through child-initiated play?
3 How can this type of play develop social skills?

The role of adults in promoting learning through play: inside and outside play

Fun play activities that promote learning take time and careful planning. Do you think it matters if a play activity is inside or outside? Do you think that children would learn more from group activities?

Organising activities

Play needs to be planned carefully in order to offer exciting and challenging opportunities to children. In a school or nursery adults can organise activities and games to promote learning and allow children to develop and meet their milestones. When planning, adults need to consider the types of activity, the location and if the activity will be for a group of children or just one child.

Some activities can be organised either indoors or outdoors. Sand play is an example of this; a sand tray can be used indoors and a sand pit can be used outdoors.

It is the role of the adult to provide children with resources that are suitable for their age and stage of development. Adults may set out activities and lead play (adult-led play), direct children towards activities and resources and engage them in play (adult-initiated play) or set out accessible resources and provide supervision so that children can choose and experience different types of play independently (child-initiated play).

Inside activities

Indoor play can include:

- messy areas
- book sharing
- small world play
- domestic corners for role play.

Indoor play is organised by adults, for example creative/messy areas, quiet areas for **circle time** and sharing books, construction or small world play, and domestic play corners.

Outside activities

Children should be given extended periods of time outdoors. Activities should allow children to make noise and move freely. As outdoor areas are usually larger, children will be able to access activities/toys they may not be able to use indoors.

Adults should create different areas for the children to play outdoors. They should plan activities suitable for the stage of development and help children to participate in all activities, as well as supervising the use of equipment and resources.

Outdoor play should include woodland and digging areas that allow children to explore and the opportunity to talk about the natural environment. Areas such as climbing frames and trikes can be used to promote physical development, while areas to make dens can be provided to spark a child's imagination. Outside activities should also be provided for babies and small children, such as giving them a soft area to play in.

Individual activities

Activities may be organised for individual children or a group of children. Individual activities can be targeted towards the development stage of a child, their interests and their individual needs.

This little girl is enjoying playing with cooked green pasta. How is that supporting her to learn through her senses?

Between the ages of 0–18 months individual activities are planned for children who are still in the unoccupied or solitary play stages. They are planned to promote development, for example rolling a ball back and forth or using a treasure basket. From around 2 years of age, individual activities can be organised based around a child's particular interest such as construction or water play.

Activities should be carefully planned for children with a developmental delay as their individual needs have to be considered. Adults should provide an individual activity that may focus on a specific area of development for that child. For example, a child that has a speech delay may take part in reading or singing a nursery rhyme with an adult. This will allow them to practice and improve their speech and communication skills.

Benefits of individual play include the following:

- time to think
- few distractions
- a chance to be creative
- a chance to use imaginative skills.
- a chance to explore on their own

Group activities

Group activities allow children from 3 years to socialise with others and develop their social skills as well as learning to cooperate and understand rules. Group activities can also include playing games such as 'If you're happy and you know it' or playing board games. They allow children to have fun together and begin to understand how games work and why they have rules. Examples of group activities include the following:

- making classroom displays
- a tallest tower challenge.
- group construction play

Sensory activities

From the moment a child is born they are constantly exploring the world through their senses. They do this by touching, tasting, seeing, smelling, hearing and moving. Babies will often place things into their mouths, small children make funny noises and older children want to touch things.

It is important that adults plan for sensory play so that children are able to learn about texture, taste and smell.

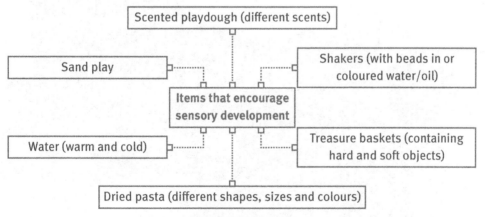

■ Figure 2.2: Items that encourage sensory development.

The role of the adult is to provide suitable sensory materials/resources for the children to use. The materials should encourage children to use a number of senses such as smell, touch and sound. During sensory activities, adults should help children to explore the resources and ask questions.

LINK IT UP

In section A2 of Component 1 you learned about physical development and the senses. Sensory play encourages children to use those senses. Take a look back to remind yourself of the senses.

ACTIVITY

Tinkerbelle's nursery is opening soon and they are planning their outdoor space. They have asked for your guidance.

1 Write a report detailing:
  a) what adults should consider when setting up an outdoor area
  b) why outdoor play is important for children's learning.

2 Create a poster for the nursery that shows activities for one day for children aged 18 months–3 years. Against each activity, outline the role of the adult.

CHECK MY LEARNING

1 Why is it important that adults plan some activities to take place outdoors?

2 What is sensory play?

3 Describe the role of the adult in adult-initiated sensory play.

The role of adults in promoting learning through play: supporting children

A key part of an adult's role in play is to make sure that learning is taking place. Helping children to understand what they need to do during an activity helps them to learn effectively. It is also important for adults to consider the personal interests of children. A child that has no interest in an activity may find it difficult to learn. Why do you think a child may not learn if they are not interested in the activity?

Explaining equipment and resources

How does a child know to spin a hula hoop around their waist? It isn't obvious. Is that the only way to play with it? When children are given an activity, they often don't know what to do. Adults need to explain what the equipment is called and what children should do as well as demonstrate how to use it safely.

■ A 2-year-old is unlikely to have the language to understand an explanation of how to stack blocks, but if they are shown how to they will usually pick it up very quickly.

There are several reasons why it is important for adults to explain equipment and resources to children:

- safety
- so children know how to use the equipment
- so children know the rules of the activity
- to help children to develop confidence.

Demonstrating equipment and resources

Sometimes, simply explaining what a piece of equipment is and how it should be used is not enough for children to fully understand. This is more so for very young children or children who have special educational needs. An activity should always be demonstrated.

Adapting activities to suit personal interests

Adults need to be able to meet the **personal interests** of children in their care. Planned activities should consider what children like to do or what they are interested in at that particular time.

If their interests are considered, children are more likely to feel valued as adults are thinking about their likes and dislikes. It also means that children will be more motivated to take part and enjoy the activities. This will promote learning, as children are more active when engaged in an activity that they enjoy.

ACTIVITY

You have just started work experience at a local nursery. The manager is concerned that some of the staff are not explaining or demonstrating the activities as they should and the personal interests of the children are not being considered. For example, some children were given time in the sand pit but not told how to play or with what equipment. The children then began to throw sand at each other. To make sure this does not happen in other activities, the manager has asked you to produce guidance on introducing a junk modelling activity to a group of children aged 3–5 years.

In pairs:

1 a) Identify the resources and equipment needed.
  b) Detail how the adult should explain and demonstrate how to use the resources and equipment.
  c) Explain how to adapt the activity for a child who has delayed fine motor skills.

2 Present your work to the rest of the class, demonstrating your explanations. Did the class understand your explanations? Could you improve them?

CHECK MY LEARNING

1 Why do adults needs to explain activities to children?

2 How can demonstrating an activity help a child to understand what they should do?

3 If an adult takes a child's personal interests into account and plans an activity, how could it affect a child's learning?

The role of adults in promoting learning through play: equipment and resources

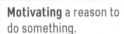
When planning play activities for children, it is important that adults select the correct equipment and resources to promote learning. Any resources that have been selected should be suitable for the age group and the interests of the children. For example, giving 5-year-olds large building blocks for a fine motor activity would not be suitable. At their age they would require something more challenging such as different sized and shaped blocks.

Choosing equipment and resources

When considering a learning activity for a child, adults should focus on equipment and resources that will promote learning. It is important that the activity allows children to want to learn and face some challenges. There are many things that adults need to consider when choosing equipment and resources.

Motivating children to engage

If you thought an activity was boring, would you want to do it? What about if the equipment or resource looked difficult to use? When creating an activity for children, adults need to **motivate** children to want to do it. They can do this in a number of ways.

▣ Why do you think these children are fully engaged in the activity?

- Adults could provide young children around 10–12 months with balls with bells or toys with wheels to encourage them to move around and explore their environment.
- If they are offered colourful and attractive resources, children are more likely to want to take part and learn.
- When children are practicing handwriting it can be helpful to try different approaches, for example using paintbrushes and paints on windows or using chalks outside. These allow children to use their imagination and could help them to engage in the activity.

Promote exploring

Children learn through first-hand experience; this can be on their own or with others. Resources should allow children to use their imagination so they are able to explore their environment and ideas freely. Children should be given a range of resources to play with so that they can choose how they want to explore.

Children like to play with water because they like how it feels. If they are given a range of different resources to use in the water, children can learn in their own way. Resources can include marbles, ping-pong balls and recycled containers. Using these, children can learn about sinking and floating.

Encourage questioning

When children ask questions they are trying to understand their world. Children will learn more from an activity if they feel they are free to ask questions about what they are doing. Asking questions is one way of improving communication and language development and encourages reasoning. There are lots of ways to use resources to enable children to ask questions.

- Select stories suitable for the age group that will capture children's imagination and encourage questions about what is happening or how the characters are feeling.

🔲 New environments can promote exploring. Taking children to a petting zoo allows them to touch the animals and see them interact with each other.

- Using resources that allow children to use their senses can also lead to questions like why? What? And how? For example, an animal listening game, where children have to guess what the noise is, can lead children to ask why a goat sounds similar to a sheep or learn the difference between a goose and a duck.

Set challenges

Equipment and resources should be chosen carefully so that they challenge children but do not make the activity unachievable. For example, giving a posting box with shapes for a child who has not yet developed hand–eye coordination will result in them becoming bored and disengaged. If the equipment or resource is too difficult then children often feel that they can't do it. A gentle challenge can encourage them to think about something in a different way and to develop and practice their problem-solving skills. For example:

- When threading beads on string, children can be given a range of different sized beads or thickness of string.
- Playing dominoes can start with matching pictures. Then, to make it more challenging, the children could move on to dominoes with dots on them. This will allow them to practice their counting. Finally, the dominoes could have numbers on them and children would need to try to remember what the number represents.

Sufficient time

Allowing children sufficient time to complete an activity gives them an opportunity to learn. If a nursery doesn't have enough resources and children must share, it can mean that not all children have enough time to play with the equipment. This can lead to some children missing out on learning opportunities. Time should be considered when planning any activity, for example:

- When planning outdoor time and using the climbing equipment, it is important that the weather is considered as this could also limit the amount of time for the activity.
- Reading takes a long time for children to master. When planning reading sessions adults should choose an appropriate book for the age of the child. Children aged 18 months–3 years are only able to concentrate for a few minutes so books for this age range should be short in length.

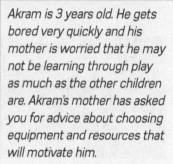

ACTIVITY

Akram is 3 years old. He gets bored very quickly and his mother is worried that he may not be learning through play as much as the other children are. Akram's mother has asked you for advice about choosing equipment and resources that will motivate him.

1 Give three reasons why Akram may not engage with the equipment and resources he is given.

2 Why is it important to choose resources and equipment that challenge Akram?

3 Give examples of equipment and resources that could encourage Akram to ask questions.

CHECK MY LEARNING

1 Identify three types of equipment/resource suitable for outdoor play and describe how these can motivate children to explore.

2 What are the disadvantages of giving children resources that they do not have time to use or explore fully?

The role of adults in promoting learning through play: social skills and health awareness

Children often try to mimic the actions of adults. This can be useful for adults as it is a good way to show children how to behave. Adults can also model specific behaviours or skills that they would like children to mimic, such as communication techniques or how to share and take turns. Why is it important that adults are careful how they behave in front of young children?

Modelling communication

Communication and language are important for a child's development and are essential for building relationships with others and making sense of the environment.

There is a difference between communication and language.
- Communication is the way messages are passed between people.
- Language is the structure for words, such as sentences and the order in which words are used.

Communication and language can be difficult for children to grasp and they will often make mistakes such as pronouncing words incorrectly, not listening and making up words.

For example, small children often have difficulty pronouncing the letter Y. They often say "lellow" instead of "yellow". Parents and childcare professionals can support them with this by encouraging the correct pronunciation early on and modelling the correct way to say Y words.

Language structure can often be a problem for children starting to form longer sentences. They are still trying to understand the rules of language and can get confused easily.

By taking time to talk to children, asking questions and listening, adults are modelling the communication behaviours they want children to mimic.

◻ When trying to say, "I went to the pet shop and saw a mouse," children may say, "I gone to the pet shop and saw mouses."

Joining in with play activities

When adults join in with play, children can understand what they need to do during the activity. It gives parents and childcare workers an opportunity to demonstrate how to play. It also gives children confidence in what they can do as they tend to feel more secure with an adult near them. Playing with children allows an opportunity for questions to be asked, which can encourage communication and further learning.
- A child under 18 months won't automatically know what to do with an activity cube and are likely to need an adult to show them. On their own, a baby is unlikely to realise that the shapes should be placed into the cube in a certain way.
- Games such as 'follow my leader' wouldn't work without a parent or childcare professional, as they are needed to lead the activity and start the game.

◻ During small world play adults could encourage a child to talk about what the animals are doing and what they think a farmer does.

Sharing

Sharing is a social skill and needs to be learned. Children often need help to enable them to share properly. Arguments between children can occur if there is not enough equipment for each child or if all of the children want to play with the same thing.

Sharing is an important part of building relationships and attachments. Young children will find it difficult to share. Modelling sharing practices will demonstrate to children how they should act.

Turn taking

Turn taking encourages sharing and is important for communication. Children who struggle with the concept of turn taking may find it difficult in the future to have a conversation without interrupting.

Baking cakes is a useful activity to encourage turn taking. A parent or childcare professional ensures safety and can pass the bowl around to each child so they get a turn at mixing the cake batter. They could also monitor children for negative behaviours such as snatching or arguments. Questions can be asked about the cakes and children can be encouraged to take turns to talk.

Examples of turn taking can include:
- 0–18 months: peek-a-boo, rolling a ball back and forth
- 18 months–3 years: hand printing, sharing ride-on toys
- 3–5 years: simple dice games, playing on a slide.

Awareness of health and safety

If parents or childcare professionals lack an awareness of health and safety, children may hurt themselves or others. There are two factors that adults need to consider. Is the toy or activity suitable for the age of the child and is it used appropriately?

Adults can check how suitable a toy or activity is based on the age of the child that will be playing with it. For example:
- Children under the age of 18 months place objects in their mouths.
- For these children bigger blocks are safer as they cannot choke on them.
- The blocks need to be wiped clean so no bacteria can get into a child's mouth.
- Smaller blocks can be given to older children, as they are less likely to put them in their mouth.

It can be a health and safety risk if children do not use toys properly or do not listen to instructions from an adult about an activity. For example, children taking part in role play may want to use a belt as a dog lead. Although this is creative and they are using their imagination, this could be very dangerous as a child could choke with a belt around their neck.

Adults should also make sure that when they give equipment to children they have the right skills to be able to use them properly. Risky items such as scissors should not be given to children who do not know how to use them in the correct way.

LINK IT UP

Safety is discussed in more detail in Learning Aim B of Component 3.

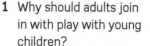

CHECK MY LEARNING

1 Why should adults join in with play with young children?

2 Give some examples of how an adult could join in with play.

3 What is the adult's role in promoting turn taking and what activities could they choose at 0–18 months, 18 months–3 years and 3–5 years?

ACTIVITY

It is UK Health and Safety week. Your voluntary placement at the nursery is coming to an end. Your team leader is keen to promote health and safety in the nursery and has asked you and other volunteers to produce an A3 poster before you leave.

The poster should focus on how the staff at the nursery should consider health and safety when planning activities. When complete, present it to the class and discuss what you included on the poster and why.

Learning aim A: assessment practice

How you will be assessed

In Learning Aim A you have learned that children have different play needs based on their age and development. Between the ages of 0–5 years there are several different stages of play that all children will go through, starting from very simple body movements (the basis of play) leading to play that requires children to socialise and communicate. You have also come to learn that adults can organise play in different ways and need to consider how to organise different play activities so children can learn.

You will be expected to show your knowledge and understanding of Learning Aim A to complete an internally assessed assignment based on the following:

- Show an understanding of the stages of play from birth to 5 years and what the role of adults is in promoting play.
- Discuss how the role of an adult could affect learning.
- Consider how the adult's role can affect how children learn.

CHECKPOINT

Strengthen
- Identify the five stages of play.
- Identify the age group linked to each of the stages of play.
- Outline the three ways play can be organised by adults.
- Describe examples of activities for each of the three styles.

Challenge
- Explain the role of an adult in promoting play and give examples to show your understanding.
- Discuss how explaining and demonstrating an activity can affect a child's learning.
- Discuss how considering health and safety in play can benefit children.
- Assess how different styles of play could benefit or disadvantage a child's learning.

TIPS

Consider what the command word is asking you to do. Think back to Component 1.

Remember that you should include examples to show your understanding of the different stages of play.

When using examples to support your explanation of the different styles of play, make sure you are clear about how they are linked to that particular style of play. Do not simply state that an activity is child-initiated. Your teacher will want to see the reasons why it is child-led.

ASSESSMENT ACTIVITY 1   LEARNING AIM   A

The manager of Happy Springs Nursery has asked that you write a guide for parents which details how children play and the role of adults at the nursery.

Produce a booklet aimed at parents that contains the following:

- Different stages of play between the ages of 0–5 years.
- An explanation of adult-led, adult-initiated and child-initiated play, with examples of activities.
- Discussion on how the role of an adult can affect a child's learning, with examples.
- Advantages and disadvantages of adult-led, adult-initiated and child-initiated play, with examples to support your assessment.

ASSESSMENT ACTIVITY 2 LEARNING AIM A

You have been taking part in work experience at a local nursery for several months. The manager is very impressed with your abilities. The local community centre, which runs a parents and toddlers group, has been in contact with the manager as they require someone to help them understand the role of adults in a nursery setting. The manager has recommended that you give a presentation at the community centre to the staff and parents.

Produce a presentation that includes the following:

1 The difference between each of the stages of play for children aged 0–5 years.

2 An explanation of the three different styles of play, with examples of each.

3 The role of the adult in organising different styles of play.

4 How the adult's role in organising play affects children's learning.

5 The advantages and disadvantages of the three styles of play.

TIPS

You are making a presentation to parents and other adults. You should consider the following:
- the style of writing – it should be professional
- examples to help their understanding.

TAKE IT FURTHER

- Compare the three styles of play and explain how they are similar in terms of their potential benefits and disadvantages.
- Create an evaluation table that shows the different roles of an adult in promoting learning through play. Include an explanation of each aspect of the adult's role with an assessment of how each aspect affects learning.

Planning play opportunities: learning in different environments at different ages

LINK IT UP

To remind yourself about the EYFS framework, go to 'How play can be organised to promote learning: adult-initiated play'.

When planning for play, adults need to consider the environment in which children will be playing. This is because the environment may not be suitable for specific activities or may not have the resources needed. How would play differ for children in a school compared to a nursery?

Learning through play in different environments

Home

A 'home' play environment could be the child's home or a childminder's house. If it is the child's home then it may also be used by siblings. If it is the home of a childminder then there may be several other children. Children feel comfortable in their surroundings as they are used to the layout and it is not as big as a nursery or school. This means that they are less likely to be anxious or worried about what activities they are enjoying and are more likely to engage with adults and others.

Home environments can have limited resources and toys as there is not always a lot of space for them to be stored.

Nurseries

Nurseries are usually run as private businesses to make a profit. Children may attend on a full-time or part-time basis. The adults in the nursery follow the EYFS framework to make sure that children meet their milestones and are developing properly. This means that adults will plan activities and select toys and games to make sure that the children are learning. Nurseries have qualified staff who are trained to work with children and promote development. There are lots of toys and activities available to all children.

Pre-school

A pre-school provides care for children of 4–5 years and helps them to learn the skills needed for starting school, such as reading and writing. Some pre-schools are part of nurseries and some are part of infant schools. Children usually attend part-time; this can include a morning or afternoon session each day. Activities will include drawing and practicing pencil grip as this will help them when they are learning to write. These skills are included in the EYFS *Development Matters* guidelines.

Reception

A reception class is the first class that children go into when they start school at around 4 or 5 years of age and they attend for the full school day. Play and learning in a reception class still follows the EYFS framework supported by the guidelines. Games and activities are planned to promote learning and development. In reception, teachers will build on the skills children have already learned. This might include listening and speaking activities, which build on the communication skills that children have already developed.

Community based groups

Community based groups for play are usually for children under the age of 5. They will often have different groups based on the age of the child. For example, baby group, toddler group or parent and tots group. This is a good way for parents or carers to play with their children and also to meet up with others. New parents who are unsure about supporting children as they learn through play can get advice and talk to others about their experiences. Community based groups often use volunteers. They often take place in churches, community halls or libraries. Typically, children will attend on a part-time basis, often two or three sessions each week. As these groups are run locally they may have less money than a school or nursery. This means that resources and toys can be limited as they may not be able to afford them. The activities may be less structured than in a nursery or reception class. Usually, children have a choice of toys they want to play with and can freely move between toys.

Learning through play at different ages

All children learn through play. The type of play and learning develops as they get older.

0–18 months

Children are more reliant on adults in this age range. Games and activities will use bright colours and noises to attract the child's attention, such as singing nursery rhymes or using a walker. Activities are used to encourage small children to explore and learn how things work and the noises they make.

18 months–3 years

Children now have a better understanding of their environment. They are interested in everything around them and have some skills in movement, such as jumping and climbing. Younger children in this range still rely on adults and may have tantrums if they do not get what they want. Play activities help children to learn some of the social skills they will need when they are older, such as sharing and taking turns. Activities that use shared resources, such as painting or using playdough, are one way of teaching children to share with others.

3–5 years

Within this age range children have already developed some of the key skills for communication and are mastering the use of their fine motor skills. The focus of play moves to letters, numbers and rhyming activities such as sing-a-longs. Activities, such as Post Office role play, help children to develop their imaginative skills; and playing outdoors on climbing equipment and using tricycles and bikes improves their physical skills, such as coordination and balance.

ACTIVITY

1 Create a mind map that shows the different learning environments and a summary of how they differ.

2 Working together in groups of three, make a list of all the nurseries, pre-schools, reception classes and community based groups in your area. Add these to your mind map.

3 Share your list with the rest of the class. Are there any similarities?

4 Make a poster to advertise the different play opportunities at one of the learning environments. You should include the name of the learning environment and how children are able to learn through play whilst there.

CHECK MY LEARNING

1 If a child is nervous about leaving their parents, in which environment do you think they will prefer to learn? Why?

2 In what way are community groups beneficial for new parents?

3 How is play in a reception class different to play in a community-based setting?

Planning physical play and learning opportunities: 0–18 months

LINK IT UP

For a reminder on the difference between fine and gross motor skills, go to section A2 of Component 1.

KEY TERMS

Hand–eye coordination coordinated control of eye movements with hand movements.

Spatial awareness understanding where you are in relation to the objects in your environment.

DID YOU KNOW?

According to the NHS, to be healthy, toddlers that are able to walk should be physically active for at least three hours a day.

◻ This little boy is trying to brush his teeth. How could it be made fun for him?

Physical play for small children supports the development of their fine and gross motor skills. To help with fine motor control children are given opportunities to interact with objects and manipulate them with their fingers. Gross motor skills are developed when children use their larger muscles to help them walk and balance. Do you think an activity that promotes gross motor skills would be the same for a 3-month-old child as it is for an 18-month-old child?

Spatial awareness

Babies have very little foot and leg coordination or **hand–eye coordination**. This is because their muscles have not developed fully enough. By the time they reach 18 months they show more control over their body and are generally able to walk. There are several ways to encourage **spatial awareness**:

- Simple ball games such as rolling a ball to a non-mobile baby will encourage them to touch and push the ball. As they try to reach it they are learning a basic understanding of distance. When they get older and are mobile, children may attempt to kick the ball or even catch it.
- Obstacle courses are a good way of improving spatial awareness. As babies begin to crawl, objects can be placed on the floor so they start to learn to coordinate their bodies. Older children will be able to negotiate an obstacle course as they learn how to get over and under objects.

Hand–eye coordination

Adults can provide children aged 3-12 months with toys with sound to help to promote hand–eye coordination. Children will look towards the sound and be encouraged to reach out and grab them. Older children, 12–18 months, can hold and manipulate objects, so will enjoy scribbling on large sheets of paper and building with blocks.

Activities to stay healthy

Staying healthy is important regardless of age. Babies are encouraged to understand their environment through movement such as crawling and walking. Being physically active is important for growth and development. Babies can be given walkers to encourage them to grasp, pull and push. At around 12 months of age children are more active and should be encouraged to take part in activities that allow them to use all their muscles such as using ride-on toys or taking part in outdoor play. Giving children space to play and run can get them moving and help to keep them healthy.

How to take care of yourself

A baby cannot take care of their own body. They rely on adults to change their nappies as well as feed and clean them. As they grow older, the basics of hygiene should be taught. Up to 18 months of age, babies will place many objects into their mouths as they do not understand what 'clean' means. The lack of understanding can lead to accidents or illness. Children could learn to take care of themselves by taking part in the following activities:

- Routines such as hand washing after a nappy change and before eating can be taught through demonstration but also through song and dance. Singing 'Wash,

wash, wash your hands' to the tune of 'Row, row, row your boat' will help children to remember what they are doing.

- Practising brushing teeth helps to develop the use of children's fine motor skills as they manipulate the toothbrush in their hands.

Gross motor skills

The movement of larger muscles and **body management** begins when a baby is born. **Body coordination** comes from a child kicking their legs and moving their arms around in an attempt to understand their body and the world around them when they are non-mobile. As they become more mobile (by around 9 months) children begin to sit unsupported. Giving toys that encourage children to sit up and to attempt to crawl will develop their gross motor skills.

▣ Table 2.2: Activities to help develop gross motor skills at different ages

Age range	Activity
3–6 months	Prop pillows will encourage children to sit up. A baby can be placed on their stomach, resting on the prop pillow. They are soft and colourful and will often make noises. This encourages the baby to try to touch and move and become more inquisitive. This helps them to explore the world around them and sparks their imagination.
6–12 months	Children have developed their balance enough to be able to sit without falling. A ride-on toy is a great way of improving balance and coordination. The muscles in the child's legs become stronger as they move and distribute their weight evenly. It can also promote the use of other areas of the body such as hands, feet and arms. In this age range, a child's hand–eye coordination and foot–eye coordination is not yet fully developed, so they will struggle with balance and coordination of their body.
12–18 months	Going to a local park is an activity that would be suitable for older children in this age range. Children can run around and attempt to pull themselves up onto some of the equipment. The different floor surfaces, such as grass to sand, will make the children think about how their walking or running has to change so they can move around. It will also spark their imagination.

Fine motor control

Children will master the control of their larger limbs before they develop control over their fingers and toes. At around 6 months old a child can hold an object, at 9 months they will use their finger and thumb to pick it up. The further the development of a child's fine motor control, the more **accurate** they are at **manipulating** objects. At around 15 months children will attempt mark-making and will hold a crayon with their hand wrapped around it. Other activities to improve fine motor control could include the following:

- Using playdough strengthens fingers, hands and wrists as children squish, poke and squeeze it. This develops their smaller muscles so they are able to work on the manipulative skills that will be needed for writing and using technology when they are older.
- Creative activities such as mark-making allow children to practice their grasp and to understand how to make marks on paper.
- To further improve grasping skills, different size crayons or paintbrushes can be used.
- Finger painting is another way in which children can develop fine motor skills, while being creative.

KEY TERMS

Body management skills used to control the body.

Bodily coordination movement of different areas of the body.

Accurate free from mistakes.

Manipulating handling or control over objects.

ACTIVITY

1 Create a table for non-mobile and mobile babies. In it, describe toys/activities that the children can use/play with to support their fine and gross motor skills.

2 Write down how an adult could make brushing teeth a fun activity for an 18-month-old. Share your ideas with the rest of the class.

3 Make a colourful and bold poster that shows a play activity for a 12-month-old that can promote spatial awareness and staying healthy.

CHECK MY LEARNING

1 A 10-month-old baby is crawling; its parents want to encourage walking. What physical activities would you suggest to help the parents?

2 How can promoting fine and gross motor skills to a child under 18 months help them to take care of themselves?

3 Which fine and gross motor skills are used when taking part in play activities that promote staying healthy? Why would these be important for a child's cognitive development?

Planning cognitive and intellectual play opportunities: 0–18 months

KEY TERMS

Imagination using your mind to be creative.

Attention skills noticing and concentrating on something.

Cognitive development information processing, memory and problem solving.

To small children everything around them is interesting. Hearing new sounds, seeing bright colours and understanding how things work and fit together: their brains are trying to make connections with every new piece of information. What do you think when you hear a siren in the street? How do you know what it is?

Planning play activities allows a child to make connections with each new piece of information.

Problem-solving skills

By 4 months old babies, are using all their senses to find out about themselves and the world around them. They have developed enough muscle control to be able to move objects towards their mouth. This is the first step towards problem solving. At around 8 months old, babies begin to see a cause and effect relationship when playing with toys. Banging and shaking can cause movement and noise. As they get older, around 12 months old, they become more interested in solving problems. The activities below require children to be active while promoting fine and gross motor skills.

- Children are naturally inquisitive. Shape sorters and simple jigsaws are a good way to support problem-solving skills. Children will begin to learn about shape and size and understand the link between the spaces available and the pieces to put in them.
- When a child has set their mind on wanting a particular toy then nothing will stand in their way. Placing colourful toys under a box that has holes in and then leaving obstacles around the room encourages children to work out how to get to the toys.

Imagination and creativity

By around 8 months old, children will begin to use their **imagination** when playing with toys and games. Providing activities that stimulate their imagination opens them up to new ideas and possibilities.

- A simple digging activity can encourage the imagination of a child aged 15–18 months. Coins or small toys hidden in sand or mud can allow a child to create a story. Adults can ask questions as children are digging to ensure that their imagination is being used.
- Playdough helps to unlock imagination and creativity. If children are also given other objects, such as blocks and sticks, they can use them all together.

Listening and attention skills

Younger children in this age range do not have the focus to pay attention for long periods of time. Early signs of listening and **attention skills** are seen when babies move their head to follow familiar sounds or when they move their arms and legs when they hear someone they know. Eventually they will become quieter when someone is talking or singing to them. Listening and attention skills can be developed through play and songs.

- Playing 'peek-a-boo' is one way of developing listening and attention skills for small babies. Children usually become quieter as they are waiting for the face to reappear from behind the hands.
- As small babies are interested in everything, their attention can move from one thing to the next quite quickly, so their focus can be held by singing songs accompanied by a rattle.

■ This child is having fun in the mud. How could this help to promote his imagination?

- Singing rhymes with actions that adults can demonstrate to children can help with focus. For example, 'Three little pigs' or 'Round and round the garden'. Children will want to copy the movement while they listen to the song and are more likely to pay attention and focus on the song.

Numeracy skills

Early on, children will begin to understand the basics of quantities; knowing if they want more or less of something. However, they will not understand quantity in terms of the number of objects. In this age range, children will imitate others when attempting to count. Activities that could help to develop numeracy skills include the following:

- Using large colourful counters or blocks can encourage numeracy development. When playing with them, adults can talk/sing the number of counters. Children will begin to mimic this, which will lead to them developing their understanding.
- Feeding and dressing a child can become a numeracy learning activity. Counting 'one arm in, two arms in' when putting on a coat or 'one spoonful, two spoonful' when feeding will encourage children to think about numbers.
- In this age range, children are also able to complete pre-numeracy activities such as comparing sizes. For example, they could be given a selection of sea shells to sort into size order.
- Matching picture cards can also be used as a way of introducing numeracy to children.

Exploration of environments inside and outside

When trying to make sense of their environment children will pay close attention to every sound, smell, touch or experience. Often they will 'explore' indoors as they navigate around their own home or nursery. However, allowing a child to be outside can help promote **cognitive development** as they learn to understand how the outside environment is different. Activities to explore indoor and outdoor environments could include the following:

- Non-mobile babies can be moved around so they are able to experience a different view of the room or outside environment. This will stimulate their interest.
- Taking a small child to the park will allow them to experience new things such as trees and ducks on the pond.
- Hide and seek is a great activity for indoor exploration. Children's toys are hidden and they have to find their favourite toy by searching through areas in the room.

Confidence using technology

Small children are beginning to recognise technology around them. From around 9 months they are using toys that have simple buttons, flaps and knobs that make sounds or have actions. These can prepare children for using technology.

ACTIVITY

To improve the numeracy skills of children in the local community centre, you have been asked by the manager to plan two play opportunities for them. They want them in a poster format so they can display these around the community centre for all volunteers to see. This means that, if staff need ideas, they can use yours.

Each play opportunity must be on a separate sheet of **A4** paper.

CHECK MY LEARNING

1 Explain how the 'This little piggy went to market' rhyme can improve a child's listening and attention skills.

2 How can a story such as 'Goldilocks and the three bears' promote numeracy skills for an 18-month-old?

Planning communication and language play and learning opportunities: 0–18 months

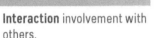

KEY TERMS

Interaction involvement with others.

Refining making changes to improve.

Lift-the-flap books have flaps on pages which show images or text underneath.

Textured stories use materials to suggest what something feels like, e.g. fur to represent animals.

▣ How could this book improve questioning?

In the first year of their life, children are busy trying to focus on the sounds they hear. They have the difficult task of trying to work out which sounds are from humans and which are not. They also need to understand what words mean. Early on, babies make lots of sounds; these are mainly babbling noises, as they are unable to form words. By the time a child is 12 months old, they are able to say a few words such as 'mama'. Do you know what your first word was?

Listening skills

Listening is an important step on the way to developing good communication and language skills. By listening, children are able to pick up on new words, and their meanings, and to begin to understand how to pronounce them and how to place them in a sentence.

At 1 month old, most babies will turn their head when they hear a familiar voice, showing that they are listening. However, as they are learning so much about the world around them, their attention is limited. This can mean that it is difficult for a child of 0–18 months to listen well and refine their speech like an older child.

- It is important that adults role model **interaction** skills such as making eye contact when they are talking and allowing for pausing. This is a foundation in later communication development.
- The repetition of nursery rhymes such as 'Twinkle, twinkle' encourages children to listen for patterns and sequences, which can help with refining their speech later.
- Listening to a song or rhyme that has a steady beat can allow children to develop their language and help them to talk.

Vocabulary and literacy skills

Vocabulary is limited early on in this age range. By the age of 6 months most children will understand the word 'no' and will babble. Within a short time (around 15–18 months) children will have learned approximately 15 words, although some may know more.

Early literacy skills are learned through listening to an adult reading a book. This interaction also allows children to **refine** their speech sounds as they attempt to mimic the words they are hearing. Questioning skills are important when exploring new words and literacy skills. Children that ask questions are practicing their language and using their question to clarify what has been said. Different types of books could improve literacy and vocabulary skills, for example:

- **Lift-the-flap books** allow children to develop their literacy and vocabulary skills. They are introduced to new language and sentence structures whilst being read to.
- **Textured stories** are another way in which small children can engage with literacy. In a book about animals, for example, children might feel the 'fur' of a bear which could prompt questions about where it lives and what it eats.

How to express and discuss feelings appropriately

Small children will find it difficult to express their feelings appropriately as they have not yet developed communication techniques. Babies cry and scream when they want attention or they feel pain, older children will have tantrums.

■ Table 2.3 Differences between children when expressing emotions

Under 12 months	12–18 months
Cry	Tantrum
Scream	Laugh
Gurgle noises	Cry
Social smile (smiles at anyone)	Cooperative when happy
Frown	Uncooperative when unhappy
Laugh	Clingy when anxious
	Wanting attention when jealous of others

There are a number of activities that can help children to learn to express emotion.

- Books with finger puppets are a good way of allowing small children to understand emotions and begin expressing them.
- Simple songs such as 'If you're happy and you know it' can be sung to and with older children in this age range.

Understanding others' experiences

Babies and very young children have not yet developed an understanding of themselves or others. To start building the foundation for understanding others' experiences adults working with young children can:

- help children to join in celebrations for different festivals
- show photographs and talk about places they know (to children around 15–18 months). They can share stories and use photographs of other children and people from different cultures and talk about them.

ACTIVITY

Lift-the-flap books are a fun way of introducing information to young children and keeping them engaged. The book follows a story and on each page there is a flap with something underneath.

In pairs, design a short lift-the-flap book for an 18-month-old child (2–3 pages). Carefully consider the topic you want to write about. The book should be colourful and the font easy to follow, and it should be at the right level for the age group. You should have a flap on every page with new information or an image under it.

When you have completed your book, get into pairs and read your story to each other.

CHECK MY LEARNING

1 Why are listening skills so important in the communication process?
2 How can improving the listening skills of young children help them improve their speech?
3 List the differences in how children of 6 months and 18 months might express emotions.

Planning social and emotional play and learning opportunities: 0–18 months

Children form attachments to those around them. When they are babies this is with their parents or carers. When they get older they also form attachments with other children and people that are important to them. In this age range, social and emotional play involves planning activities that allow children to begin to understand how to interact with others and the rules of sharing and turn taking that will help them form relationships in the future. How would you feel if someone took a pen from you as you were writing with it? Would you want to be friends with them?

Social play and learning

Developing relationships

Relationships are limited during this age range as children are usually not confident with strangers. Babies will develop strong **social** and **emotional bonds** to their primary caregivers and this will be shown when separation anxiety emerges. As a child becomes mobile and is more active in play, anger and frustration can occur when they can't get what they want. Having a reliable, familiar person to carry out play activities with can help to calm them and help them to feel at ease. Play activities, such as the suggestions below, can help to build stronger bonds and trust between adults and children.

- Although friendships do not emerge in this age range, it is important that adults allow children to watch during activities with others. This will then form the basis of them understanding how to interact in the future and form relationships.
- Singing in groups such songs as 'Five little monkeys' teaches children about having fun with others.
- A calming play activity for babies can be based around massage. Adults can sing or talk to the baby as they massage legs and arms. This helps to build trust and strengthen emotional bonds.

Sharing, turn taking and compromise

Children 0–18 months old find it difficult to share with others and to understand the concept of taking turns. They want everything their own way and struggle with understanding social skills such as compromise. Activities to build sharing and turn taking could include the following.

- From around 6 months a child will actively hold a toy; simple sharing can be encouraged by passing the toys back and forth between the child and adult.
- Getting children to make prints of their hands and feet for a group collage on the nursery wall is one way to encourage social skills. Children may have to wait their turn to share the resources.

Emotional play and learning

Expression of feelings

Sometimes it can be difficult for younger children to express themselves as they do not fully understand their own emotions. Practising recognising their own facial expressions can help them identify how they feel.

- Younger babies can have a place to be calm where they can have special toys and comfort blankets.
- By 18 months, children have more understanding. Finger puppets or dolls can be used to show expressions of feelings.

Build on relationships

- Young babies are attached to their caregiver and will often show distress when they leave. Adults can use carpet time to show photos of and talk about people who are special to them. Adults can also have one-to-one time with children to create stronger bonds.

Self-confidence, self-esteem and self-awareness

At the age of approximately 15 months, children will begin to develop a sense of who they are; they will also begin to develop self-confidence and self-esteem. There are several ways adults can help with this.

- Playing with children 0–18 months old and paying full attention to them, using safe play mirrors and talking about them can encourage self-confidence.
- Self-esteem can be encouraged by making a child feel involved in decision making. When choosing an activity to play, giving a choice to the child and allowing them to 'choose' will make them feel important (even if the decision is actually the adult's).

■ Children do not begin to develop self-awareness until around 15 months old. What could she be thinking? How could an adult help her understand?

Promoting independence

Children under 18 months tend to be very attached to their main caregiver, and rely on them for everything; because of this they are not very independent. Having independence is an essential life skill that is needed for confidence. It is important that young children are given activities that promote independence so that, in the future, they are less reliant on adults.

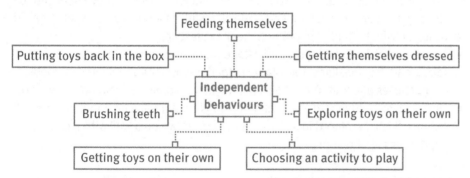

■ Figure 2.3: It is important that young children are given activities that promote independence.

Puppets can help to promote independent behaviours. Finger puppets or dolls can be used to show children how to feed themselves and what not to do when eating dinner. Children around 18 months will try to mimic this behaviour.

ACTIVITY

1 Write a script for a puppet show that you will perform to the rest of the class. It should be based on an independent behaviour you want to promote in a child. You will need to design your puppets from paper and make them large and colourful.
2 Evaluate how well you performed your puppet show. What can children learn from it?

CHECK MY LEARNING

1 How can an adult involve a child aged 10 months in a sharing activity?

2 How can taking part in sharing activities help to promote the social development of children aged 18 months?

Planning physical play and learning opportunities: 18 months–3 years

LINK IT UP

More information about physical development, including gross and fine motor skills, can be found in Learning Aim A of Component 1.

LINK IT UP

A balanced diet and the right nutrients are important for a growing child. Look back at Learning Aim B Component 1 for a reminder of how diet can affect growth and development.

■ Helping with food preparation can encourage children to want to snack on healthier foods.

At 18 months most children will be able to walk without any help. Their gross motor skills are developing and over the course of the next 18 months they will be able to run, climb, throw a ball and pedal a tricycle. As well as promoting physical skills, these activities will promote other areas of development such as cognitive skills and social skills. What type of gross motor skills do you think are needed to use a tricycle?

Spatial awareness

A child's sense of spatial awareness becomes more developed from 18 months. Children now have a better idea of where objects are in relation to them. This makes kicking a ball easier as foot and leg coordination are now improved. Being able to see the ball and know where to kick shows that hand–eye coordination has also improved. Children will still miss the catch, or stumble when trying to kick, but these skills will further develop with practice, and the following activities could help:

- Bat and ball games will further improve spatial awareness and allow children to practice their hand–eye coordination as well as balance. A 'T ball' game set uses oversized bats and balls and allows children to practice hitting the ball off a T.
- Foot and leg coordination can be improved with 'walk the line' activities. An adult can draw a line outside in chalk and children have to stand on it and walk.

Activities to stay healthy

Between 18 months and 3 years, children can be picky eaters and will sometimes not eat if they feel uncomfortable about what is put in front of them. It is important that children see mealtimes as a relaxed event and not a time where they are forced to eat foods they don't like. If mealtimes become stressful, children will not want to eat. The following activities could help promote healthy lifestyles:

- Role play can allow children to understand more about living a healthy lifestyle. Taking part in a 'mealtime' role play can open discussions about different foods, such as vegetables and fruit. These help children to feel comfortable around new foods.
- Making a 'food cupboard' with children can get them thinking about healthy food options. It can be placed in a real cupboard or drawn on a wall with a piece of paper to act as the door.

How to take care of yourself

At this stage children may be beginning to go to the toilet independently and will be learning about washing their hands and being hygienic. They may not yet understand the reason why they need to wash their hands. However, they will be becoming familiar with the routine. Adults can make it clear when children need to wash their hands and model how to do it properly.

Children could help with food preparation, enabling adults to discuss with them which foods are healthy and which are not. Children can be introduced to a range of fruits and vegetables, which they can peel and cut.

Resting is important. Sometimes children are so involved in play and what is going on around them that they don't realise they are tired. Children can move to a quiet area of the room and rest their eyes and listen to a story. The story can be read by an adult or can be an audiobook. Being in a calm environment and concentrating on the sound of the story will encourage some children to fall asleep.

Gross motor skills

Physical play gives children a chance to become more coordinated in their movements as they develop their gross motor skills even further. It also gives children the opportunity to play with others and develop their social skills, which builds self-esteem.

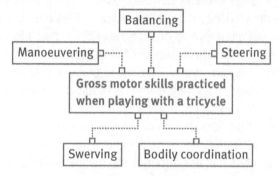

Figure 2.4: Gross motor skills practiced when playing with a tricycle.

Activities to improve gross motor skills could include the following:
- To strengthen arms and core muscles in the body, children can crawl around.
- Squatting and bending improve strength and balance. Playing hide and seek with toys encourages children to search for them and squat to pick them up. This activity can also promote cognitive development as it encourages children to be curious.
- Climbing frames encourage children to coordinate their body while they hold onto bars and climb. When other children are using the climbing frame at the same time, children can practice their skills of manoeuvring as they move around each other as well as improving their social skills.

Fine motor control

Accuracy and manipulation of objects has improved, as children have got older. At 18 months they should be confident in using a palmer grasp to build a tower of bricks and are likely to enjoy scribbling with crayons. By the time they are 2½ years old, children often show a hand preference and start to use a simple tripod grasp for holding a crayon.

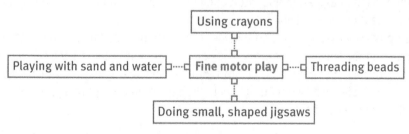

Figure 2.5: Fine motor skills practiced during play.

Activities to improve fine motor skills could include the following:
- A sand table or sand pit allows children to use different tools to manipulate the sand. Scooping and raking will strengthen the small muscles in the hand and wrist.
- Wax crayon etching is a colourful way to develop fine motor skills.

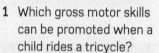

ACTIVITY

1 Which gross motor skills can be promoted when a child rides a tricycle?

2 Create a mind map to show how riding a tricycle can promote each of the other areas of development (social, emotional and cognitive).

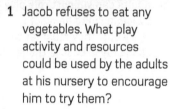

CHECK MY LEARNING

1 Jacob refuses to eat any vegetables. What play activity and resources could be used by the adults at his nursery to encourage him to try them?

2 Bella damaged her hand several months ago. She is not as developed as others for her fine motor skills. What activities could Bella try to promote her learning and development of fine motor skills?

Planning cognitive and intellectual play and learning opportunities: 18 months–3 years

You learned in 'Planning cognitive and intellectual play and learning opportunities: 0–18 months' that younger children are very interested in everything around them but lack attention and listening skills. Do you think that changes between 18 months and 3 years? If so, in what way?

Problem-solving activities

Children in this age range are likely to have a tantrum or show their frustration if the activity they are working on doesn't go to plan. They are not as resilient as older children and will often give up on an activity if they find it too challenging. Problem-solving activities could include the following:

- Counters and weights can introduce a child to problem solving in maths and science. A child could hold a weight while an adult encourages them to find objects in the nursery that are lighter or heavier.
- Puzzles such as magnetic puzzle boards can encourage children to be creative as well as practice their problem solving. Magnetic puzzle boards contain different shapes and characters that are colourful and magnetic. Children use these shapes to create pictures on the board. They need to be able to understand how the shapes fit together and how to create an image that fits the space given. In what way could these types of activity promote fine motor skills too?

Imagination and creativity

Between 18 months and 2 years, many children will use their imagination and act out pretend games. Usually, these are based on home-life situations, answering the 'phone' to daddy or mummy, going to work, doing laundry and looking after a 'baby'. Children might create a 'play' but it will usually be based on what they have witnessed at home. Adults can help with this by providing a role-play area with costumes. Pretend play can help children to build friendships as they play alongside and with other children, sharing and communicating with them.

From 2 years of age upwards, children will use their imagination to pretend items are different objects.

- Using the environment inside or outside can spark imagination in children. An empty cardboard box could be a rocket ship! An outdoor hose could be a snake! When using imagination and interacting with others, children have the chance to enhance their social skills.
- Using natural resources found outside is one way of encouraging imagination. Children may see a twig or branch as part of a tree but, when they have enough of them, they could begin to build a fort. Adults can suggest ways in which they could use them safely whilst encouraging children to come up with their own ideas, which will boost their self-esteem.

■ Adults can support role play by joining in to help act the story out. They must let the child stay in charge though.

Listening and attention activities

Children in this age range can often seem to ignore adults. This is a busy time for children as their brains are in overdrive as they develop. To be able to listen effectively, children need a quiet area free from distractions. The following activities could help develop listening and attention skills.

- Adults can play a pattern or shape activity with **wipe boards**. The adult can show the pattern or shape to the children and encourage them to copy it on their wipe board. They then answer questions about what they have heard and understood. This is something that could be done later in the day, with adults asking the children to match the pictures on a sheet based on what they are saying.
- There are some apps that can promote listening and improve attention in children, such as phonics apps. Phonics apps aim to help children with their language development. The apps keep children's attention by using fun characters, songs and rhymes. Children need to listen carefully to be able to learn new vocabulary and how to say it.

Numeracy activities

By 2 years old, most children will know what 'one' and 'two' mean and they will be able to show how old they are using their fingers. When playing with water, they are able to show which container has more water in it. 'Numeracy' isn't just numbers but also shape and number patterns. Other activities could help to develop numeracy skills:

- Puzzles can develop numeracy skills as children are looking at shapes and moving them to fit.
- Counters can be used to support learning of numbers. Children can use different coloured counters in several ways. Adults could ask younger children around 18 months–2 years to try to sort the counters by colour. Children around 2–3 years old could be asked to count.

Exploration of environments inside and outside

A child's environment, whether it is inside or outside, is a useful tool for learning new things. There are a range of objects and new experiences that can promote learning between 18 months and 3 years.

- Using outdoor material can allow children to explore size and weight. Adults can ask children to collect stones and pebbles. They can then do a comparison game where children are asked which is the biggest, the longest or the heaviest.
- Children like to feel and smell and try to work out what objects do. Placing a tent outside (or even inside) and setting up camping equipment is one way of encouraging children to learn about new things and allowing them to explore. Children can walk through the tent and work out what the items are and how they are used.

Confidence using technology

Children may not be confident at using technology at this age but they will have been introduced to it. Technology can be used in learning activities to support other areas of development.

- A drawing program on a tablet can promote confidence with using technology whilst allowing children to practise their fine motor skills. Children can draw shapes and create pictures either by using their finger or using the electronic stylus/pen.
- Using a tablet can also allow children to access colours that they may not be able to mix with paint. When using paint, children have limited access to the colours on their table. However, with a computer/tablet, there are a range of colours and different shades.

◩ Children can use their imagination to play games inside a tent.

Planning communication and language play and learning opportunities: 18 months–3 years

GETTING STARTED

Talking to children in different ways can encourage them to develop their vocabulary and improve their language. Using a toy telephone can be a fun way for children to start conversations. How could this improve fine motor development? How could it promote social development?

LINK IT UP

For more detail on how children's communication and language develops, look back at Learning Aim A in Component 1.

KEY TERMS

Listening walk being silent whilst walking in order to hear what is going on around you.

■ Having a strong vocabulary allows children to feel confident when they are asking questions and promotes cognitive development.

Language and communication skills have improved significantly by the time a child reaches 18 months old. It is important that adults plan activities that make the most of children's language abilities in order for them to improve and develop new skills in all five areas of their development. Did you ever struggle to say a particular word? How do you think adults can help children that have speech difficulties? How important is language for building friendships?

At 18 months, the majority of children are already saying a few short words and can understand simple requests such as "get your book". By the time they reach the age of 2, most children will have developed approximately 50 words and will be learning several new words per week. Sentences at this point are simple and will usually consist of two words placed together such as "drink gone". By 2½ years, the average child will have developed approximately 200 words and be able to ask simple questions such as "What's that?"

Listening skills

Between 18 months and 3 years, children are learning lots of vocabulary so listening is important. Good listening skills will enable children to master new words and have confidence in what they say. Interaction with others is an essential part of the communication process, as children will refine their speech as they listen to, and later understand, new words. Listening to each other can promote social development by helping children to build friendships. Other activities to develop listening skills could include the following:

- Reading storybooks with children allows them to use their imagination. It also allows them to use the vocabulary that they have learned as they talk about the book.
- Books that are not familiar to children will encourage them to learn new words. As children begin to learn new words, adults can help to refine speech by pronouncing words in the correct way. This supports children as they master the word.
- To encourage listening skills, adults can take children on **listening walks**. On a listening walk a child visits a wooded area and they are asked to be silent and listen to what is going on around them. By not talking, children can hear the wind in the trees, birds and other woodland noises. This will encourage discussions about what they hear and see.
- Simple action games such as the 'Five little ducks' allow children to practice the rhyming of words and improve their listening skills as they focus on the instruction of the song.

Vocabulary and literacy skills

Typically children will match the sounds of an object that they are playing with, such as a 'moo' when playing with a toy cow. They are very good at copying the sounds from adults but need specific help when trying to pronounce words.

By 3 years old, children may ask a lot of questions. These questions are a way of finding out about the world from a person that they trust.

Children can now form sentences that can be fully understood and should be encouraged to use their vocabulary and build upon it with new words. Singing nursery rhymes and songs will allow children to practice the words they know and learn new ones.

Mixing with children of different ages can improve vocabulary. Adults can mix age groups for a role play activity. Younger children can learn from older children and pick up new words.

Older children may find it difficult to understand some younger children who may not have developed their vocabulary as much. Because of this, the older children will have to think of new ways of expressing themselves in order for the younger children to understand them.

Expressing and discussing feelings appropriately

At around 18 months, children will seek out immediate attention. As they can't always get what they want or have trouble in expressing themselves, they can have tantrums and become argumentative. By 2–3 years, children can become jealous of their peers or siblings, especially when they are getting adult attention. This can stop children developing friendships and relationships as well as learning. By 3 years, children are becoming more rational and will begin to appreciate the needs of others; the following activities could help them develop their skills in this area:

- Role-play activities such as 'dress up' can allow children to express themselves safely without fear. Encouraging children to act out their feelings towards others in a safe environment can lead to them overcoming any frustrations they have.
- Using books, children can develop their knowledge of emotions. Stories such as 'The Angry Ladybird' or 'The Happy Bear' allow them to explore feelings.

Understanding others' experiences

Children are now asking more questions about who they are and how other children and families might be different to them. They are at an age where they are able to understand basic concepts so it is important to teach them about different cultural and religious experiences in a positive way.

- Cooking activities can help children recognise that food differs across cultures. Adults can cook simple (child friendly) recipes to give children a chance to see different foods and learn about the stories behind them and how they are made. With simple recipes children can get involved in the process and use their sense of touch, feel and taste when taking part.
- To make children aware of religious festivals, they could help to create a display and talk about what happens at each.

ACTIVITY

Quinn and Harvey are 3 years old and are twins. They were born prematurely and this affected their learning abilities. They are struggling with their communication and language and find it difficult to say words or understand what the words mean. One of their favourite songs is 'Old MacDonald'. They don't know all the words to the song but they love to make the animal noises. Gemma is the nursery nurse in charge and she has decided that it is important for all children to learn to associate the noise of an object with the sound it makes. She tells you that this basic association can lead to new vocabulary and improved speaking skills. Gemma has asked you to create a poster to help children like Quinn and Harvey.

1 Create an A3 'word-sound' poster. Pick one of the following themes:
   - animals
   - transport

You should draw pictures of the theme you have chosen and include a word that best describes the sound it makes.

2 How will the poster help to develop Quinn and Harvey's communication skills?

3 How would the poster help to promote Quinn and Harvey's social and emotional development?

CHECK MY LEARNING

1 How can sharing stories with each other promote communication and intellectual development?

2 If you were a nursery nurse, how would you get a 2-year-old to calm down and try to express their feelings in an appropriate way?

Planning social and emotional play and learning opportunities: 18 months–3 years

■ This child is trying to comfort her friend who is upset. How can comforting one another build on relationships?

Children are well on their way to developing a sense of themselves and understanding who they are. As they learn they can often get frustrated and jealous of others, which can lead to tantrums. Around the age of 2½, children begin to react well to praise and positive attention when it is given by adults and will try to do their best to get it. Have you ever been shopping and seen a small child screaming at their parents? Why do you think some children do this?

Towards the age of 3, children are not as easily frustrated if they do not get immediate gratification as they now find it easier to wait. They find it easier to share and take turns and usually show concern for others when they are upset.

Social play and learning

Development of friendships and relationships

Through parallel and associative play, children have had some interaction with their peers. At 3 years, children lack some social skills but are beginning to develop friendships with others. They are likely to have a sense of trust with a familiar adult. As children are more comfortable around others they will ask questions; this can be seen during associative play. Adults should start introducing activities that encourage children to work together.

Many nurseries have their own garden area for planting. This is a beneficial activity for the future development of friendships between children. They are becoming aware of each other and the activity can lead to questions. This can promote cognitive development as asking questions can develop problem-solving skills and imagination.

Sharing, turn taking and compromise

Children in this age range crave immediate gratification and this can mean limited sharing and compromise with peers. To support the development of social skills, adults can plan activities that encourage sharing and compromise with others.

By the end of this age range, most children will have learned to share and enjoy playing with others. Adults can plan activities to build on these skills. This encourages children to think about their feelings and the feelings of others.
- At around the age of 2½, children can kick a ball. Children could take turns in rolling or kicking the ball to other children or an adult.
- Using 'sharing bins' in role play can help children to understand sharing. The bin contains different props and all children are told that anything in the bin can be used by anyone in the nursery. When one child takes a prop, other children will learn that they can no longer use it and learn to compromise by using something else instead.

Promoting independence

At 18 months, children are still heavily reliant on their caregivers. As children want to be independent, frustration can arise. Children at this age should be guided into becoming independent and given activities that can promote it without overwhelming them. Having a sense of independence can lead children to develop a sense of self and begin to be more aware of themselves. It can also help children to build friendships with others. Activities that could help to promote independence include the following:

- Role play or pretend play is a useful activity to show children different ways of becoming independent. Pretending to have a family meal will encourage setting the table, serving food and self-feeding.
- Role play that uses dress up encourages the child to undo their zip or buttons and work out how to take clothes off and put them back on.

Understanding culture and values

It is important that children have an understanding of the diversity of culture. At this young age, children rarely have an understanding of themselves but they can still be introduced to other cultures and value systems through some simple activities.

- Circle time is a good opportunity to talk to children in a relaxed atmosphere. At the end of the day when children are winding down, discussion about culture can take place. Books that reflect diversity can be read and questions asked.
- A dancing activity can teach children the differences in dance from a range of cultures. Video clips of different dances can be shown and the children have to copy the moves.

Emotional play and learning

Expression of feelings

Children can have some issues with controlling their behaviour and feelings in this age range. That is because they are not fully aware of how they feel or the appropriate way of dealing with it. Activities to encourage expression of feelings include the following:

- **Emotion face** activities can begin the process of children linking a facial expression to a feeling. At this stage of development, children will find this difficult so it is important that adults take the lead and prompt questions.
- During circle time children can be given a teddy to pass around. The children can talk about 'how teddy feels today'. This can encourage children to express their own feelings.

Improving self-confidence, self-esteem and self-awareness

Children often appear as though they are full of self-confidence; however, a lot of the time they are struggling to understand their own emotions. To try to encourage children to tackle their shyness and worry, they need to know what those feelings look like and what could be done to help cope with them.

Finger puppets can be used to show children how a child might act if they were upset in a specific situation. "Look, Alice is feeling sad today because she misses her mummy." Adults can use characters to show children what can be done in that situation. This will teach them how to improve their own confidence but also how to be self-aware and aware of others.

Building on relationships

Although children can have tantrums and be argumentative they are learning that it is more important to get along with others as there will be a reward. This reward can be spending time with someone they like or taking part in a fun activity. Children begin to develop empathy and will help others if they see them in distress. They are also more likely to stop a tantrum if they know it upsets someone else.

Children have started having a preference as to who they want to play with. Activities should encourage group work using role play in order for children to build on the relationships they already have.

ACTIVITY

Jariyah is 2½ and her behaviour has recently changed. Her baby brother has started at her nursery. Since he started, Jariyah has become argumentative, has tantrums and wants to be near the adults all the time. She doesn't like it when they pick her brother up to feed him. She no longer plays with her friends and, when playing with shared resources, she refuses to share.

1 Why might Jariyah's behaviour have changed?

2 Describe how emotion faces could help.

3 How can using emotion faces promote Jariyah's emotional and communication and language development?

KEY TERM

Emotion face showing different emotions on your face. This can be done by a child or adult, or shown through images or video.

CHECK MY LEARNING

1 Describe how group activities can promote compromise.

2 How can activities that promote compromise also promote social development?

3 Olivia is 2½, is very shy and barely talks to the other children or staff. What activities do you suggest the nursery could provide so that she can gain some confidence?

Planning physical play and learning opportunities: 3–5 years

Between 3–5 years of age, children's fine and gross motor skills advance rapidly. Children improve in their balance and coordination and have a good sense of their surroundings when playing. Being physically fit and healthy is important as it promotes all other areas of development.

By taking part in a physical activity with others, children are able to build on relationships and friendships, which can promote communication and language skills. Can you think of other areas of development that physical play can help to develop?

Spatial awareness

Spatial awareness has developed quickly. Children can sense where an object is in relation to them. Their foot and leg coordination has improved significantly as they can now kick a ball with some force, hop on one foot and are able to walk along a line. They are able to catch and throw a large ball, showing their hand–eye coordination has also improved.

Hand–eye coordination

Fine motor play activities can help children to coordinate their eye movements with their hand movements. Children will need to have well developed hand–eye coordination to be able to draw and write; the following activities can help to develop this:
- Using a plastic needle (these are blunt and cannot hurt the child) to thread beads onto string can help to improve a child's hand–eye coordination.
- A creative activity such as making cards using paints, crayons and scissors also requires hand-eye coordination.
- To further improve coordination and control, children could be introduced to bicycles. By around 4 years, children are usually confident with riding a tricycle. At 5 years, when ready and confident with tricycles, children can be introduced to bicycles. Stabilisers or balance bikes can be used to help with balance. This will help with their coordination and improve control.

Activities to stay healthy

As children are more active in this age range, they are using all of their bodies and keeping fit. Besides being taught about physical fitness through play activities indoors and outdoors, it is important to consider other aspects of staying healthy. Children need time to rest, to eat healthy foods and to be able to take care of their bodies through washing and brushing their teeth.

In a nursery, pre-school or school, adults can ask children to choose the fruits and vegetables they would like for snack time. They could pick them from their garden area (if they have one). Children can help to wash and cut the fruit and vegetables while having discussions with the adults.

How to take care of yourself

Most children have a good sense of how to take care of themselves, as they are likely to be self-feeding, but they should be reminded about hygiene. At this age a lot of activities will take place outdoors to improve gross motor skills. This means that children can often play in the mud or pick things up that could have germs and

◪ Using crayons requires children to be accurate when colouring as crayons are often chunky, which could lead children to colour over the lines of the picture.

bacteria on them. Good hygiene, such as washing hands after playing outdoors and after using the toilet, should be taught to the children.

Knowing which foods are high in sugar can also be useful for children, as well as an awareness that too much sugar can be bad for their teeth.

Adults can help children learn about healthy and unhealthy food in group activities. In groups, child can place two hoops overlapping each other on a table. There can be a selection of food (real or plastic) on the table too. Children can discuss in their groups where to place the food: healthy in one hoop and unhealthy in the other. Anything they are unsure about can go in the middle. Adults can then open up discussions about eating healthy.

Gross motor skills

When a child is between 3–4 years old they can jump from a low step, run, kick a large ball and stand on one leg for a moment. By 4–5 years most children can run, avoid obstacles and swerve around things as well as skip. They are significantly stronger and have better control over their bodies. They are confident in running, hopping and skipping and they have refined their balance so they can stand on one foot for longer than ten seconds without falling.

Through physical activity, children develop the gross motor skills that will help them develop in other areas. Being able to run and play outside can promote emotional development as children will feel good about themselves. Taking part in physical games together, such as the following, can promote cognitive skills such as problem solving:

- Using a climbing frame, swings and slides allows children to have control over all of their body. They will stretch, reach, swing and pull themselves up.
- Bat and ball games encourage the movement of swinging, balance and bodily coordination.

Fine motor control

At 3–4 years, children are usually able to button and unbutton, can generally use scissors, thread beads and use a knife and fork well. At 4–5 years, children will be able to form letters, write their name and colour pictures in more accurately, plus colour within some lines. Further development of fine motor control can be learned through activities.

- Construction toys using different materials that allow children to push, pull and twist can encourage the use of fingers and also promotes imagination.
- Further activities that are useful for strengthening the hand muscles include creative play with crayons, pens, paintbrushes and scissors. Junk modelling encourages children to feel textures and different materials and then to manipulate them to create something. This also promotes cognitive development as it sparks their imagination.

■ As children step and jump their balance and coordination is improved.

ACTIVITY

A new nursery has just been set up and they are planning to buy new outdoor play equipment. The manager is keen on prompting learning through physical play and wants children aged 4–5 to improve their gross motor skills such as balance, strength, bodily movements and coordination.

The manager has asked that you write a proposal for the nursery that describes the equipment that should be bought.

Your proposal should:

1 include one or more resources

2 outline two activities that children could take part in using the resources

3 choose one activity and describe how it can promote gross motor skills and social and emotional development.

CHECK MY LEARNING

1 Discuss how role play can promote a child's learning across all areas of development.

2 Describe the motor skills used when a child is colouring or painting.

Planning cognitive and intellectual play and learning opportunities: 3–5 years

Between 3 and 5 years, children become more sophisticated in the way they think. They can usually count, have better problem-solving skills and are able to use their imagination in new ways. Children's cognitive and intellectual learning depends on the adults around them. New topics or learning opportunities need to be pointed out to children as they may not realise they have an opportunity to learn. If you were outside and saw a slug, would you see the learning opportunity? Can you think of ways it can promote each area of development?

Problem-solving skills

Problem-solving skills are becoming well developed. Children are usually more confident and are less likely to have anxiety over new situations. They are more likely to be tackling things head on and trying to solve problems rather than giving up. It is still important for adults to continue with the development of this skill.

Simple maths problems such as counting money in shop role play are one way to develop Problem-solving skills further. They will also help with the understanding of numbers and number patterns, which will be needed for school.

Creativity and use of imagination

Creativity and imagination are more than just fun for children; they are a way of expressing emotions and building friendships. As time goes on, children become more creative and experiment with games, toys and other resources. They will begin to make up their own games with their own rules and become interested in sharing the world of their imagination with others.

- At 3–4 years, children enjoy building with large cardboard boxes and imagining they are castles or boats.
- Children around 4–5 years will be developing their skills ready for school. One way to support this, and also benefit their creativity, is for them to use wipe boards. Children can practice writing skills on the boards and remove mistakes easily. They can draw characters and tell a story to adults.

Listening and attention skills

At approximately 3 years, children show an interest in listening to stories and talking about what is happening in the pictures. Their attention can be held for longer. When there is a story that they love, they are happy to hear it repeated many times. Around 4 years of age, children are able to use their listening skills to follow three step directions.

Activities to help improve listening and attention skills could include the following:

- As children now have better listening and attention skills, adults can make the most of going on trips and visits. This could include visiting the zoo, where children can listen to animal sounds, discuss the animals and listen to the zookeepers as they give information about the natural habitats of the animals there.
- Taking children to a museum encourages them to practice being quiet and listening when an adult is talking about a display.

Taking children out sparks their interest and encourages them to listen and ask questions. It is also important that they learn to listen to the rules and stay safe.

Numeracy skills

At 3 years old, a child can tell if an object is heavy or light, is able to arrange objects into categories and can understand the term 'more than'. By the time they reach 5 years, children can usually count accurately up to ten, are able to add two sets of objects together and can understand matching of equal objects. Activities that could help practice numeracy skills include the following:

- Using play money in role play situations can improve numeracy skills. Playing 'shop' or 'post office' allows them to use simple maths sums for the 'money'.
- Wipe boards can be part of a quick basic numeracy activity like adding and subtracting. Adults can ask numeracy questions and children can guess the answer and write it on the board.

Exploration of environments inside and outside

The exploration of inside and outside environments continues in this age range. As children are more confident in their body management, can communicate effectively and are able to express themselves, activities that support exploration should be more challenging. Challenging activities will allow children to think carefully about what they are doing, which will help them to learn.

- In 'loose parts play' there are different materials in an outside play area. Children are encouraged to explore that environment to find the objects and to play with them. A pipe could be turned into a pirate's spyglass or an old cable reel could be a bird's nest on a boat. Children might not use their imagination with the objects they find; they may simply want to find as many as possible. It is up to them.
- A woodland walk can allow children to explore the natural environment of some animals. Children can feel different textures when touching leaves, twigs and the bark of trees. This promotes questioning and sparks the imagination as well as promoting the development of fine motor skills.

Confidence using technology

Different technologies can be used to help children to understand their world. Children should be encouraged to use a range of different technologies so they are more familiar with them. As well as electronic items like digital cameras, tablets, PCs, computer games and apps, more traditional items, such as mechanical toys/pulleys and construction kits, can also be used.

- Children enjoy playing in sand using mechanical toys and pulleys.
- There are a range of computer games for children to use that can help to improve their numeracy, problem-solving skills or attention skills. Using technology, such as manipulating pulleys or using apps on a tablet, promotes physical development and hand–eye coordination. Adults should monitor children when they use computer games to make sure they stay on task with them.

ACTIVITY

Using sheets of paper, create a set of memory cards that will help a child develop their problem-solving abilities. They should not contain too many words and should look simple and colourful.

Don't forget that you should have six matching pairs (12 cards).

Once you have made your cards, swap with someone else in the room and try theirs.

CHECK MY LEARNING

Caleb is 4 years old and finds it difficult to concentrate and listen during story time.

1 How can taking Caleb to the local zoo help to develop his attention and listening skills?
2 Explain why the development of listening skills is important for cognitive and social development.

Planning communication and language play and learning opportunities: 3–5 years

Children's language has now become more fluent; this is important for them as communication and language is one of the main ways that children will learn. As they develop emotionally and socially, communication becomes a key part in the development of friendships and relationships. Children need to be able to communicate so they can express themselves without feeling frustrated. Sentence structure will start to become more complex as they get ready to start school. Imagine that you had tape over your mouth; how could you tell someone you were upset or hungry if you couldn't speak?

Listening skills

Children between 3–5 years often have difficulty when pronouncing words. Words such as 'spaghetti' are often pronounced as 'pasgetti' and animal as 'aminal'. This is common in young children and should not be a concern to adults unless it continues after the age of 5. Play in this age range should be aimed at refining speech sounds through interaction with others. Playing with other children and talking to adults allows children to practice their communication skills but also allows them to refine how they say words.

Many children at this age will already know nursery rhymes and songs. The rhythm encourages children to refine their speech to help them to pronounce the words correctly. Having a singing session while acting out the rhyme will allow children to have fun whilst learning how to say the words correctly.

Older children can be recorded while singing. When it is played back to them they will be able to hear themselves, which they will often find quite funny. It is a useful way to pick up on any mispronounced words.

As children are more active and are able to pay attention for longer periods, action games such as 'Simon says' can develop listening skills. As the adult gives out commands such as 'touch your toes' or 'spin around' the children have to use their listening skills to work out if the adult has said 'Simon says' at the beginning of the sentence. If they do not listen properly, and make a move, they would be disqualified from the game.

Vocabulary and literacy skills

This adult is using a large book to read to the children. Why do you think it is important to let children see the pages of the book?

By the age of 3 most children have a good understanding of words such as 'on', 'under' and 'in' and are able to use pronouns such as 'I', 'we' or 'you' and are able to use some plurals. Most sentences are easily understandable and children now use questions to gain further knowledge and to expand their vocabulary.

By the age of 5, children can usually use complex sentences with words such as 'because' and 'can' and talk about what has happened in the past and what might happen in the future. They are more articulate and are also able to argue with others and to answer back. Literacy skills have developed and most enjoy listing to and talking about storybooks and will make an attempt to read and write. By the time a child is 5 years old they begin to match words to what is being said and can usually recognise letters and their sounds.

Story sacks are a great way to get children to develop their literacy skills and vocabulary. A story sack will have a theme based around a book (for example a train driver). It will also contain supporting material based on that theme, such as train themed snap cards, pictures that could be coloured in or a simple comprehension task based on the book. Children can choose their story sack.

How to express and discuss feelings appropriately

Children will now know some basic feelings and are likely to apologise if they have done something wrong. They are beginning to use more complex words to describe their feelings like 'embarrassed'. Children are usually better at managing their emotions and tend not to have tantrums as much, but they still need help. The following activities could be useful:

- Puppets are a good way for a child to address any emotional issues they may be having. For example, some children may feel anxiety when away from parents or parents may be going through a difficult time (for example a divorce). Children can hide behind a screen to feel more comfortable talking about their feelings.
- Picture books that depict emotions can also help children identify which emotions they are feeling if they are unable to say them. These books show pictures of children with different facial expressions. Usually under each facial expression it will give the emotion that the child has. It may also have a story to describe the feeling.

Understanding of others' experiences

Children are now more inquisitive as they are able to talk about new things and have discussions about what they have heard and seen. If something is not the 'norm' for a child they will want to learn more about it and will do so by asking questions. The following activities could help to improve understanding of others' experiences.

- Allowing children to cook different foods encourages them to understand other cultures. Children can take part in cooking rather than just tasting foods. At Christmas, children can make star shaped biscuits or mince pies. Around Chinese New Year, children could make simple Chinese dishes such as noodles and sticky rice cakes.
- It is important that children learn about different religions. Having group discussions about religions can help children to understand the importance of respecting others' beliefs and traditions.

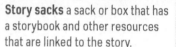

KEY TERMS

Story sacks a sack or box that has a storybook and other resources that are linked to the story.

ACTIVITY

Work in small groups to write a list of words that children may struggle to say.

1 Using your word list, describe how adults can help to promote communication and language through play, in order to help children to say the words correctly.

2 How can supporting speech help to promote a child's intellectual, social and emotional development?

CHECK MY LEARNING

1 Why is it important to listen carefully when playing a game like 'Simon says'?

2 How can puppets help a child that may find it difficult to control emotions?

Planning social and emotional play and learning opportunities: 3–5 years

Children are now becoming more independent. If they are with someone they know, being away from their primary care giver is much easier. Children are less likely to have tantrums and will usually deal with situations in a more cooperative way. Emotions have become more complex, with some children showing embarrassment and excitement.

Around 3–4 years, children will show a preference for a friend but will only develop close friendships around the age of 5. Sharing with others has become much easier and children can usually understand the rules of games, although they will often fail to follow them. What games did you play with other children when you were younger? Did you ever try to change the rules?

Social play and learning

Developing friendships and relationships

Children have moved away from simply observing others as they play and moved towards forming relationships. Bonds with other children are built on trust and sharing and develop into friendships. The majority of friendships at this stage are same sex. As children are more emotionally developed, they understand when a friend is upset, shy or needs help. Activities to develop friendships and relationships could include the following:

- Setting up team games and activities that allow children to work together and cooperate will develop trust between them and deepen their friendships. For example, children can pass a balloon to each other using their knees to hold it. This will also help to develop balance and coordination.
- A treasure/scavenger hunt can build bonds as children work together to find the hidden objects.
- Shop role play will require children to cooperate and talk to each other. It will also promote speaking and listening skills.

Sharing, turn taking, compromise

In this age range, sharing and turn taking has become easier for children. They are less likely to have a tantrum and cause an argument when they do not want to share as they have more of an understanding of others' feelings. However, there can be times when some children choose not to share or take turns. At this point, adults should act as a role model or suggest a solution.

- Board games such as 'snakes and ladders' are particularly good for developing turn taking skills. As each child's turn is short the game keeps their interest.
- Have you ever played 'keep it up' with a balloon? This group activity can encourage sharing as there is only one balloon with a group of children. Children stand in a circle and the balloon is thrown into the air. Only one child at a time can hit it to keep it up. Some children may reach out to hit the balloon but realise that another child is doing the same thing. They will learn to compromise and let the other child hit the balloon, in the hope that they can hit it the next time.
- A joint project of a collage based on the current season, such as autumn, can also help children with sharing resources and compromising.

These two children are sharing the blocks. If one child wanted to use all the blue blocks, what do you think would happen? How do you think an adult could help in that situation?

Understanding culture and values

Children are very quick to notice when something is different. It is important that adults explain that everybody is different and emphasise that this is a good thing. This will help them when forming friendships.

- Sharing stories and rhymes in children's home language(s) so that others hear can help them understand that children belong to different cultures and speak different languages to themselves.
- Role-play resources can reflect the different cultures of the children. The 'home' corner can have different cooking pots or a different cooker. This activity will also promote language skills and extend a child's vocabulary.

Emotional play and learning

Expressing feelings

By the time a child reaches the age of 5 they are more aware of how to self-manage their feelings. They are less likely to argue back and have tantrums as they have learned to express themselves. It is important that adults continue to promote the expression of feelings so that children can express themselves in a positive way rather than a negative way.

- Some dolls have been specifically made to help children express their emotions. The dolls show an emotion on their face. If a child is sad, they may want to play with the sad doll. This will help adults identify that the child is upset but it also helps the child as they try to understand their own feelings.
- A 'how I feel today' mirror can encourage children to look at their own faces and say how they feel. The mirror needs to be large enough so children can see all of their face. On the mirror it says 'how I feel today'. As children look into the mirror, the words encourage them to think about how they feel while looking at their facial expression. Adults can support them with new vocabulary that expresses their feelings such as 'frustration' or 'anger', while they form links between new emotions and their facial expressions.

Improving self-confidence, self-esteem and self-awareness

Being self-aware requires children to think about their feelings and how they think others see them. Having a strong self-awareness will allow a child to gain confidence and self-esteem as they are able to recognise their strengths and weaknesses, can understand their own behaviour and can identify what they need to do to complete a task.

- At circle time children can be asked to stand and talk about what they did during the day. Adults can ask each child to nominate one other child for doing something good. As each child takes a turn, they praise someone else. This activity makes children feel good about themselves and increases their self-esteem as they praise other children but it also increases the self-esteem of the children who have been praised.
- When a child is confident they are more likely to take part in activities and more likely to make friends with others. Creating an 'I can do' play for children to take part in encourages them to think about what they are good at. They then get to dress up, sing or dance and show others what they can do well.

ACTIVITY

The local pre-school is keen on making sure that every child has a friend and doesn't feel left out. They want to make sure that, as the children turn 5 and are getting ready for school life, they have the skills to make friends so they don't find it difficult when they start school.

The manager has asked you to create a leaflet that includes several activities that staff can plan for children in order to improve their friendship skills.

Your leaflet should include:

1 different activities

2 any resources needed

3 an explanation as to why building friendships is important for all areas of development.

CHECK MY LEARNING

Rory, aged 4, has just started nursery and does not know anyone. She is finding it difficult to express her emotions in a new environment.

1 Explain how circle time could help Rory with her emotions.

2 What could adults do for Rory to promote friendships through play?

Planning play opportunities to promote more than one area of development

Many activities promote a number of different areas of development at the same time. Here are a few examples. Can you think of others?

Type of play and learning	Age range		
	0–18 months	18 months–3 years	3–5 years
Physical development	• Using a rattle that is colourful and noisy is one way for babies to improve their grasp. It will also encourage their cognitive and intellectual development as they begin to develop their listening and attention skills. • An obstacle course for babies can help them improve spatial awareness and promote their gross motor skills as they crawl around objects in front of them. It also encourages them to problem solve as they work out how to get around an object.	• Playing outdoors on a tricycle can develop balance, bodily coordination and steering skills. It also encourages children to socialise and builds confidence and self-esteem.	• Using a plastic needle, children can thread beads onto string. This will help to improve their hand–eye coordination. The activity will allow children to share the beads with each other and to problem solve if they find it difficult to thread the bead. Children may also discuss with others what they are making or the colours they are choosing to use.
Cognitive and intellectual development	• A digging activity, searching for coins or hidden toys, can allow children to use their imagination to create a story. Communication and language are also promoted as children talk about what they have found.	• Magnetic puzzle boards can encourage children to be creative as well as practice their problem-solving skills. Manipulating the magnetic pieces is one way of improving dexterity and promoting fine motor skills.	• Children can practise their writing skills and improve pencil grasp and dexterity whilst writing on a wipe board. As mistakes can easily be removed, it will help improve a child's confidence and self-esteem.

Type of play and learning	Age range 0–18 months	18 months–3 years	3–5 years
Communication and language	• Lift-the-flap books can allow children to develop their literacy and vocabulary skills as they are introduced to sentence structure. As a child helps to turn the pages, this activity can also help to develop their fine motor skills.	• Action songs such as 'Five little ducks' allow children to practice rhyming and improve their listening skills as they need to focus on the instructions. It is also one way of enabling children to work together as it can be sung in a group. This means that children are able to begin to build friendships with others as they sing.	• Children's literacy and vocabulary can be improved when using story sacks. As a story sack can also contain puzzles and comprehension tasks, children can also develop their problem-solving skills and social skills as they work with others when completing the puzzles.
Social	• Making prints of hands and feet for a group collage on the nursery wall will promote sharing and turn taking but also allow children to use their gross motor skills.	• Group gardening activities, such as planting vegetables, allow children to develop friendships as they tend the soils and plant seeds and bulbs. It is also a great way for children to use their cognitive skills, such as problem solving, when placing seeds. The activity can also lead children to ask questions about the vegetables they are planting.	• Team games, such as children passing a balloon only using their knees, will allow children to work together and cooperate. It also helps to develop a child's balance and coordination.
Emotional	• Using finger puppets or dolls to show expression of feeling can also allow a child to use their fine motor skills and their communication skills as they attempt to say how they feel.	• Emotion face activities can allow a child to link facial expressions to emotions. As adults will help with this activity it can lead to children talking about emotions and also answering questions. This activity can take place during circle time with other children, allowing everyone to share in the time they talk and to begin to develop friendships.	• Allowing children to have 'share time' where they can share what they like about their favourite game allows them to improve their self-awareness. It can also develop friendships as they find other children with similar interests, while improving their communication skills as they discuss in a group setting.

Learning aim B: assessment practice

How you will be assessed

In this learning aim you have considered the different learning environments in which play can occur. You have also studied the ways that adults can demonstrate how learning can be supported through play, covering three age ranges. It is important that you are fully aware of these age ranges as your assignment will ask you to cover all three. You should know how children require different activities based on their age and ability.

You have learned about the different types of play opportunities including physical, cognitive, communication and language, and social and emotional play. You have also explored different activities and resources. You will need to know how children learn through taking part in these activities and how they can promote learning across all five areas of development.

You will need to produce an assignment to assess your understanding of Learning Aim B. Within this assignment you will need to do the following:
- Know the activities and resources needed to promote learning for three age groups:
  - o–18 months
  - 18 months–3 years
  - 3–5 years.
- Know how play can promote learning.
- Give examples of activities and resources that can support learning.
- Come to a conclusion about how play activities promote learning across the five areas of development.

CHECKPOINT

Strengthen
- Identify the five areas of development.
- Describe how play can promote physical development across the three age groups:
  - ☐ 0–18 months
  - ☐ 18 months–3 years
  - ☐ 3–5 years.
- Identify two activities and resources used to promote gross motor skills.
- Describe how play can promote communication and language across the three age groups.
- Outline two activities and resources that could be used to promote learning for emotional development.

Challenge
- Assess how activities/resources for different age ranges could promote learning for social development.
- Assess how physical activities can promote learning across communication and language development.
- Assess how social activities can promote learning across emotional development.

ASSESSMENT ACTIVITY 1 | LEARNING AIM B

- Ashlee, the manager of Sweet Ted's Nursery, is concerned that there is a missing report from the filing cabinet. The report was about play opportunities and how they are used to promote children's learning. Ashlee has asked that you write the report as it is needed for new staff members starting next week.
- Your report will be based on children aged 0–5 years in the nursery.
- You should:

1 describe how play can promote learning across the five areas of development across the three age ranges

2 discuss how two activities for two different age ranges can promote learning across different areas of development

3 assess those activities and resources and decide which has the most benefit.

TIPS

You need to consider how the activities can link to other areas of development. For example:
- Books to encourage literacy and communication can also encourage physical development as the child manipulates the pages with their fingers.
- Using tricycles to develop coordination and steering can also allow children to develop socially as they interact with others when outdoors.
- Role play can allow a child to understand language and learn new vocabulary while encouraging a child to develop their emotions and be able to express them.

When writing about the activities you should also think about how they benefit the child.
- Problem-solving activities such as computer games can promote listening and questioning skills because they spark children's imagination.
- Developing socially when taking part in team games or board games with others is beneficial as it means children can form friendships and relationships. It also benefits them because they can talk to other children, which will improve their communication and language.

TAKE IT FURTHER

- Evaluate how the use of construction blocks can develop fine motor skills and a child's imagination.
- Evaluate how beneficial role play is at supporting communication and cognitive development.
  - Example: Role play is very beneficial to a child when they are learning new vocabulary as it can allow them to practice new words and sentence structures.
- Assess the extent to which board games can support the development of friendships.

03 Supporting Children to Play, Learn and Develop

Introduction

In this component, you will understand how physical, cognitive/intellectual, communication and language, and social and emotional circumstances can impact on children's learning and development. This includes the impact on all areas of development as a whole as well as the separate areas of development.

You will consider how both the inside and outside environment, in the home and in childcare settings, can be adapted to meet the needs of children with individual circumstances who require support to play, learn and develop.

You will learn how to adapt activities for children with individual circumstances to promote their learning and development.

You will consider the needs of children: 0–18 months, 18 months–3 years and 3–5 years.

This component builds on the knowledge, understanding and skills you developed in Components 1 and 2, so you will need to revisit these. At the end of this component, you will take an external assessment, completing activities related to children's play, learning and development, and supporting children with individual needs.

LEARNING AIMS

In this component you will:

A	Investigate individual circumstances that may impact on learning and development.
B	Create safe environments to support play, learning and development in children aged from birth to 5 years.
C	Adapt play to promote inclusive learning and development.

Physical circumstances that may impact on learning and development

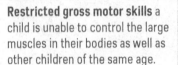
There are several different physical circumstances that children may face that may impact on their learning and development. Some children have sensory impairment, which means they have difficulty seeing or hearing. This can create many challenges for the child, affecting all areas of their learning and development. Children's physical development can be restricted, which means they are unable to move in the same way as other children.

In Component 1, you learned that children acquire skills at varying rates in different areas of development and that not all children develop at the same rate physically. Some children's gross and fine motor skills may be delayed, which means these skills are not developing as quickly as they are in other children the same age.

Can you think of any reasons why children's physical development may be delayed?

Sensory impairment

If a child has a sensory impairment this means that they have difficulty in seeing (visual impairment) or hearing (hearing impairment). These can have a significant impact on all areas of a child's development and learning.

KEY TERMS

Restricted gross motor skills a child is unable to control the large muscles in their bodies as well as other children of the same age.

Restricted fine motor skills a child is unable to control the small muscles in their hands and fingers as well as other children of the same age.

Delayed gross motor skills the large movements of a child's body are not progressing as quickly as other children of the same age.

Delayed fine motor skills the small movements of a child's hands and fingers are not progressing as quickly as other children of the same age.

■ Table 3.1: The possible impact of sensory impairment

Area of development	Possible impact of visual impairment	Possible impact of hearing impairment
Physical development	Motor development can be affected as a child may be reluctant to move because they are unsure what is around them. They may not move towards things because they cannot see them. A child aged 0–18 months who can see well may be stimulated by a bright coloured ball and reach out to try to grab it. A child with a visual impairment may not be able to see the ball clearly, or at all, so will not reach out.	Some conditions that cause hearing impairment may cause discharge from a child's ears. Some children may need to tilt their heads or lean forward in order to hear properly which can affect their posture.
Cognitive and intellectual development	If a child is not moving around much, they will not fully explore the environment, which is important for the brain to develop. This may mean that they do not develop concepts such as shape or space.	A child may have difficulty with reading and mathematical concepts.
Communication and language development	A child may have difficulty learning to talk because they cannot read lips and notice the way adults' mouths are moving.	A child may have difficulty learning to talk because they cannot hear the sounds required in order to speak.
Social development	If a child is unable to make eye contact this will affect their ability to engage in social situations. Social interaction includes non-verbal language such as body language and facial expressions. Children who cannot see will not pick up on these, which will make it difficult for them to read social situations.	Restricted language can affect communication with others, which can prevent a child from interacting socially.
Emotional development	A child may be less independent because they rely on adults to complete tasks for them. This can affect their self-esteem and make them feel they cannot do things.	The effects on the other areas of development can cause a child to have low self-esteem and feel left out because they cannot communicate effectively.

■ Which areas of a child's development and learning could visual and hearing impairment effect?

Restricted gross motor skills

If a child has **restricted gross motor skills**, they may have a disability or medical condition that limits the amount of large movements their body can make. This can mean that they are unable to use equipment and join in with activities that are suitable for children of the same age. A 4-year-old who cannot walk and uses a wheelchair will be unable to use the same climbing frame as other 4-year-olds.

Restricted fine motor skills

If a child has **restricted fine motor skills** they are unable to control the smaller muscles in their hands and fingers as well as other children of the same age. They may struggle with activities such as using a knife and fork, fastening buttons or holding a pencil.

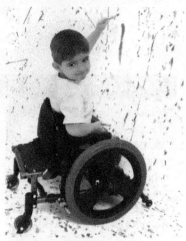

How might being in a wheelchair restrict a child's gross motor skills?

ACTIVITY

1   Plan a website for new parents explaining how the following can impact on children's learning and development:

   a sensory impairment

   b restricted gross motor skills

   c restricted fine motor skills.

Produce a fact sheet for professionals working with children aged 3–5 which includes information on the impact of the following on children's learning and development:

   a delayed gross motor skills   **b** delayed fine motor skills.

Delayed gross motor skills

If a child has **delayed gross motor skills** the large movements made by their bodies are not progressing as quickly as other children of the same age.

Most play incorporates physical movement. A child with delayed gross motor skills may find it hard to explore the environment, which can affect other areas of development.

- **Communication and language development**: a child who finds it hard to explore the environment will not have opportunities to talk about what they are experiencing.
- **Social development**: a child may have limited opportunities to join in with other children's play, which means they may not make friends easily.
- **Emotional development**: a child's self-esteem may be affected as well as the way they see themselves (self-concept); they will be aware that they cannot do things that other children the same age can do and this may make them feel inadequate.

Delayed fine motor skills

If a child has **delayed fine motor skills** the movements of their hands and fingers are not progressing as quickly as other children of the same age. A child with delayed fine motor skills may find it hard to explore new materials using their hands.

Children can usually hold a crayon and draw simple shapes by the age of 3. A child who has delayed fine motor skills may not be able to do this at 3, which can make them feel frustrated and delay them starting to form letters and write.

LINK IT UP

To remind yourself that children acquire skills at varying rates in different areas of development, go to Component 1, section A.

To remind yourself of the growth and development across the ages of birth to 5 years, go to Component 1, section A.

To remind yourself of the different physical factors that affect growth and development, go to Component 1, section B.

CHECK MY LEARNING

1   List the different physical circumstances that can affect a child's learning and development.

2   Explain what is meant by 'sensory impairment'.

3   Explain the difference between 'restricted development' and 'delayed development'.

Cognitive and intellectual circumstances that may impact on development

There are several cognitive and intellectual circumstances that may impact on children's learning and development.

Some children have **poor concentration levels**. We all have times when we find it difficult to concentrate but, if this is happening regularly, there can be a significant impact on a child's learning and development. Do you ever find it hard to concentrate? What prevents you from concentrating?

Some children may have **delayed literacy skills**, which means they do not learn to read and write as quickly as other children the same age. Can you remember learning to read and write? How old were you?

It is important that adults understand the expected concentration levels and literacy skills for children across different age ranges in order to recognise if these skills are delayed.

Poor concentration levels

Some children have a short attention span and find it hard to focus on what they are doing. This can lead to disruptive behaviour, which will be looked at later in 'circumstances that may impact on learning and development'.

- Children who find it hard to concentrate may talk a lot and interrupt people. This can affect their communication and language development and also their social development, as they find it difficult to take turns in a conversation.
- Children with poor concentration levels can be restless or fidgety. They may not persevere with learning a new physical skill like riding a tricycle because they lose interest quickly. This can affect their physical development.
- There is a significant impact on cognitive development as children find it hard to pay attention, follow instructions and complete activities. This can affect children aged 3–5 years significantly as this is the period within which they start full-time school.

Remember children's levels across the age ranges will be very different and you should consider their ages and stage of development before coming to the conclusion that they have poor concentration levels.

 **Table 3.2: Concentration levels across the different age ranges**

Age range	
0–18 months	Children have a very short concentration span and become distracted easily because everything is very new to them.
18 months–3 years	Children are still learning about the world and exploring. Their levels of concentration will still be developing but they are usually able to concentrate for a few minutes.
3–5 years	Children can usually sit still for longer periods and concentrate for long enough to complete a task or activity.

Delayed literacy skills

If a child has delayed literacy skills, this means their reading and writing skills are not progressing as quickly as those of other children the same age.

A child who is left-handed may have delayed writing skills as they struggle to find a comfortable grip when holding a pencil and their grip can be awkward when they are starting to make marks and write. This may mean it takes them a little longer than other children to form letters.

A child with delayed literacy skills may develop learning difficulties or behavioural problems. If a child's literacy skills continue to be delayed as they get older, they can be at risk of dropping out of school and being unemployed later in life. This is why it is important to support children whose literacy skills are not meeting the expected milestones.

It is important to understand the development of children's literacy skills across the different age ranges in order to determine if there is a delay.

▣ **Table 3.3: Literacy skills across the different age ranges**

0–18 months	Children are developing their hand-eye coordination skills ready for writing by picking up objects and using toys such as shape sorters. They may begin to make marks with brushes and chunky crayons. Children this age will enjoy looking at simple books and will learn which way up books are held and which way the pages are turned.
18 months–3 years	Children will be starting to show a preference for a particular hand for writing. They will use a palmer grasp to hold crayons and pencils which means they grip with the palm of their hand. Children this age are learning that print has meaning, for example that the sign outside the supermarket actually says its name.
3–5 years	Children grip crayons and pencils using a tripod grip which means three fingers are used. They make shapes and start to form letters and write their own name. They can usually read their own name too and recognise other familiar words such as names of family members and names of their favourite snacks or television programmes.

▣ **How could being left-handed delay a child's writing skills?**

ACTIVITY

Sundeep is completing work experience at a childminders. There are children aged from 0 to 5 years of age. The childminder has asked Sundeep to observe the children's literacy skills. Sundeep is unsure what should be expected at each age group.

Create a set of information cards to help Sundeep to recognise how children's literacy skills should be developing at:

- 0–18 months
- 18 months–3 years
- 3–5 years.

You will need to create one card for each age group.

Test out your cards by giving them to a partner to review. Would the cards enable your partner to recognise where children's literacy skills may be delayed?

CHECK MY LEARNING

1 What are 'poor concentration levels'?

2 Which areas of a child's development can be affected by poor concentration levels?

3 What are children's expected concentration levels at:
   - 0–18 months
   - 18 months–3 years
   - 3–5 years?

4 How would you know if a child had delayed literacy skills?

LINK IT UP

To remind yourself of cognitive and intellectual development across the ages of birth to 5 years, including the development of attention span, go to Component 1, section A.

To learn about social and emotional circumstances that may impact on a child's development and learning, including disruptive behaviour, go to 'Disruptive behaviour' in this component.

To remind yourself of planning play opportunities for children, including vocabulary and literacy skills, go to Component 2, section B.

Communication and language circumstances that may impact on learning and development

One important circumstance that may impact on a child's learning and development is if they are learning **English as an additional language**.

Many children are learning English alongside a different language because their parents do not speak English or their parents can speak more than one language.

Some children attend childcare settings where the staff and children may not speak the language the child uses at home. This can create many challenges for the child and can have a negative impact on their learning and development. However, it is important to remember that being able to speak more than one language is a gift and that the impact of this on a child's learning and development can also be very positive. How many different languages can you speak? Can you think of the benefits of being able to speak more than one language?

Cognitive/intellectual skills are developed if children think in more than one language. Their problem-solving and creativity skills are developed.

Languages spoken are often associated with culture and religion, therefore children develop a strong sense of self-identity which can lead to high self-esteem.

Benefits of children learning English as an additional language

Children's memory skills develop which makes it easier for them to retain information and learn other languages easily.

Speaking the same language as parents enables the child and parent to have a closer bond which is good for the child's emotional development.

Children learn more than one language so they can socialise with different family members or members of the community in which they live. Children may communicate with family members who are abroad.

Figure 3.1: The benefits of children learning English as an additional language are varied

As well as the positive impact that learning English as an additional language can have on a child, there can also be a negative impact.

A child who enters a setting where all the other children speak a different language:

- may be frightened – they will not understand why others cannot understand them and why they cannot understand others
- may feel different to other children and that can have a negative effect on their self-esteem
- may take a long time to settle in because they will need to tune in to the language around them and make sense of it – this means they may find it difficult to leave their parents when starting a new care or educational provider.

A child may lose the ability to speak their 'home' language because they are exposed to English more than the language spoken at home. However, this can depend on their age and the amount of time they have spent away from their parents. Here are some examples about two different children.

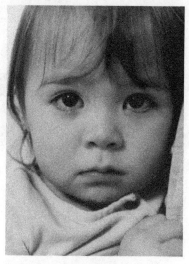

Radikha

Radikha aged 18 months is cared for in a nursery five days per week because her parents work full-time. This means that, during the week, Radhika spends more time awake at the nursery than at home. Radikha's parents speak Punjabi at home.

Radikha is using English words much more than words in Punjabi because English is the language she hears the most.

Canan

Canan aged 3 is starting nursery. This is the first time he has been away from his parents. At home Canan and his parents speak Turkish.

Once in nursery Canan begins to pick up the words for things in English very quickly, however he still speaks Turkish to his parents when he goes home.

■ Why might a child be distressed when they cannot understand the language around them?

A child learning English as an additional language may have gaps in their English vocabulary (the words that they know in English).

Sometimes a child who is learning English as an additional language may develop a speech delay. This can happen when different languages are spoken to them by the same person.

Speech may become delayed because it will take more time to process the different words and phrases than if only hearing one language.

LINK IT UP

To remind yourself of children's communication and language development across the ages of birth to 5 years, go to Component 1, section A.

DID YOU KNOW?

Many settings employ adults who can speak different languages so they can communicate with children who are learning English as an additional language to support their learning and development.

ACTIVITY

You have been asked to appear on a television documentary called *The Impact of Learning English as an Additional Language*.

Prepare some notes for your television appearance.

You should include:

- the positive impact of learning English as an additional language on children's learning and development
- the negative impact of learning English as an additional language on children's learning and development.

Practice reading out what you will say with a partner.

CHECK MY LEARNING

1. Give three benefits to children's development of learning English as an additional language.

2. Give three ways in which the impact of learning English as an additional language can negatively affect children's learning and development.

3. Explain how the amount of time a child spends hearing different languages can determine what becomes their preferred language.

Social and emotional circumstances that may impact on learning and development

Adults are a very important influence on children's social and emotional development. Children learn by observing adults and will copy them. This means it is important that adults are not **negative role models** and do not set a bad example.

Part of being a good role model is interacting positively with children and giving them the attention they need. It is also important that adults are good role models in developing children's understanding of **social norms and values**. Adults should provide play opportunities to enable them to be happy and to develop in all areas.

The amount of time children spend playing has changed over time. Think about your memories of playing as a child. What about children today? Are their opportunities for play the same as yours? What has changed?

KEY TERMS

Negative role model someone who does not set a good example.

Social norms and values attitudes and behaviours that are considered normal in society.

Bond an emotional tie between two people.

Limited interaction with adults not much communication and contact with adults.

Limited interaction with adults

Children begin to interact with adults as soon as they are born. They enjoy spending time with adults and soon learn how to respond positively to play experiences and develop skills such as taking turns. Playing with adults helps to create a **bond**.

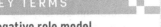

Table 3.4: Adult interactions with children differ across the age ranges

0–18 months	Children will prompt adults to play with them, for example by putting up their hands to show that they want to be picked up.
18 months–3 years	Children often follow familiar adults around and may tug on their clothing or call their name in order to get their attention. They will start to transfer the skills they have learned from playing with adults into play with other children.
3–5 years	Children will sometimes ask adults to play with them. Children this age need support to play fairly and follow the rules.

It is very important that adults give children the attention they need, or there can be a significant impact on children's learning and development. **Limited interaction with adults** can mean that children:

- have a lack of interest in things
- do not learn how to join in and play with other children
- behave unacceptably in order to gain the adult's attention
- do not develop their language skills (because they are not being spoken to by adults).

How does interaction with adults support children's learning and development?

Poor awareness of social norms and values

The expression 'social norms and values' refers to the attitudes and behaviours that are expected in society. For example, in society it is expected that we will: queue at the counter in a shop rather than push in, not interrupt when people are talking.

Some children have a poor awareness of social norms and values, which means they often display inappropriate and unwanted behaviour in social situations and public places. They may be disruptive. This can make it difficult for them to concentrate and to make friends. They may become withdrawn and not join in with others because they feel different and have low self-esteem.

Difficulty forming bonds with adults

By the time children have reached 18 months they have usually formed bonds with familiar adults; however, some children can have difficulty with this due to individual circumstances.

◨ Table 3.5: Some children have difficulties forming bonds with adults

Premature birth	Children born prematurely may need care away from home, for example they may spend their first days in an incubator at the hospital which may prevent them from building an attachment to their parents.
Postnatal depression	This can affect the mother's ability to cuddle, show affection and interact with her baby, which can prevent her building an attachment with the child.
Child's health	If a child spends time away from home, for example in hospital, they may not spend as much time with their parents as other children.
Parents' health	If a parent/parents are ill, they may not spend a lot of time with the child and play with them, which could mean relationships are not developed.
Abuse	Some children are abused by their parents. This can mean they do not build positive relationships with them.

If a child has difficulty forming bonds with adults, this will have an impact on their learning and development.

Limited experience of play

Play is important for children's health, wellbeing and development. However, some children may have limited experience of play. This could be for a number of reasons such as: overcrowding in the childcare setting or home, lack of outdoor space, not having the opportunity to mix with other children.

It is the role of the adult to provide play opportunities that support all areas of learning and development and to play with children, being a positive role model.

If a child has not been given enough opportunities to play this can have an impact on their learning and development. Without play children will:

- not be given opportunities to find out what they like and are interested in
- find it difficult to control their emotions
- be unable to make friends and learn to get along with others
- not learn how to use resources and equipment
- not progress in all areas of development
- find it difficult to adapt to different situations.

Children are happy when they are engaged in play, therefore limited experience of play can lead to anxiety and depression.

ACTIVITY

Sophie is attending work experience at the local playgroup with children aged between 2 and 4. This is her first time working with children and she is not sure what is expected. She has spent the morning looking on her mobile phone and ignoring the children.

Write down the answers to the following questions.

1 How is Sophie being a negative role model?

2 How could the limited interaction with the children affect their development?

Make some notes about the advice you would give to Sophie to enable her to be a more positive role model.

LINK IT UP

To remind yourself of social development and emotional development of children across the ages of birth to 5 years old, go to Component 1, section A.

To remind yourself of the different factors that affect growth and development, including socio-economic factors such as poor relationships with significant adults, go to Component 1, section B.

To remind yourself of the role of the adult in promoting learning through play, go to Component 2, section A.

CHECK MY LEARNING

1 State what is meant by social norms and values.

2 Explain the impact on children's development if they have difficulty forming bonds with adults. Give two examples for each area of development.

3 Explain the impact of limited play opportunities on children's learning and development.

Friendships

Friendships are important to children as they grow and develop. Friendships enable children to have positive interaction with other children and show children they are accepted, giving them confidence. Friendships form easily if children have well developed social skills and the confidence to interact with others. However, some children have difficulty forming friendships with other children and, because children learn a lot by playing with others, this can affect their learning and development.

Think about your own friendships and why these are important to you. At what age did you first develop friendships? How did friendships support your learning and development growing up?

Difficulty forming friendships with other children

Children's expected social development is shown in Table 3.6. But some children do not find it easy to make friendships. This can be for a number of reasons.

- A child may not have the skills required to form friendships, for example delayed social skills, making it difficult for them to share and take turns.
- A child may not have formed strong bond with adults, which makes it easier to make relationships with others and form friendships because they have learned to trust and to understand the needs and feelings of others.
- A child may have delayed language skills or may be learning English as an additional language, which means they find it difficult to communicate with other children.
- Some children's personalities mean they like to take the lead, do things their own way or win at games. They may not be tolerant of others and may respond inappropriately when there is a disagreement. This can put other children off from wanting to play with them.

◼ Table 3.6: Expected social development across the age ranges

0–18 months	Children will look at other children, get excited when they see them and begin to play alongside them.
18 months–3 years	Children usually start to form friendships at the end of this period.
3–5 years	By this time children have usually developed one or two close friendships and may have a best friend.

 How can you tell that these two children have developed a friendship?

ACTIVITY

Ruby is 4 and likes to tell the other children what to do when they are playing. She often gives each child a role that they must take, for example baby, mum or dog. Sometimes Ruby pushes the other children to make them do what she wants them to do. Today, she began to scream and cry loudly when another child said they wanted to go and play somewhere else. She hit the other child and threw some toys and equipment around. She then 'sulked' in the corner.

Write down your answers to the following questions.

1 Why might other children not want to play with Ruby?

2 How might Ruby's behaviour affect her ability to make friendships?

3 If Ruby doesn't make friendships, how might this have an impact on her development?

LINK IT UP

To remind yourself of social and emotional development of children across the ages of birth to 5 years old, go to Component 1, section A.

To remind yourself of planning social play and learning opportunities for children, including development of friendships, go to Component 2, section B.

CHECK MY LEARNING

1 Explain why forming friendships is important to children's learning and development.

2 Give two reasons why children may find it difficult to form friendships.

Disruptive behaviour

You have just learned about friendships and how some children can have difficulty forming these. One of the reasons children may find it difficult to form friendships with other children is that they have **disruptive behaviour**. This is attention-seeking behaviour that disturbs and interrupts activities. If a child has disruptive behaviour this will affect not only their learning and development but will have an impact on the children around them too. Imagine someone in your class is behaving disruptively. How do you think this would affect you?

Several types of disruptive behaviour are shown in Figure 3.2.

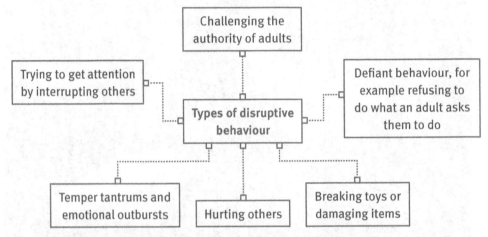

▪ Figure 3.2: Disruptive behaviour disturbs and interrupts activities

It is important to remember when recognising disruptive behaviour that expectations for behaviour change across the age ranges, as shown in Table 3.7.

▪ Table 3.7: Expectations for behaviour across the age ranges

0–18 months	Children do not understand the needs of others and do not understand that toys may belong to others.
18 months–3 years	Children are easily frustrated and may have tantrums. They do not like attention being given to other children.
3–5 years	Children can follow simple rules and play more cooperatively with others. By 5 children usually understand the difference between right and wrong.

A child may display disruptive behaviour for a number of reasons. For example, they may have difficulty forming friendships because of delayed language, sensory impairment or poor concentration levels.

▪ At what age do children usually have temper tantrums?

If a child is displaying disruptive behaviour this can mean they may not make friendships with other children. A child may continue their behaviour because they feel they have 'nothing to lose'.

A child with disruptive behaviour may find it difficult to concentrate. This will have an impact on their cognitive/intellectual development and eventually on their academic performance.

◪ How is the girl in this photo being disruptive?

LINK IT UP

To remind yourself of the stages of play, go to Component 2, section A.

ACTIVITY

Sally, who is an early years practitioner, tells off Kieran, aged 2, for pouring his juice all over the table. Some of the other children start to pour their juice on the table because they know it will get Sally's attention.

1 How is Kieran showing disruptive behaviour?

2 How can disruptive behaviour impact on a child's learning and development?

3 Why have the other children copied Kieran's behaviour?

CHECK MY LEARNING

1 Give three examples of disruptive behaviour.

2 Give one reason why a child may display disruptive behaviour.

3 Explain how the disruptive behaviour of one child can affect the learning and development of other children.

A child experiencing a transition

GETTING STARTED

Discuss, in a group, the different transitions you have experienced in your lives.

How did these impact on your learning and development?

Write down your ideas.

KEY TERMS

Transition changes in children's lives.

Care or educational providers settings that provide formal care or education for children.

Sibling a brother or sister.

Significant family member a close family member such as a parent, sibling or grandparent.

Family structure the way in which a family is organised.

▣ How might starting school be an exciting time for children?

A **transition** is a change in a child's life. There are several different transitions that a child may experience between 0 and 5 years.

A transition often brings a new environment or a new relationship to a child, which can have different effects on different children. During a transition, a child may experience a range of feelings which can impact on their learning and development. A child may feel stressed, anxious and nervous.

Children like things in their lives to stay the same (be consistent) as this helps them feel safe and secure, therefore changes can be unsettling. Often transitions mean that a child will be separated from their parent/s. The effects of this can depend on the child's age and stage of development.

Can you remember the first time you were separated from your parents/carers? How old were you? How did you feel?

Starting care or educational providers

Almost all children will experience this transition.

▣ Table 3.8: Starting day care across the age ranges

0–18 months and 18 months–3 years	Children may attend a day care setting because their parents work.
3–5 years	Children in this age group will be starting school.

Starting a **care or educational provider** can be exciting for a child but can also be a stressful time. They will be nervous and will not know anyone or where anything is. They may suffer from separation anxiety, which is a form of distress caused when children are separated from their parents/carers.

Reactions of children to this transition depend on their age and stage of development. For example, children aged 0–18 months may cry and become clingy, whereas older children may ask lots of questions such as people's names and where things are, for example the toilets or their favourite activities.

Moving between care/educational providers

Sometimes children move between care or educational providers. For example, they leave the childminding setting because it is time to start school.

This can be a distressing time because the child will have formed bonds with their previous carers. These bonds will be broken, and they will need to form relationships with new people and make new friends. This may cause them to feel unsafe and insecure. The routine at the new setting could be different to the previous one, which can be confusing for children and make them feel unsettled.

Birth of a new sibling

A new baby in the family is a huge adjustment for a child. They may feel that the new baby is going to take their place. Many children experience feelings of jealousy towards a new **sibling** and they may start to behave like a baby to get the adult's attention, for example cry and have tantrums or wet themselves even though they are toilet trained. This is called regression. A child may behave aggressively and may try to hurt the baby by hitting them or taking toys from them.

Death of a significant family member

Many children will find death difficult to understand. When a **significant family member** such as a parent, sibling or grandparent dies, a child will struggle to understand why the person is no longer there and why they cannot see them.

The child may cry and feel angry. They may become clingy to other significant family members because they are worried they too will die. Some children become withdrawn and stop speaking and begin to play alone. Their eating habits could also be affected, which could lead to them becoming ill. This will have an impact on their physical development.

Change in family structure

The way in which a family is organised (the **family structure**) can change through divorce, separation or death. This means that there can be new additions to families. For example, children can find themselves with a new step-parent or step-sibling. As with the birth of a new sibling, a child may experience feelings of jealousy or resentment to the new additions to the family.

The family may need to move house or the child may be spending time at two different homes, which can be confusing and make them feel unsettled. This can also disrupt their sleep patterns, therefore they may find it difficult to concentrate, which can have an impact on their cognitive/intellectual development.

Moving house

Moving house can be an exciting time for a child but can also be distressing, particularly if the new house is a long way from their old home and they have to move to a new care or educational provider and get used to new adults and children.

There can be an impact on the child's emotional development, as they may feel sad because there is a sense of loss. Their routine is likely to be disrupted during the move, which will make them feel anxious. They may become clingy to significant family members and regress in their development. They may even feel angry about the move.

> **DID YOU KNOW?**
>
> Some children who are looked after and 'in care' (for example, living with a foster family rather than with their birth parents) are likely to experience multiple transitions in their lives.

> **ACTIVITY**
>
> *You are completing your work experience in a children's centre where many of the children are experiencing different transitions. You have been asked to create a section of a staff training guide to explain to staff the effect of transitions on children's learning and development.*
>
> The training guide must cover the following:
> - starting care/educational providers
> - moving between care/educational providers
> - birth of a new sibling
> - death of a significant family member
> - change in family structure.

> **LINK IT UP**
>
> To remind yourself of the social and emotional development of children across the ages of birth to 5 years, go to Component 1, section A.

> **CHECK MY LEARNING**
>
> 1 Give three examples of transitions that a child may experience.
> 2 Explain the effects of starting care or educational providers on children of different ages.
> 3 Explain how the impact of the birth of a new sibling can be similar to a change in family structure.

How individual circumstances may impact on learning and development

GETTING STARTED

Working in pairs, make a list of milestones expected in the following age groups:

- 0–18 months
- 18 months–3 years
- 3–5 years.

How do you think children's learning and development can be affected if they are not meeting expected milestones?

Write down your ideas.

KEY TERMS

Expected milestones development that is expected at a particular age.

All areas of development physical, cognitive/intellectual, communication and language, social and emotional.

Initiate play to start play.

DID YOU KNOW?

Observations of children are carried out in settings to check children's development against milestones.

It is important to remember that no two children the same age, even identical twins, will develop at the same rate.

DID YOU KNOW?

Some children's development is ahead of expected milestones. This is called being 'gifted' and/ or 'talented'.

There are several different circumstances that may impact on children's learning and development in all areas of development – physical, cognitive/intellectual, communication and language, social and emotional.

Milestones are aspects of children's development that are expected at particular ages. Milestones have been decided by professionals who have studied large groups of children and reached a conclusion about the normal pattern of development for different ages. Think about the following milestones. At what age is the development expected?

- Starting to walk
- Starting to talk
- Riding a tricycle

Milestones are used to measure children's development to see if they are developing at the expected rate. In Component 1, you learned about the growth and development of children across the ages of birth to 5 years old and what is expected at different ages.

Not meeting expected milestones

A child may not be meeting **expected milestones** because they have additional needs known as 'developmental disorders', which prevent them from developing at the expected rate in one or more areas of development.

If a child's rate of progress across **all areas of development** is a lot slower than what is considered 'typical' for their age, this is called 'global development delay'.

Some children have a delay in one aspect of one of the areas of development.

Where children are not meeting the milestones in one area of development, this can impact on other areas of learning and development, as shown in Table 3.9.

 Table 3.9: The impact of not meeting milestones

Impact of not meeting physical development milestones	• May find it hard to explore the environment • Limited opportunities to play with others, impacting on language and social development • Feelings of frustration leading to low self-esteem, poor self-concept and effects on behaviour
Impact of not meeting cognitive/intellectual development milestones	• May find it hard to learn language • May struggle with shapes which will affect reading and writing development • May play differently to others, affecting social development • Low self-esteem as may feel excluded from play
Impact of not meeting communication and language development milestones	• May be unable to express feelings • Fewer opportunities to interact with others, impacting on social development • Impact on cognitive/intellectual development as may find it hard to organise their thoughts
Impact of not meeting emotional development milestones	• May not understand the needs and feeling of others • Miss out on opportunities to play with other children • Unable to manage behaviour appropriately • Poor concentration – so find it difficult to learn
Impact of not meeting social development milestones	• Unable to develop friendships • Can affect physical development • May not learn language easily • Impact on self-esteem • Poor behaviour

Not initiating play

When children **initiate play**, they choose resources, how to play with them, who to play with and how the play develops. Some children may not be able to initiate play, which means they are less likely to be confident and independent. This could be for a number of reasons, for example:

- low self-esteem
- delayed social development
- delayed language development
- lack of experience of play.

Their learning and development can be affected in several ways, as shown in Figure 3.3.

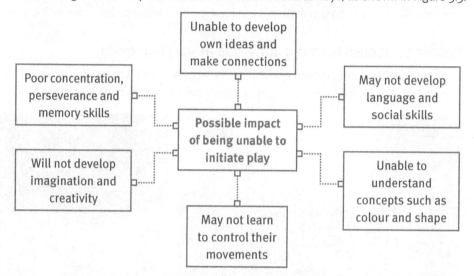

Figure 3.3: Possible impact of being unable to initiate play

LINK IT UP

To remind yourself of growth and development of children across the ages of birth to 5 years, go to Component 1, section A.

To remind yourself of the factors that affect growth and development, go to Component 1, section B.

To remind yourself of child-initiated play, go to Component 2, 'How play can be organised to promote learning, child-intiated play'.

ACTIVITY

You are working in a large day nursery. Some of the children appear to not be meeting expected milestones.

Produce a booklet to explain to the staff the impact of not meeting expected milestones in children's physical development.

Your booklet should focus on the impact on other areas of development.

CHECK MY LEARNING

1 Describe what is meant by 'expected milestones'.
2 Give one reason why a child may not be meeting expected milestones.
3 Give two reasons why being unable to initiate play may impact on a child's ability to socialise.

Why might some children find it difficult to initiate play?

How individual circumstances may impact on physical learning and development

There are several individual circumstances that may impact on children's physical learning and development. Some children have difficulty with their gross motor movements, which means they are unable to access learning activities at **varying levels** or **navigate** their way around play areas and activities. Some children's fine motor development means they are unable to pick up and grasp small objects or manipulate materials to use them correctly. What impact do you think this can have on their physical development?

Unable to access learning activities at varying levels

In both the indoor and outdoor environments, activities and resources may be situated at varying levels. The pictures below show some examples of varying levels.

■ How many different 'levels' can you see in these pictures?

A child who has a sensory impairment or restricted or delayed gross motor skills may be unable to access learning activities at varying levels because their physical skills of coordination and balance are not as good as other children. This can have an impact on their learning and development, for example on their:

- physical development – they may not develop stamina
- social development – they may not develop friendships.

Unable to grasp small objects or manipulate materials in a constructive way

Some children have restricted or delayed fine motor skills. This means they may be unable to grasp small objects such as buttons or beads because the movements of their hands and fingers are not as well developed as other children. They may find it hard to manipulate materials such as clay, playdough, paint, building bricks or jigsaw pieces to make something **constructive**. This can have an impact on children's learning and development, for example on their:

- cognitive development – they may find it hard to think and make choices
- emotional development – they may find it hard to express their emotions and may lack a sense of achievement.

Some children may find it difficult to manipulate equipment and resources too, so they will find it hard to handle these skilfully enough to use them in the way they are intended to be used. Examples that they may struggle with include fastening buttons and cutting with scissors.

May tire easily and not be able to sustain involvement in activities

It is not uncommon for children to feel tired occasionally. However, some children tire easily, and this can affect their ability to **sustain involvement** in activities, which means they are not involved in activities for long before needing a rest.

There are several reasons why children may tire easily. They may be going through a transition or not getting enough sleep. In 'How resources can be organised and the use of specific areas' and 'Health and safety considerations for outside environments' you learned that, when looking at health and safety considerations for inside environments, the indoor and outdoor environment should provide quiet, comfortable spaces for children, so they can rest when they are tired.

◻ **Table 3.10: How children's learning and development can be affected if they tire easily**

Physical development	May lack the energy to take part in physical activities
Cognitive/intellectual development	May struggle to learn and remember things
Social and emotional development	May be irritable and moody which can affect relationships

May be unable to navigate the play areas and activities

Some children may find it difficult to navigate round the setting. Children with restricted or delayed gross motor skills or a physical disability may find it difficult to control their movements to gain access to the play areas and activities. Those with a sensory impairment may be unable to see clearly, making it hard for them to explore the environment. Children's learning and development can be impacted if they are unable to navigate play areas and activities.

- physical development – children may move less because they find it difficult to control their movements
- cognitive/intellectual development – children's learning could be affected if they cannot access activities and resources
- social and emotional development – children may not play with other children because they cannot move in the same way as them. This could affect their self-esteem.

Adults should ensure that furniture and equipment is positioned to allow all children to navigate to play areas and activities.

ACTIVITY

Write a report about how individual circumstances may impact on physical learning and development. Your report should include information about children who:
- are unable to access learning activities at varying levels
- are unable to grasp small objects or manipulate materials in a constructive way
- may tire easily and not be able to sustain involvement in activities
- may be unable to navigate the play areas and activities.

You will need to include headings in your report to check you have covered everything.

LINK IT UP

To remind yourself of physical development across the ages of birth to 5 years, go to Component 1, section A.

To remind yourself of sensory impairment, restricted and delayed fine and gross motor skills, go to 'Physical circumstances that may impact on learning and development' in this component.

DID YOU KNOW?

Most children aged 18 months–3 years still need an afternoon nap. This usually stops when they reach 3–5 years.

CHECK MY LEARNING

1 Explain what is meant by varying levels.

2 Give three examples of materials that children who struggle with their fine motor skills may find difficult to manipulate.

3 Give a reason why children may tire easily.

How individual circumstances may impact on cognitive and intellectual, and communication and language, learning and development

You have already learned about children's cognitive/intellectual and communication and language development across the age ranges of birth to 5 in Component 1, but did you know that they are closely linked together?

Language allows us to process our thoughts. If children struggle with language this means their thinking skills will be affected, which can have an impact on their ability to communicate and socialise with others.

Language is the way in which we communicate our **preferences** and choices, for example how we are feeling or what we want. Some children have difficulties with this, which can lead to them being frustrated. Language difficulties can also prevent children from building friendships. For these children play with others may be limited, as they may be **perceived** as not wanting to play due to **lack of responsiveness**. Other children may think a child is ignoring them when really they do not understand what has been said. This could be because they have English as an additional language, or communication needs or that the stage of development they are at means they do not understand some words yet or the rules of language.

Cognitive and intellectual learning and development

Difficulty understanding the rules in play

Some children have difficulty understanding the rules in play because they have not learned these. This could be because they have poor awareness of social norms and values or limited experience of play.

In some types of play, children need to understand they have to wait, take turns, share or listen to others. This type of play will require children to:
- take turns at the different roles, which may involve waiting
- listen when others are speaking
- share the resources
- be respectful of the opinions, choices and preferences of other children.

Where children have limited experience of play, they may not have been given opportunities to develop skills such as sharing and turn taking. They may find it difficult to join in with other children as they may come across as being disruptive or not playing fairly. Figure 3.4 shows some of the rules of play that some children may find difficult to understand.

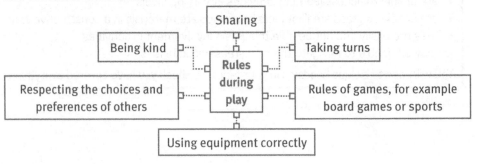

■ Figure 3.4: Children may miss out on play if they do not understand the rules. This can affect their cognitive and intellectual development.

Communication and language learning and development

Difficulties communicating preferences and choices

Depending on their age and stage of development, some children find it hard to communicate their preferences and choices. This means they do not have the language to be able to tell people what they want. Where this happens children may use other ways to express themselves.

Children who are not meeting the expected milestones in their language or children who have English as an additional language may also struggle to communicate their preferences and choices. This can impact on their emotional development as it can lead to them feeling frustrated, which can have an effect on their self-esteem.

Some children have communication needs, which means they have difficulties with speaking and listening and with the process of making sense of information.

Play with others may be limited

If a child is having difficulty communicating, they may not understand what other children are saying to them and may also have problems reading body language. Other children may perceive this as meaning that the child does not want to play. They may stop inviting the child to play, which can lead to the following:

- feelings of isolation, which can lead to a poor self-image
- limited opportunities for play, which could affect the development of physical and cognitive skills
- limited opportunities for social development, which could mean children do not develop friendships
- feelings of frustration, which could lead to disruptive behaviour.

🔲 Why might some children have difficulty communicating?

ACTIVITY

Gabriel, Ibrahim and Leah, aged 3, are on their way outside to play.

"Come on, let's go make a den!" says Gabriel.

Leah does not know the word 'den' and does not understand what this means, therefore she stays inside. Also, she would much prefer to do a painting but does not have the language yet to explain this.

"Let's go!" says Gabriel to Ibrahim. "Leah is not coming."

1 What assumption has Gabriel made about Leah?

2 What could be the impact on Leah's social and emotional development.

3 Why might Leah have found it difficult to communicate her needs and preferences?

How individual circumstances may impact on social and emotional learning and development (1)

KEY TERMS

Isolate cause a person to be alone/apart from others.

Emotional resilience a person's ability to adapt to stressful situations.

Some children may find cooperative play difficult. This could be because of their stage of development. Children who are used to 'getting their own way' at home may try to take the lead and dominate the play. This can be off-putting for other children and could cause them to **isolate** the child. However, isolation may be the child's choice or they may find it difficult to join in group or team activities.

Emotional skills come more easily to some children than others. This could be due to their age and stage of development but also a range of other factors.

Think about the things that make you stressed and how you cope with this. How might your reaction be different to someone else's?

Children may find cooperative play difficult

From 3 to 4 years of age children begin to play well with their peers and learn to share and take turns. They often engage in the same play. This stage of play is called cooperative play. You have already learned about the stages of play in Component 2.

Some children may find cooperative play difficult. This could be because they:

- cannot negotiate as they like to have 'their own way'
- are unable to recognise the needs and feelings of others
- have not learned to respect the choices and preferences of others
- do not understand the rules of play
- have delayed language or social development
- have not learned to be patient.

Children who find it difficult to play cooperatively:

- will be less confident about interacting with others.
- may feel unwanted, which will impact on their self-esteem (the way they feel about themselves) and their self-concept (the way they see themselves). They may display inappropriate behaviours because they feel left out.
- may miss out on the development of language because playing cooperatively enables children to listen and talk to other children and practise language in their play.

Children may have poor emotional resilience

Children with poor **emotional resilience** find it difficult to cope with stressful situations. The degree of emotional resilience a child has depends on their age and stage of development. For example, babies and toddlers cannot express their feelings and manage these as well as older children.

Poor emotional resilience can also be affected by many factors:

- transitions
- abuse
- parental depression
- bullying
- family stress, such as divorce/ separation.

■ Why might some children find it difficult to play cooperatively?

Stress takes its toll on the brain and the body, therefore it can have a negative impact on children's learning and development. Stress can instil feelings of fear and make children more dependent on adults. Children with poor emotional resilience may develop problems such as anxiety and depression.

Children may isolate themselves or be isolated by others

Some children may isolate themselves from others. This could be because they enjoy their own company and may like to complete activities by themselves or it could be that their social skills are lacking.

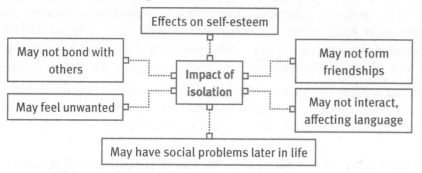

■ Figure 3.5: The possible impact isolation can have on a child's learning and development

You have already learned that some children may not understand the rules in play. Rather than take the risk of being rejected by others, a child may choose to play alone.

Children may isolate another child because they:
- behave disruptively
- interrupt/spoil the play
- want their 'own way'.

Sometimes, if children are being isolated by others, this could be a sign of bullying.

Children may refuse or find it difficult to join in team or group activities

Team and group activities such as board games or sport enable children to develop social skills and the confidence to interact with others; however, some children refuse or find it difficult to join in these types of activities. This could be because they do not understand the rules of play or their social skills are not yet developed.

Children who do not like these kinds of activities or find it difficult to join in may need support from an adult to help them to engage. Without this support they may not:
- form bonds and friendships
- learn about differences
- learn to respect others
- learn to negotiate and cooperate with others.

All these skills are important for later life.

ACTIVITY

Create a poster to be displayed in your classroom to show how individual circumstances may impact on social and emotional learning and development.

Your poster will need to include information on the following:

1 children who may find cooperative play difficult

2 children with poor emotional resilience

3 children who may isolate themselves or be isolated by others

4 children who may refuse or find it difficult to join in team or group activities.

LINK IT UP

To remind yourself of children's social and emotional development across the age ranges of birth to 5 years, go to Component 1, section A.

To remind yourself of the stages of children's play, go to Component 2, section A.

To remind yourself of children who may not understand the rules in play, go to 'How individual circumstances may impact on cognitive and intellectual development and communication and language learning and development' in this component.

CHECK MY LEARNING

1 Explain what is meant by 'cooperative' play?

2 Give a reason why a child may:
   a) isolate themselves from others
   b) be isolated by other children.

3 Assess the benefits of team and group activities to children's learning and development.

How individual circumstances may impact on social and emotional learning and development (2)

Some children may find it difficult to build **positive relationships** with adults. This can have a significant impact on children because adults are important in children's play and positive relationships with adults enable children to be confident and explore.

Emotional development refers to the way children develop and control their feelings and the way they feel about themselves – their self-esteem. Children express their feelings in their language, facial expressions and behaviour; however, some children have limited **expression** of thoughts and feelings. This can make them frustrated and cause disruptive behaviour; you have already learned about this in 'Friendships' and 'Disruptive behaviour'.

Routines are very important for children's social and emotional development. Some children find it difficult to cope with changes to their routine. Think about your own routine. How would you feel if this suddenly changed?

Children who have limited expression of thoughts and feelings

Just like adults, children experience many different feelings, for example:

- fear
- happiness
- frustration
- jealousy
- anger
- sadness.

Some children are able to express their feelings through their language, but some children do not find this easy because they may have limited vocabulary or communication needs. Children can be overwhelmed by their thoughts and feelings which, because they cannot explain what they are thinking or what they want, can result in:

- temper tantrums
- disruptive behaviour
- aggression towards others.

Children who find it difficult building positive relationships with adults

Children need to make relationships with other adults who may be caring for them. It is important that these adults are approachable as this will make it easier for positive relationships to be built.

Adults can show they are approachable by:

- showing they are interested in children's interests
- having open body language
- making eye contact with children
- being sensitive to children's needs and feelings
- smiling at children
- showing children respect.

If a child finds it difficult to build positive relationships with adults, they may:

- have difficulty developing relationships with others
- be unable to trust people
- be unable to form friendships
- have difficulty understanding the needs and feelings of others
- be unable to control behaviour and emotions
- lack confidence and independence to explore and try new things.

Why do children need positive relationships with adults?

Children who find it difficult to cope with change, routines and new situations

Change and new situations can be difficult for children to cope with. They get used to having a regular routine and this enables them to feel safe and secure.

Children learn routines from a very young age. For example, a baby soon learns that the sound of a tap running means it is bath time.

Routines make children feel emotionally safe and secure because they enable their lives to have predictability, which means they know what is going to happen next. When routines are changed, children become confused and unsettled, which can have a significant impact on their emotional development.

Low self-esteem

Self-esteem is how we feel about ourselves. Some children have low self-esteem, which means they do not feel good about themselves. Low self-esteem can be caused by a range of factors, such as:

- how others react to us
- comparing ourselves to others or being compared to others
- poor relationships with others
- not understanding rules in play
- delayed or restricted development
- not being praised
- not feeling accepted
- feeling of not belonging.

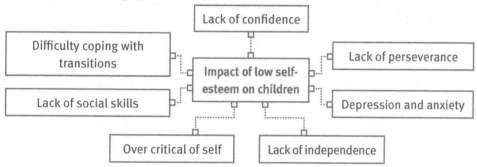

Figure 3.6: Possible impact of low self-esteem on children's social and emotional learning and development

LINK IT UP

To remind yourself of the social and emotional development of children across the ages of birth to 5 years, go to Component 1, section A.
To remind yourself of transitions children may experience, go to 'A child experiencing a transition' in this component.
To remind yourself about children who have disruptive behaviour, go to 'Disruptive behaviour' in this component.

How do routines such as this one help children?

CHECK MY LEARNING

1 Give one impact on a child's learning and development of being unable to express thoughts and feelings.

2 List two reasons why children may find it difficult to build positive relationships with adults.

3 Explain why routines are important for children's learning and development.

ACTIVITY

You have been invited to a job interview at a children's centre. To prepare for the interview, you need to make some notes on the possible impact on learning and development of the following:

- children who have limited expression of thoughts and feelings
- children who find it difficult to build positive relationships with adults
- children who find it difficult to cope with change/routines/new situations
- children with low self-esteem.

You will need to organise your notes with headings.

Ask a partner to check through your notes. Have you missed anything?

Learning aim A: assessment practice

How you will be assessed

In this component you will be assessed by an external assessment worth 60 marks. This will be completed under supervised conditions. It will be a question paper with space to write your answers. You will complete activities related to children's play, learning and development, and will plan how to support children with individual needs.

There will be three sections to the paper: Section A, Section B and Section C.

Section A will test your knowledge of A: Investigate individual circumstances that may impact on learning and development. You will be asked to give examples, explain the effects of things and identify the effects of different circumstances. Some questions will have multiple-choice answers.

CHECKPOINT

Strengthen
- Ensure you know what you need to do to clearly give examples of individual circumstances that may impact on learning and development.
- Ensure you understand the word 'explain'.

Challenge
- Make sure that you can demonstrate a high level of understanding of how individual circumstances may impact on learning and development.
- Make your explanations of how individual circumstances may impact on learning and development as clear as possible.

1 Give one example of a physical circumstance that could affect a child's learning and development. (1 mark)

2 Identify two potential effects of disruptive behaviour on social and emotional development of a 3-year-old. (2 marks)

Choose two answers from the following.

A Difficulty making friends   D Low levels of self-esteem

B Restricted gross motor skills   E Delayed literacy skills

C Poor concentration levels

3 Mary, aged 4, has a visual impairment, which is an example of a sensory impairment. Complete the table to give a possible impact of visual impairment on each area of Mary's development. (4 marks)

Area of development	Impact of visual impairment
Physical	
Cognitive/Intellectual	
Communication and language	
Social and emotional	

4 Identify two social and emotional circumstances that may be experienced by children from the following. (2 marks)

A Poor concentration levels

B English as an additional language

C Poor awareness of social norms and values

D Difficulty forming friendships with other children

E Delayed fine motor skills

5 Explain two possible effects of moving house on a child's learning and development. (2 marks)

6 Starting a care/educational provider is an example of a transition a child may experience. Give an example of one other transition a child may experience. (1 mark)

7 Many children are learning English alongside a different language. Give two examples of the impact learning English as an additional language can have on children's learning and development. (2 marks)

TIPS

Make sure you spend the right amount of time on each question. Generally, questions with higher marks need you to provide longer answers.

Ensure you read the questions carefully, checking the area of development and child's age if this is given.

Check you are giving enough examples. Are you being asked to give one example or two?

TAKE IT FURTHER

- Check your answers. Your answers should take into account the command words, for example 'give' or 'explain'.
- 'Give' means to provide examples or reasons.
- 'Explain' means that you need to give details of the subject and go on to give reasons for your view or argument.
- Check your understanding of the different areas of development.

Managing risks and hazards of environments and activities

KEY TERMS

Risk likelihood of an environment, activity and/or resource causing harm.

Hazard potential for an environment, activity and/or resource to cause harm.

Risk assessment a process of evaluating what might cause harm to people (the potential risks) and making sure things are in place to manage the risk and prevent harm.

Children under 5 years of age need a safe environment in order to support their play, learning and development. It is the role of the adult to ensure all children are safe when engaging in play and learning activities. It is important when choosing resources for children that they are appropriate for the children's age and stage of development so that there are no   to children and no **hazards** that could harm them. It is important that we are aware of any potential risks and hazards to children and that we ensure these are minimised to keep children safe. How dangerous something is to a child depends on a child's age and stage of development, for example small beads could be dangerous to children aged 6–12 months as children this age put everything in their mouths and could choke, whereas these would be less dangerous to a 5-year-old child as they are less likely to put them in their mouth. How can we ensure that toys and activities are safe for children of different age groups?

Considering risks and hazards

We can minimise risks and hazards by ensuring that the environment is safe and that toys and activities are not dangerous and are suitable for the age of the child.

Children 0–18 months explore by putting everything in their mouths. This is known as 'mouthing'; this means that small items that are suitable for older children to play with, for example building blocks, can be dangerous for babies and toddlers.

Children aged 18 months–3 years often take part in what is known as exploratory play, which can consist of gross motor movements such as opening and closing doors; this means that adults need to ensure that there is not a risk of accidents such as trapped fingers.

Children aged 3–5 years are becoming more independent in their play and they seek opportunities to play away from adults, therefore adults need to ensure that any areas where children may be out of sight such as dens or tents are safe.

Although it is important to ensure that all children are safe, we must remember there should be a balance between the potential risk of harm and the benefit of children participating in activities. Children need to have experiences in order to help them learn and develop and to support them to manage risks for themselves.

For example, if we stop children 18 months–3 years from climbing then they may not develop to their full physical potential. We can ensure that the children are given age appropriate climbing frames to climb on and that measures are in place to stop them being hurt.

You can minimise the amount of risk by carrying out **risk assessments** to identify potential hazards that could harm children and what you can do to prevent this from happening. For each activity that children take part in adults should list all the things that could be dangerous in the activity and then consider what they can put in place to stop these being a risk to the children's safety.

Choosing age and stage appropriate resources

All toys and resources provided for children must be safe for them to play with and must be appropriate for their age and stage of development. There are a number of symbols that can be found on children's toys, which show they are safe. Adults should look out for these when buying toys for children.

- The British Lion Mark indicates that toys have been tested.

- The age advice symbol. This means that the toy is not suitable for children 0–3. This could be because it has small parts that very young children could choke on.

- The CE mark is a declaration by toy manufacturers that the toy is safe.

- The BSI Kitemark™ indicates that safety requirements have been met.

- The fire resistant symbol is attached to items that have passed a scientific control test showing that they are resistant to fire.

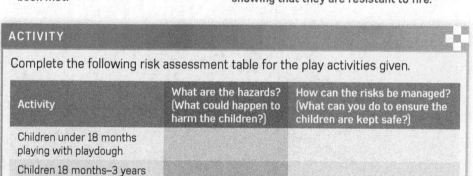

ACTIVITY

Complete the following risk assessment table for the play activities given.

Activity	What are the hazards? (What could happen to harm the children?)	How can the risks be managed? (What can you do to ensure the children are kept safe?)
Children under 18 months playing with playdough		
Children 18 months–3 years playing with a play kitchen		
Children aged 3–5 playing in a tent		

For each activity write down the benefits of the activity to children's development.

LINK IT UP

To remind yourself of the characteristics of children's development from birth to 5 years, go to Component 1, section A.

To remind yourself of what children learn from different types of play, go to Component 2, section B.

CHECK MY LEARNING

1 Why is it important to check the symbols on children's toys?

2 Give two reasons why it is important to manage risk and hazards when supporting children's play, learning and development.

3 Assess the importance of the balance between the potential risk of harm and the benefit of children participating in activities.

Positive risk taking and the role of the adult

GETTING STARTED

Make a list of reasons why playing outside could be risky to children.

How would you encourage children to be safe when playing outside? Consider this for children aged:

- 0–18 months
- 18 months–3 years
- 3–5 years.

Write down your answers.

KEY TERMS

Positive risk taking balancing the potential risk of harm against the benefit of children participating in activities.

Adult to child ratio the number of adults to the number of children.

You have already learned that a risk is the likelihood of something causing harm. Taking a risk can be dangerous but there is such a thing as '**positive risk taking**'. This is where we balance the potential risk of harm against the benefit of children taking part in an activity. For example, we may think that children playing outside can be dangerous. However, if they do not do this they will not have access to fresh air and will not get any exercise, which is not good for their development. Imagine a world where children never experienced the outdoors. What would this be like?

There should be enough adults to enable children to carry out activities safely and it is the role of the adult to support children in their play, whether it is led by adults or initiated by the children, to ensure children are safe; however, this does not mean that we need to make the play less exciting.

Positive risk taking

You have already learned in 'Managing risks and hazards of environments and activities' that activities, resources, areas, toys and equipment should be risk assessed to consider what the risks are and how these can be prevented.

Rather than being overly concerned with safety, adults should also allow children opportunities to explore. Life is full of risk so the best way to prepare children for life is to ensure that they learn how to judge risk for themselves.

It is important to teach children how to be safe in public areas. Children from 2 years of age can be taught simple rules about personal safety. Older children (for example, 3–5 years) can be taught to cross roads safely, and be taught their address and parent/carer's telephone numbers in case of an emergency.

LINK IT UP

To remind yourself of different play structures: adult led play, adult initiated play and child initiated play, go to Component 2, section A.

To remind yourself of the characteristics of children's development from birth to 5 years, go to Component 1, section A.

◼ How can adults teach children to use scissors safely?

The role of the adult

Implementing adult-led play, adult-initiated play or child-led play

In section A2 of Component 2, you learned about adult led play, adult initiated play and child initiated play.

Adult led play is when adults plan and organise children's play and the adult takes the lead in order to teach children particular concepts or skills. For example, the adult may plan to build train tracks with the children aged 18 months–3 years and count the pieces to teach them to count to ten.

Adult initiated play is when adults plan and organise children's play to allow children to explore. It is the role of the adult here to organise toys and resources in ways that will encourage children to play with them. The adult should allow the children to explore but also they should introduce new materials and concepts to the children. For example, after setting up a painting activity for children aged 3–5 years, the adult may introduce some different sized brushes to the children and may suggest that they mix the colours.

Child initiated play is when children choose what to play and how to play. The role of the adult here is to ensure that the children lead the play and decide what to do. The adult should observe and show that they are interested but should not interfere. For example, if children aged 18 months–3 years are building a tower, the adult should not suggest that they knock it down and build something else.

Planning adult to child ratios

It is the role of the adult to ensure that all play is suitable for the children's age, stage of development and abilities. There is a legal requirement for there to be enough adults to support children's play and learning. This is called the '**adult to child ratio**'.

The younger children are the more adults are needed. This is because younger children (for example, 0–2 years) are less independent than older children (for example, 3–5 years) and need more adult care to meet their needs.

There should be a minimum of two adults at all times, for example if there were only three children aged 0–2 years, there would need to be two adults as it is unlawful for one adult to be left alone with a group of children.

◨ **Table 3.11: Current adult to child ratios**

Age of children	Adult to child ratio
0–2 years	1 adult to 3 children
2 years	1 adult to 4 children
3–5 years	1 adult to 13 children

ACTIVITY

You are working with a group of children on a cutting and sticking activity. Francesca, aged 4, is reluctant to join in. She tells you that her daddy told her off at home for picking up the scissors and told her "Never touch scissors; they are sharp and dangerous!"

1 Answer the questions, working in pairs, and write down your answers.
   a) Why do you think Francesca's Dad has said this?
   b) How will using scissors support Francesca's development?
   c) What are the hazards with this kind of activity?
   d) How can the risks be minimised?

2 Role play what you would say to Francesca's dad to explain to him the benefits of risky activities.

CHECK MY LEARNING

1 Explain what is meant by 'positive risk taking'.

2 If a nursery has 24 children between 0 and 2 years, how many adults will they need?

Supporting children's play

GETTING STARTED

Make a list of all the things you have learned from an adult by observing and copying them.

Why is it important that adults are good role models? Discuss with a partner and write down your thoughts.

Children need adults in their play to support them, to ensure the play remains safe. It is the adult's role to model appropriate behaviours and responses and to supervise the children without interrupting or spoiling their play. Think about when you were a child and an adult interrupted your play. How did this make you feel?

However, it is not always possible for adults to stand back. There are times when adult intervention is needed to ensure that children do not hurt themselves or become bored. Adults can offer children new ideas and resources or give alternative suggestions to them in order to maintain the children's **stimulation** and to keep them safe. Overall it is important that all play is suitable for the children's ages, stages and abilities, including levels of confidence and how easily and quickly they get bored.

Role modelling appropriate behaviours and responses

During play, adults should **role model** sharing, taking turns and helping others. This will encourage children to be caring to others in their play. Adults should teach children to use resources safely and should be a role model for correct use.

KEY TERMS

Stimulation giving something interest, enthusiasm or excitement.

Role model a person looked to by others as an example to be imitated.

Available being there to supervise.

Intrusive causing disruption or annoyance through being unwelcome or uninvited.

Supporting children's play

It is important that the adult is **available** to supervise and support the children but they need to judge when it is best to leave children to get on with their play by themselves.

If the adult is **intrusive** and interferes too much this could affect the children's development. For example, if you rush to stop a toddler opening the cupboard in the play kitchen and open it for him because you are afraid he might trap his fingers, this has stopped him from being independent and developing his physical skills.

Appropriate intervention

Sometimes adults may need to intervene if something is not safe or to help children to be respectful of others.

■ Why would an adult need to intervene in this situation?

DID YOU KNOW?

For most children, the most important role models are their parents and caregivers.

It can be easy to stop children from playing dangerously by distracting them with a new resource or idea.

Offering new ideas and resources or alternatives

Sometimes adults may need to give children some new ideas or resources to ensure that their play remains safe and to enable accessibility for the encouragement and stimulation of play. For example, an adult might discretely replace a broken toy with another one or add some water to the sand so that it is less likely to get in the children's eyes.

The adult may suggest that children change what they are doing without making it obvious that this is a safety precaution.

Ensuring that all play is suitable for children's ages, needs and abilities

Play should not only be suitable for the children's ages but adults also need to take the children's needs and abilities into account. Some children may be less confident than others and may need reassurance from an adult to join in. Others may need the play to be made more exciting because they are ahead in their development and are becoming bored.

Adults also need to understand that play activities may need to be adapted in order to meet the needs of children who have additional needs. For example, having larger crayons in the mark making area for a child who has weak fine motor skills.

■ Adults should model how to carry scissors correctly with the hand clasped around closed blades.

ACTIVITY

Paul works in the local day nursery. He is having difficulty keeping the children's interest in the construction area. The children have been throwing the building bricks around and he is worried that the area is becoming unsafe.

Write down what advice you would give to Paul. Your advice must cover the following points:

1 role modelling appropriate behaviours and responses
2 supporting children's play – being available but not intrusive
3 offering new ideas, resources and alternatives
4 ensuring the play is suitable for the children's ages, stages and abilities.

Role play with a partner with one of you taking on the role of Paul and one of you the role of the advisor.

LINK IT UP

To remind yourself of the role of the adult in promoting learning through play, go to Component 2, section A.

CHECK MY LEARNING

1 Give two examples of when it is appropriate for an adult to intervene in children's play.
2 Give three roles of the adult in keeping children's play safe, one for each age group: 0–18 months, 18 months–3 years and 3–5 years.
3 Explain how an adult can be a good role model to children in their play.

Teaching children how to use internet enabled technology (1)

Why do adults need to teach children how to use tablets safely?

The internet is wonderful. It opens up a world of exciting possibilities and enables us to learn, create and connect with people all over the world. Very young children now go online.

Children 0–18 months may be given a phone or tablet to watch a cartoon or listen to soothing music.

Children 18 months–3 years may be starting to play games and use apps.

Children 3–5 years may be chatting online to friends and family.

The benefits of children using technology

Children not only have access to technology through devices such as computers, tablets and mobile phones, but as technology advances there are now many more resources that can enable children to be introduced to technology such as smart watches (wearable technology), app enabled toys and toys with voice recognition. **'Smart' devices** can wirelessly connect to other devices or networks that open up endless opportunities for us to interact with others online.

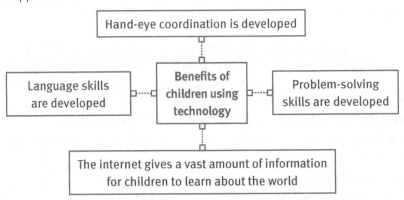

Figure 3.7: Children can benefit from using technology in many ways

Using the internet can be beneficial for children if used appropriately, for example there are lots of apps available that encourage children's learning and creativity. Unfortunately, the internet can also be a risky place for children.

Table 3.12: Risks associated with children using the internet

Cyberbullying	This is bullying that takes place online and through social networks, games and text messages.
Online abuse	This is abuse that happens online. It can include cyberbullying, sexual abuse or exploitation, grooming or emotional abuse.
Sharing private information	Children may share personal information online, for example their home address or photographs/videos of themselves.
Phishing	Children may receive messages asking them for personal information such as passwords. The messages might look like they are coming from someone the child knows.
Falling for scams	Children may see offers on websites that promise them things, for example a new game in exchange for their parents' credit card information.
Accidentally downloading malware	This is software that is specifically designed to gain access to or damage a computer without the knowledge of the owner. Children may accidentally click on something that downloads a virus.
Inappropriate posts	Anything a child posts on the internet cannot be permanently deleted. Children need to be aware that things they post online could be seen for years to come.

How to be safe online

Adults can set up **parental controls** on phones, tablets, games consoles, laptops and computers to keep children safe online.

Parental controls will filter what children can see online, such as those shown in Figure 3.8.

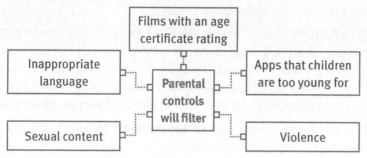

■ Figure 3.8: Adults can set up parental controls to keep children safe online

They also stop children sharing personal information.

Blocking children from social networking sites will reduce the risk of children talking to people they do not know online or tagging themselves in posts, which will reveal their location to strangers.

Controls put in place by adults

Parental controls can:

- limit the time of day children can go online, reducing this to day time only so as not to disturb children's sleep
- limit how long a child is online for; it is not healthy for children to spend too long on **internet enabled** devices because it can limit the amount of exercise they do
- block children from spending money online. For example, some game apps allow players to buy characters or features ('**in app purchase**'), which can be very expensive. Children aged 18 months–3 years may pay for something accidentally if the parent/carer's credit/debit card details are registered on the device. Older children may deliberately pay for something they want without realising how much it actually costs! Adults can make sure there are no credit/debit cards attached to the app so children will not be able to buy anything and parents/carers' card details will not be available online, which stops the risk of theft and fraud.

Teaching children how to use internet enabled technology (2)

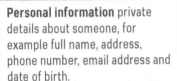

KEY TERMS

Personal information private details about someone, for example full name, address, phone number, email address and date of birth.

Inappropriate content information or pictures online that could upset a child, material that is directed at adults, that might lead a child into unlawful or dangerous behaviour. This could be pornographic or violent material, or inappropriate language.

How can we talk to children about internet safety and teach them to recognise when something is not appropriate for them to see?

When talking to children about internet safety, adults need to take the child's age and stage of development into consideration. We want to keep children safe but not to frighten them. The conversation could include what apps and games they like, what makes them feel uncomfortable and what to do if they see something that upsets them. Adults should also discourage children from sharing their **personal information** online.

Adults should be aware of what is age **inappropriate content** for children and should report this using the appropriate channels.

Talking to children about internet safety

It is important that adults talk to children about how to stay safe online. Adults should be aware of what apps, games or websites children are interested in and should tell children if they are worried about any of these.

Children should be encouraged to tell an adult if they see anything online that scares them or makes them feel uncomfortable. This can include cyberbullying.

Adults should teach children what personal information means and that it is important not to share this information online.

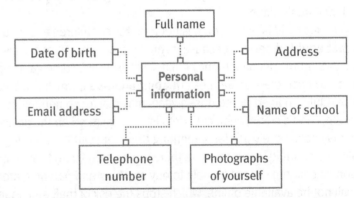

☐ **Figure 3.9: Adults should teach children what personal information means**

Explain to children that it is easy for people to disguise themselves online, for example an adult could pretend to be a child. Children should be aware that if they are talking to someone online who genuinely knows them (such as a family member) they shouldn't need to ask for personal information.

If children are using social media sites, adults should teach them:

- how to block someone
- how to report someone
- not to reveal their location
- not to give their full name.

 How could the adult in this picture teach the child to stay safe online?

Recognising and reporting age inappropriate content

Some websites can have content that is inappropriate for children. This could include images or comments that could upset a child, material that is directed at adults, for example sexual content, violent images or inappropriate language. It is important that children are taught to recognise when something is not appropriate for them to see.

Adults have a duty of care to report age inappropriate content online. There is a facility for this on social media sites. There may also be times when it is necessary to contact the police.

ACTIVITY

Design a poster aimed at 3–5-year-old children to encourage them to stay safe online.

Consider the age of the children. The poster needs to be simple enough for this age to understand and should not aim to frighten the children. It should include:
- pictures of devices, games and apps that children this age may use
- simple information on how to keep safe online that will not frighten the children.

Compare your poster with the person sitting next to you. Is there anything you have forgotten to include?

CHECK MY LEARNING

1 Give three examples of personal information that children should be discouraged from sharing online.
2 Explain how adults can help children stay safe on social media sites.
3 Explain what an adult can do if they see children looking at something inappropriate online.

Health and safety considerations for inside environments

GETTING STARTED

With a partner, get down on the floor and move around at a level to enable you to see things from a child's perspective. Write down how your classroom would need to be adapted to ensure young children were safe.

Children's surroundings have a significant impact on their development. Adults should give great care and attention to the room layout, furniture and floor coverings to ensure children are safe when indoors. Think about your childhood memories: What made you feel comfortable as a child? What made you feel safe in a room?

Width of doorways, aisles and corridors

- Doorways should be wide enough to accommodate prams and pushchairs for children aged 0–18 months and also wheelchairs for children, parents/carers or staff who have a disability.
- Aisles and corridors should be kept clear and should be wide enough to give children and staff easy access to different rooms and areas. There should be enough space to accommodate more than one person at a time, for example children aged 3–5 years often play in groups and may be moving around together, but children aged 0–18 months will be accompanied by an adult when moving through aisles and corridors, which may involve them being carried or transported in a pram or pushchair.
- In the event of a fire, aisles and corridors need to allow as many people as possible to move out in one go.

Layout of furniture

- Furniture should be positioned so that there is a clear pathway to enable children to move around easily to access activities and resources.
- Furniture should be positioned so it does not block the children's view. For, example, children aged 18 months–3 years are not as tall as older children so items such as high shelving units could restrict their vision across the room.
- The layout of the furniture should allow enough space for individual and groups of children to move around freely.

Types of furniture used

All furniture should be child sized and strong with rounded edges to prevent accidents. For example, children under 18 months who are crawling and starting to walk are likely to walk into things so any sharp corners could be dangerous.

Chairs

- Chairs being used for children should be sturdy and the right height to enable children to have their feet flat on the floor so they can sit comfortably and control their bodies.
- It is a good idea to have chairs that have sides to support children under 18 months who may still be unstable when sitting.
- The setting will need chairs for adults that are low enough for them to sit and interact with children and strong enough to provide support for them as they are heavier than children.

Tables

- Tables should be the right height to match the chairs. The posture of 3–5-year-old children could be affected if they are leaning down to work on low tables.

- Tables in childcare settings are often used for a range of purposes, for example eating as well as activities, therefore they need to be light and **movable** as they may be transported around for different purposes.
- It is a good idea to have adjustable tables so the height can be altered to enable children in the 18 month to 3-year-old age group or 3–5-year-old age group to stand up when taking part in activities.

Some furniture in the setting such as storage units that are wall fixed may be heavy and **immovable**. This is to stop children being able to push them and stops items being knocked over if children run into them.

◻ What makes this furniture suitable for children?

Types of flooring and floor coverings

- Children spend a lot of time on the floor so this is a very important indoor play surface.
- There should be carpeted areas for babies aged 0–18 months who move around by rolling and crawling and for some activities for older children such as role play.
- Washable flooring is also required in some areas, particularly toilet and sink areas, eating areas and messy play areas, as it is likely there will be spillages here.
- Hard flooring should be durable and non-slip to ensure children are kept safe.
- Some floor coverings are not suitable for young children, for example laminate flooring or tiles, as pieces can become dislodged causing a **trip hazard**.

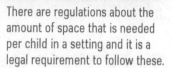

KEY TERMS

Movable capable of being moved.

Immovable fixed and impossible to move.

Trip hazard object(s) on the floor that could cause someone to trip and possibly fall.

DID YOU KNOW?

There are regulations about the amount of space that is needed per child in a setting and it is a legal requirement to follow these.

LINK IT UP

To remind yourself of the characteristics of children's development from birth to 5 years, go to Component 1, section A.

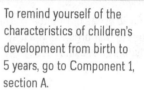

ACTIVITY

Design a leaflet to advise a newly opening nursery on the health and safety considerations for inside environments.

The leaflet must cover:
- width of doorways, aisles and corridors
- layout and types of furniture
- types of flooring and floor coverings.

You must give advice for all the following age groups:
- 0–18 months
- 18 months–3 years
- 3–5 years.

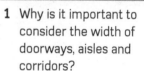

CHECK MY LEARNING

1. Why is it important to consider the width of doorways, aisles and corridors?

2. List two things that should be considered when planning the indoor environment to ensure children are safe, for each of the age groups:
   - 0–18 months
   - 18 months–3 years
   - 3–5 years.

How resources can be organised and the use of specific areas

Resources should be **organised** in a way that enables children to find things easily. Think of a time when you have been unable to find something that you wanted. How did this make you feel?

Childcare settings should be well organised not only so everyone knows where everything is but also to minimise the risk of accidents and to keep children safe.

Many settings are split into **specific areas** separating the different resources and activities. Each area has its own risks and safety considerations depending on the kinds of resources being used there and the types of play taking place. It is the adult's role to ensure that all areas are kept safe and are suitable for the ages of children using them.

How resources can be organised to enable children to find things easily

- Adults should consider how resources are stored and displayed for the children. It is good practice to store toys and resources in organised sets so that children can find things easily.
- Drawers, shelves and boxes where resources are kept should be at the correct height for children to enable them to find things easily.
- For younger children, aged 0–18 months, drawers, shelves and boxes can be labelled with a picture to show children what is in there. For example, a picture of building blocks on the box where these are kept.
- There should also be the word displayed for children aged 18 months–3 years who can recognise letters and children aged 3–5 years who may be starting to read.
- Having the resources organised in this way makes it easier for children to tidy up, which can prevent trip hazards.

▣ How is this adult helping the children to find things easily?

Use of specific areas for play activities and routines

A good way to support children's learning through play is to divide the room into activity areas.

LINK IT UP

To remind yourself of the different play opportunities for children, go to Component 2, section B.

◼ Table 3.13: Common areas and the safety aspects that adults should consider

Role play area	This area should have enough space for children to move around, dress up and act out situations and stories. There should be sufficient storage for dressing up items and props and child sized light and moveable furniture as the areas could be turned into anything from a home to a play shop or doctor's surgery!
Book area	Ideally, the book area will be in the corner of the room, enabling children to relax and have some quiet time. Soft seating should be available to create a homely environment. The book shelves should ideally be heavy and immovable. However, the shelves where the books are stored should be at varied heights with some low enough for children aged 0–18 months and 18 months–3 years to reach and some slightly higher for the 3–5-year-old children.
Messy area	This may cover painting as well as gluing and sticking and materials like sand, water, playdough or gloop. It is important that this area is near to the sink to provide handwashing facilities for the children and to enable spillages to be cleaned up quickly. There should be a mop and a sweeping brush available nearby to prevent trip and slip hazards.
Construction and small world area	This area consists of building materials such as different types of blocks and small imaginative play resources such as toy animals, people, cars and trains. This area needs to be spacious as children will be playing on the floor. There should also be lots of storage to prevent trip hazards. This area is best situated in a corner of the room to stop children using it to gain access to other areas. This will protect children from being bumped into and stood on when they are on the floor.
Mark making area	Pencils, crayons, felt tip pens and chalks should be organised into separate containers and be easily accessible to the children. There should be enough space for the children to work, for example children aged 0–18 months or 18 months–3 years may need to work on large pieces of paper so will need plenty of room so they do not knock other children around them or poke them in the eye with a sharp pencil.
Baby and toddler rooms	Children aged 0–18 months have different needs to older children. They learn by exploring with their senses and through physical movement. Rooms for children of this age should have plenty of space for babies who are rolling, crawling or starting to walk but also quiet secluded areas where babies who cannot yet move by themselves will be protected from older babies who may bump into them. There should be a suitable space for changing babies' nappies with consideration of the height of changing tables to ensure babies do not roll onto the floor.

◼ Why should baby rooms have a carpeted area?

DID YOU KNOW?

Children learn more and feel safe and secure when things are in order and their indoor environment is well designed.

ACTIVITY

Write an article for a childcare magazine that gives advice on:

1 how resources can be organised to enable children to find things easily

2 the use of specific areas for play activities and routines.

You must give advice for the age groups:

- 0–18 months
- 18 months–3 years
- 3–5 years.

Remember to include some pictures as examples!

CHECK MY LEARNING

List two benefits of organising resources for children.

Explain how well organised resources can impact on children's learning.

Health and safety considerations for outside environments (1)

It is considered good practice for children to have as much access to outdoor environments as they do to indoor ones. Outdoor play can take place in the setting's outdoor area but may also be away from the setting, for example on an outing. Outdoor play is very beneficial to children's development; however, there are safety considerations that need to be taken into account. Hazards in the outdoors can be very different to those indoors. How can you ensure that the outdoor environment is safe for children to play in?

There are many things that need to be taken into account to ensure children are safe in outside environments. Adults need to consider the different types of weather and how to plan for these. Children's hunger, thirst and **toileting needs** will also need to be taken into consideration.

Appropriate clothing

Children should have access to outside environments all year round and in all weathers. This means that children need to be wearing **appropriate clothing** in order to stay safe when playing outside.

▣ **Table 3.14: Clothing for different weathers**

Clothing for sunny weather	Sunglasses Sun hats Long-sleeved t-shirts to protect arms from the sun *High SPF sun screen should also be applied to protect children (with permission from their parents/carers)
Clothing for rainy weather	Rain coats with hoods Waterproof trousers Waterproof all in ones for children aged 0–18 months Wellington boots Umbrellas
Clothing for cold weather/snow	Warm padded coats Warm padded all in ones for children aged 0–18 months Hats Gloves Scarves Warm socks Wellington boots/snow boots Lots of layers such as fleeces and jumpers underneath coats

Planning ahead

Clothing changes

The weather in the UK can be very unpredictable! It is good practice when children will be playing outdoors for adults to regularly check the weather forecast and ensure they are prepared for any sudden changes. This is particularly important if planning an outing for children, for example rain covers may need to be taken for pushchairs for children aged 0–18 months in case of a sudden downpour. The temperature can get colder later in the day and we get colder the longer we are outside, therefore coats, gloves and hats will need to be available just in case children start to feel cold.

Toileting needs

When taking children on an outing, adults will need to check there are toilet facilities and nappy changing facilities. Children should be given plenty of opportunities and reminders to go to the toilet and potties should be taken for children aged 18 months–3 years who may still be toilet training. Spare clothing should be available in case of any accidents and also disposable gloves, wipes and plastic bags for soiled clothing.

Hunger and thirst

When in outdoor environments children should drink plenty of water, particularly on hot days. Adults should monitor how much children are drinking to ensure they do not get dehydrated. There should also be snacks available in case children are hungry.

 What else may need to be considered when taking children outdoors on a rainy day?

DID YOU KNOW?

Outdoor learning is a major part of the curricula in the UK for children aged 0–5 years. Children should play outside every day in all types of weather.

LINK IT UP

To remind yourself how exercise affects children's growth and development, go to Component 1, section B.

ACTIVITY

You are working at 'The Children's Choice' day nursery and have been asked to plan an outing to the park for a group of children.

Create a plan which includes the following:
- appropriate clothing
- planning ahead for:
  - clothing changes
  - toileting needs
  - hunger and thirst.

You must show you have considered the age ranges:
- 0–18 months
- 18 months–3 years
- 3–5 years.

CHECK MY LEARNING

1 List appropriate clothing for sunny weather, rain and cold weather/snow.

2 Explain two things that need to be considered when planning an outing for children.

3 Explain the importance of planning ahead when taking children outdoors.

Health and safety considerations for outside environments (2)

When playing in outdoor environments, adults should consider **accessibility** by ensuring that children can enter and exit buildings and outdoor spaces safely and that the different outdoor surfaces and levels are safe for children to play on. The outside environment should be planned to accommodate both noisy and quiet play.

Outdoor play resources should be suitable for all children, taking into account different ages and stages of development. Remember that many activities that are carried out inside can be adapted to be taken into the outdoor environment.

Look back at 'Health and safety considerations for inside environments'. How could the different areas be duplicated outdoors?

Accessibility

It is good practice for children to be allowed to move freely from inside to outside and vice versa to develop their play, and they need to do so safely.

◼ Table 3.15: Accessibility considerations for children in the different age groups

0–18 months	There should be **ramps** available where there are stairs.
18 months–3 years	Hand rails should be provided on stairs for children who may still be unsteady on their feet.
3–5 years	Doors should be open so children can move in and out freely.

Open doors should be safe to ensure that they cannot slam shut, trapping children's fingers.

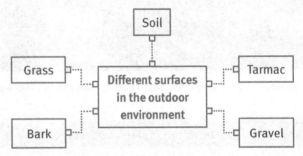

◼ Figure 3.10: It is important to plan the surfaces for outdoor environments

- It is important to plan the outdoor environment to ensure that the surface closest to the door is smooth, to prevent accidents when children step outside.
- Adults should check the outdoor area is safe and there is no litter, broken glass or animal faeces.
- Adults should have salt available to put down when it is icy to prevent children from slipping.
- The outdoor area should be secure with fences and locked gates so that children cannot escape and also strangers cannot get in.

Choice of outdoor play resources

The outdoor play resources should cater for children of all ages and stages of development.

- **0–18 months.** Children like to explore natural materials like sand, water, gravel and mud.
- **18 months–3 years.** Children like items such as magnifying glasses for looking at insects. Plant pots and gardening tools enable them to explore nature.
- **3–5 years.** There should be items such as cardboard boxes, plastic crates, tyres, play tents and sheets to enable them to make dens and hideaways.

Wheeled toys

Wheeled toys should be available and these should be suitable for children's different ages and stages of development.

- **0–18 months.** There should be sit and ride toys and push along toys as they are still learning to walk and control their bodies.
- **18 months–3 years.** Children will be able to ride a tricycle and push a toy pram.
- **3–5 years.** Children are more advanced in their physical development and two-wheeled bicycles could be introduced for those who are ready.

Physical circumstances

Adults will need to consider children who have physical circumstances. Ramps may be required and items such as climbing frames may need to be adapted to cater for children with mobility needs.

Choosing quiet or noisy play spaces

Outdoor play areas should be split so that there are large areas where children can run around and make noise but also quieter corners for activities like gardening, looking for insects or making a den. There should be areas providing shade from sunshine and rain. The large area needs to be spacious enough for children to move around freely and not too cluttered. Older children should be encouraged to 'park' up their wheeled toys so that these do not become a hazard to children who are running around. There should be space for adults to push children aged 0–18 months around in their prams or pushchairs.

Levels

It is good practice when children are outdoors to enable them to experience different **levels** to develop their physical skills of balance and coordination. This could include: stairs, climbing frames, low walls and logs. There should be ramps and slopes to enable children to ride wheeled toys both uphill and downhill.

Labels and maps

Labels can be used to support children in the outdoor area. For example, laminated pictures of tricycles to show children aged 18 months–3 years where to park these and words for children aged 3–5 years who are learning to read. Labels and signs can be used to point children in the right direction of the different areas, for example 'Garden' or 'Sand pit'. When taking children on outings, children aged 3–5 years will benefit from being given a simple map of the area and shown where to go if they get lost.

ACTIVITY

Design an outdoor area that is suitable for children aged:
- 0–18 months
- 18 months–3 years
- 3–5 years.

Draw your design on a large piece of paper and label the different areas and resources. You should show you have considered:
- accessibility
- outdoor play resources, taking into consideration age and stage of development
- quiet and noisy play spaces.

CHECK MY LEARNING

List two suitable outdoor resources for each age group:
- 0–18 months
- 18 months–3 years
- 3–5 years.

Explain why children need both noisy and quiet play spaces in the outdoor environment.

Learning aim B: assessment practice

How you will be assessed

Section B of the external assessment will test your knowledge of B: Create Safe environments to support play, learning and development in children aged 0–5.

Section B covers how the environment can be adapted to meet the needs of children with individual circumstances who require support to play, learn and develop. You learned about adaptations that could be made in the home and in early years settings and you considered how the adaptations could be made for the age groups:

- 0–18 months
- 18 months–3 years
- 3–5 years.

In section B of the external assessment you will be asked to state reasons for things, match items and give explanations.

> **CHECKPOINT**
>
> **Strengthen**
> - Ensure you know what to do in order to explain how the environment can be adapted to meet the needs of children with individual circumstances who need support to play, learn and develop.
> - Ensure you understand the words 'risk' and 'hazard'.
>
> **Challenge**
> - You need to be able to demonstrate a high level of understanding of adaptations that could be made in the home and childcare settings.
> - Ensure you consider the needs of children in the different age groups: 0–18 months, 18 months–3 years and 3–5 years.

1 State one reason why adults need to choose age and stage appropriate resources for children. (1 mark)

2 There is a legal requirement for there to be enough adults to support children's play and learning. This is called the adult to child ratio. Match the age group to the correct ratio. One has been completed for you. (2 marks)

Children 0–2 years   1 adult to 4 children

Children aged 2 years   1 adult to 13 children

Children aged 3–5 years   1 adult to 3 children

3 Explain two benefits of positive risk taking to children's learning and development. (4 marks)

4 Explain two ways that adults can ensure children aged 3–5 years stay safe online. (4 marks)

5 State two factors that need to be considered when buying furniture for children. (2 marks)

6 Explain two ways in which the environment can be organised in a way that helps children to find things easily. (2 marks)

7 Give two benefits of adults planning ahead for play in outdoor environments. (2 marks)

8 Outdoor play resources should cater for children of all ages and stages of development. Complete the table below to show:

a) an example of a suitable resource or activity that could support children in each age group

b) the reason why each resource or activity is suitable for the age group. (6 marks)

Age range	Suitable resource/activity	Reason
0–18 months		
18 months–3 years		
3–5 years		

TIPS

You need to interpret the questions correctly. Check which age range the questions are asking you about.

Read the questions carefully to find the command word in the question, for example 'state', 'give' or 'explain'.

In 'explain' questions you should use words such as 'because', 'due to' and 'therefore' to make sure you have given reasons.

TAKE IT FURTHER

- Check your answers. Where you have been asked to 'explain', are your explanations clear? Remember 'explain' means you need to show you understand a topic and give reasons to support your answers.
- Have you given clear reasons for the outdoor resources/ activities you have given for each age range?

Adapting play to promote inclusive learning and development

Consider the following scenarios.

- Only girls can play with the dolls and prams.
- Only older children can play outside.
- Some children cannot access the sand area because they have a disability.
- A child cannot understand the story because he is learning English as an additional language.
- A child is excluded from a Christmas card making activity because she is not a Christian.

1 Discuss with a partner how these are examples of not being inclusive.

2 Why is it important that all children can access all activities?

3 Write down your ideas.

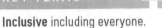

KEY TERMS

Inclusive including everyone.

Right to learn a moral or legal entitlement to have an education and learn.

The United Nations Convention on the Rights of the Child a statement of children's rights that must be followed.

Adapt make something suitable for all children.

Adults need to adapt play to promote **inclusive** learning and development. This means make changes to activities for all children to ensure they can take part and learn. For example: adding a ramp to the outdoor area to ensure that children with a physical disability can access the area. Can you think of any other examples?

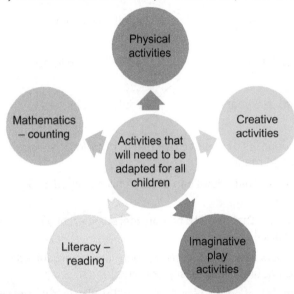

◼ Figure 3.11: Being inclusive covers ensuring activities are adapted for all individual circumstances and age groups

Being inclusive also covers ensuring activities are adapted for all individual circumstances and for the different age groups:

- 0–18 months
- 18 months–3 years
- 3–5 years.

It is important to recognise that every child has a **right to learn** and within this right is the need to promote all the five areas of development.

Adults will need to understand how to adapt all activities to ensure that all areas of development are promoted to include all children.

Recognition that every child has a right to learn

Every child has a right to learn. This means they have a moral and legal entitlement to have an education. The United Nations International Children's Emergency Fund (UNICEF) is a charity working in many different countries across the world to defend children's rights.

In 1989, UNICEF produced The **United Nations Convention on the Rights of the Child**. This is a statement of children's rights and it has been approved all over the world.

The United Nations Convention on the Rights of the Child has 54 articles that cover all aspects of a child's life and sets out the rights that all children everywhere are entitled to.

One of these articles states that 'every child has the right to an education'. This means that we have a legal responsibility to ensure that every child learns.

You have already learned in Component 2 that children from birth to 5 years old learn through play. To ensure that every child learns through play, adults need to **adapt** activities for children with individual circumstances to promote their learning and development. By individual circumstances we mean:

- physical circumstances
- cognitive/intellectual circumstances
- communication and language circumstances
- social and emotional circumstances.

Promoting five areas of development for all children

When considering a child's right to learn adults need to understand that this covers all five areas of development, which are interrelated. You have already learned about these in Component 1.

◨ Table 3.16: The five areas of development

Physical development	Control over the body Development of the senses Gross and fine motor skills
Cognitive/intellectual development	Development of information processing Memory Problem-solving skills
Communication and language development	Development of speech sounds and language skills Listening and attention skills Social skills Formation of sentences
Social development	Development of relationships Building confidence and self-esteem Development of friendships
Emotional development	Development of bonds and trust Independence Development of emotional resilience

All the areas of development are as important as each other, therefore adults need to ensure that all children are given opportunities to learn and develop in each of the five areas.

The five areas are all interrelated, which means one area of development is dependent on the others. For example, a child cannot learn to write until they have developed their fine motor skills to hold the pencil and their language skills to understand letters and words.

This means that adults need to adapt activities for all children to ensure that all areas of development are covered, and that development is seen as being holistic rather than separated into the different areas.

ACTIVITY

'Butterflies' Day Nursery looks after 60 children.
- *There are a mixture of boys and girls.*
- *The nursery has rooms for children aged 0–18 months, 18 months–3 years and 3–5 years.*
- *There are children from a range of different ethnicities speaking a range of different languages. Some of the children are learning English as an additional language.*
- *The nursery has several children who have individual circumstances.*

1 Explain why it is important that the nursery ensures that every child has the opportunity to learn. You must refer to the United Nations Convention on the Rights of the Child.

2 Explain why it is important that the nursery promote all five areas of development for all children.

3 Write down your answers.

LINK IT UP

To remind yourself of holistic development, go to 'Development' in Component 1.
To remind yourself of the five areas of development across the ages of birth to 5 years old, go to Component 1, section A.

CHECK MY LEARNING

1 Explain what is meant by the right to learn.

2 Give two examples of how a setting can be inclusive.

The role of the adult

GETTING STARTED

Draw a picture of yourself and list all the things that make you different.

Share your picture with a partner and discuss the things that make you different from each other.

Discuss why it is important to celebrate differences.

It is the role of the adult when working with children to promote inclusion to ensure all children can join in with organised activities. This involves having a positive attitude to difference and coming up with solutions to barriers that can stop children participating, rather than excluding them.

Adults can promote inclusion by role modelling **desired behaviours** when interacting with children who have **additional needs**. It is also the adult's role to cater for children's different interests and preferences. You have already learned in Component 2 about child initiated play, which is where children choose what to play with and how to play. Imagine being told what to do all the time and not being given a choice. How would this make you feel and how would it affect you?

Promoting inclusion

Inclusion means to include everyone regardless of their:

- ethnicity
- gender
- age
- religion
- language
- abilities
- additional needs
- disabilities.

To promote inclusion, adults need to ensure that all children can join in organised activities. This will sometimes require adaptations to the environment or new equipment or resources to be brought in for particular children. This will ensure there are no barriers to children learning and developing.

Some examples include the following:

- special seats on outdoor swings so children with physical disabilities can take part in physical activities
- different sized paintbrushes available for children of different ages and stages of development so they can all join in with creative activities
- books in different languages so all children can develop their literacy/reading skills
- counting in different languages so all children can develop their mathematics/ counting skills
- dressing up clothes and cooking utensils from different cultures so all children can take part in imaginative play
- soft balls with bells inside for babies with visual problems.

KEY TERMS

Desired behaviours the way in which we want children to behave.

Additional needs a term used to indicate that a child requires extra support or services to enable them to participate fully in activities.

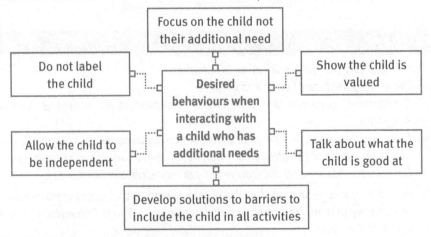

Figure 3.12: Ways in which adults should interact with a child with additional needs to be a good role model to other children

Role modelling desired behaviours

Interacting with children who have additional needs

In the past, children with additional needs were given negative labels and were separated from other children. Today, things are very different and children with additional needs are included and given the same opportunities as other children.

It is important when adults are interacting with children who have additional needs that they role model desired behaviours, in other words, behave in the way we wish other children to behave.

Giving children a choice

It is important that children are given a choice when both planning and choosing activities.

Children can plan their own activities if adults spend time with them talking about what they want to do and allowing them to choose their own materials and resources.

To facilitate this type of approach, it is important that resources are organised to enable children to find things easily. You have already learned about this in 'How resources can be organised and the use of specific areas'.

Giving children choices supports their learning and development as it allows them to:
- learn to make decisions for themselves
- develop independence skills.

However, it is important that the degree of choice given is appropriate for the age and stage of development of the children. Table 3.17 shows some examples of how children in different age ranges can be given choices.

Table 3.17: How children in different age ranges can be given choices

0–18 months	Children can be given a treasure basket containing different items and they can choose independently which items to explore.
18 months–3 years	Children can be asked to choose a book that they would like to look at with an adult.
3–5 years	Children can be given a choice of what they would like to eat and could serve themselves at the table.

ACTIVITY

Andreas is starting his first job working with children aged 3 to 5 years. He is unsure of his role in adapting activities for the children who have individual circumstances.

Create a help guide for Andreas to support him.

The help guide must include:
- promoting inclusion
- role modelling desired behaviours when interacting with children who have individual circumstances
- giving children choice.

DID YOU KNOW?

It is a legal requirement for settings to be inclusive.

LINK IT UP

To remind yourself of how resources can be organised to enable children to find things easily, go to 'How resources can be organised and the use of specific areas' in this component. To remind yourself of child initiated play, go to Component 2, 'How play can be organised to promote learning, child-intiated play'.

CHECK MY LEARNING

1 Give three examples of how adults can promote inclusion.

2 Give an example for each age group of how children can be given choices at:
- 0–18 months
- 18 months–3 years
- 3–5 years.

3 Assess the impact on 3–5-year-old-children's emotional and social development of being given choices.

Responding to children

KEY TERMS

Praise express approval.

Reward something given to someone to recognise their efforts or achievements.

It is the role of the adult to respond positively to children in their play, learning and development. These responses include **praise** and **rewards**.

Children use their behaviour to get the attention of the adults around them. Praise and rewards are needed for children to understand how to get the attention of adults in positive ways.

It is important that adults recognise when children are becoming bored or losing concentration. Think about an occasion when you have found an activity difficult. What did you do? What did the adults around you do?

Responding positively to desired behaviours in children

Praise

When adults praise children they are expressing their approval. This helps children to understand what desired behaviours are and they are more likely to repeat the behaviours.

If children are not praised for their behaviour, they are less likely to repeat it. This is why praise can be effective in supporting children to behave well. Sometimes it is a good idea for adults to ignore a child's unwanted behaviour because if children realise the behaviour is not getting them any attention they are likely to stop it. Obviously, some behaviours cannot be ignored, for example a child hurting another child.

Praise can impact children's learning and development by:
- helping children to feel good about themselves, building self-esteem
- building confidence.

Rewards

Adults sometimes use rewards as a way of responding positively to desired behaviours. Stickers and gestures from adults are two examples.

The rewards given to children will need to be carefully considered to ensure they are appropriate for the child's age and stage of development. For example, it would not be effective to give a 1-year-old child a sticker as they may not understand what this is. A clap would be a much more effective way of rewarding a child of this age.

Just like praise, rewards can help children to understand what is desired behaviour and they are likely to repeat something if they are rewarded.

Rewards work well if they are used at the time of the desired behaviour. If they are given later, children may forget what they have done. Giving out certificates at the end of the week for good behaviour would not be effective for a group of 18 month–3-year-old children as they may have forgotten what happened earlier in the week.

Rewards can also be ineffective if they are used too much as children may behave in a certain way just to get the reward rather than because it is the 'right thing to do'.

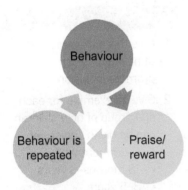

Figure 3.13: Desirable behaviour is likely to be repeated if children are praised or rewarded for it

Recognising when children are becoming bored, losing concentration or finding activities difficult

It is important that adults recognise when children are becoming bored with an activity or are losing concentration. This can be shown in disruptive behaviour (see 'Disruptive behaviour').

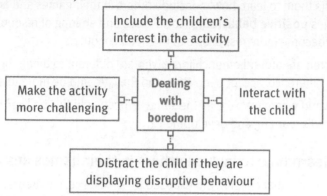

■ Figure 3.14: Adults should recognise when children are becoming bored with activities and deal with the boredom

Children can become bored because they are losing concentration. Adults can interact with the children to help them focus and avoid distractions, for example put the activity somewhere quiet, move other children who may be interrupting the activity.

There may be times when children are finding activities difficult. To avoid this it is the role of the adult to:

- ensure activities are appropriate for the children's ages and stages of development, for example an 18-month-old would not be able to play a board game involving mathematical sums
- divide up big tasks into smaller ones, for example while gardening the activity should focus on filling up the plant pot first, before putting in the seed
- allow sufficient time for children to engage in the activity, for example a child couldn't complete a jigsaw in the same amount of time as an adult
- support children by introducing different resources, for example in the creative area if a child is struggling to use a paintbrush they could be given some different sized brushes to hold.

LINK IT UP

To remind yourself of disruptive behaviour, go to 'Disruptive behaviour' in this component.

ACTIVITY

You are going to appear on a radio programme about supporting children's behaviour.

The programme will be covering:

- responding positively to desired behaviours using praise and rewards
- recognising when children are becoming bored, losing concentration or finding activities difficult.

Make some notes of what you will say on the programme. You will need to refer to children of different ages:

- 0–18 months
- 18 months–3 years
- 3–5 years.

Practice with a partner what you are going to say.

CHECK MY LEARNING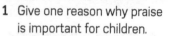

1 Give one reason why praise is important for children.

2 Give an example of a reward suitable for a child aged 0–18 months.

3 Assess the possible impact of rewards on the self-esteem of a child aged 3–5 years.

Benefits to other children of adapting activities

In 'Adapting play to promote inclusive learning and development' you learned about how to promote inclusion. This is where adults adapt activities for all children in play learning and development. Providing an inclusive environment has many benefits to children.

- It supports them to learn how to include others in their games and activities.
- It promotes **positive behaviours**, social skills and sharing of resources.
- Children become more responsive to the needs of others.

Where children are around other children who are different to them, they learn to understand difference, accept people for who they are and be more tolerant of others.

Imagine a world where we were all the same? What would this be like? How would this affect children's learning and development?

Children learn how to include others in their games and activities

If the environment that children are exposed to is inclusive, children will learn how to include others in their games and activities. They will recognise that other children learn in different ways and will be able to adapt their play to accommodate others.

Where children are around other children who have different needs, they begin to understand that some children learn at a different pace to themselves or that they have some limitations to what they are able to do. This results in children being sensitive to the needs of others and they start to ensure that other children have equal chances to join in.

Children learn to become:

- adaptable
- patient
- tolerant of others

which supports their social and emotional development.

It is important to remember that children's ability to include others in their games and activities depends on their age and stage of development. For example, children aged 0–18 months do not yet understand the concepts of sharing or waiting. You have learned about development across the ages of birth to 5 years old in Component 1.

■ What do children learn from being in an inclusive environment?

Promotes positive behaviours

When play and learning activities are adapted for all children this promotes positive behaviours as children learn to be sensitive to the needs of others. This supports them to be caring and enables them to improve their social skills, for example:

- sharing and turn taking
- learning from each other
- accepting that everyone is different
- building up a good rapport with others
- making friendships with children from different ethnicities, religions and with different abilities
- socialising with both girls and boys
- less likely to discriminate against others when they are older.

Also, children's emotional development is supported as being kind and accepting of others makes children feel better about themselves, which increases their self-esteem.

Children become more responsive to the needs of others

In an inclusive environment, children will become aware of different **communication methods** and will learn to respond to other children using these in order to meet their needs.

- *Adam, aged 3, speaks Punjabi and is learning English as an additional language. His friend Elliot has learned to say 'Hello' in Punjabi as he has picked this up from Adam.*
- *Claire is 5. In her class at school there are several children with a hearing impairment who use sign language to communicate. Claire has learned the signs for 'Yes', 'No' and 'OK' so she can respond to the children.*
- *The children at 'Oakwell Pre School' have learned to sit still and not shout at the table at snack time as they are aware that any sudden noise or movement could upset Billy, who has a visual impairment.*

These examples show how being in an inclusive environment has supported the children to understand the needs and feelings of others. This is called empathy.

How do you think adding bubbles to the water in this picture has supported the children to behave positively?

LINK IT UP

To remind yourself of development across the ages of birth to 5 years, go to Component 1, section A.

To remind yourself of promoting inclusion, go to 'Adapting play to promote inclusive learning and development' in this component.

ACTIVITY

Fatima, aged 3, will soon be starting at the school nursery where you are a student. She is learning English as an additional language.

1. Create an information sheet to inform Fatima's parents about how activities will be adapted for her at nursery.
2. Explain how adapting activities for Fatima can benefit the other children in the nursery.

CHECK MY LEARNING

1. Give an example of how adapting activities for all children in play, learning and development supports children to include others in their games and activities.
2. Name three social skills that children may develop from activities being adapted for all children.

Adapting activities and resources to support a child with physical needs

GETTING STARTED

Look around your classroom and assess it.

Consider how the environment would need to be adapted to support someone with physical needs.

How could the resources and equipment be adapted?

In 'Health and safety considerations for inside environments' you learned about health and safety considerations, including the layout of furniture and accessibility, and the physical circumstances that may impact on learning and development such as restricted or delayed gross motor skills. Can you think of any other physical needs that children may have?

Children with physical needs may need **adjustments** to be made to the environment so they can access activities and resources. Adults should select appropriate resources to support **grasping**, **holding**, **releasing** and **transferring**.

Making adjustments to the environment

Children with physical needs will need adjustments to their environment to enable them to use resources and take part in activities.

Space

Adults should ensure that there is **sufficient space** available for a child with physical needs to carry out activities safely.

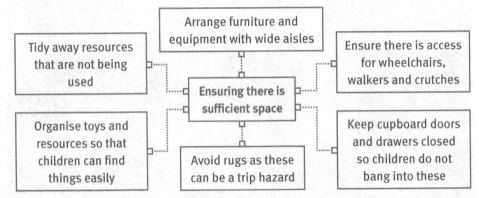

Figure 3.15: Adults should ensure that there is sufficient space available

Most of the advice in Figure 3.15 applies to all children but it is important to remember that children with physical needs may be more likely to knock into furniture than other children and they need more support to ensure they can move around freely and not trip over.

Lighting

To enable children with physical needs to move around easily, the amount of lighting may need to be adjusted to improve **visibility**.

If children can see where they are going, they are less likely to bump into things or trip. Whilst this is important for all children, it is especially important for children with physical needs as they may require more light than other children to ensure they keep safe when moving around the activities.

Adults should ensure that activity areas are well lit and should add lamps if needed. Some settings use dimmer switches, so the light can be adjusted easily.

KEY TERMS

Adjustments alterations or movements made to achieve a desired fit, appearance or result.

Grasping the movement of grabbing something by closing the fingers around it.

Holding to have a grip of something.

Releasing the movement of letting go of an object that has been grasped.

Transferring moving something from one hand to another.

Sufficient space enough/ adequate space.

Visibility the state of being able to see or be seen.

Why is it important for children with physical needs to be given enough space?

Choosing resources that are age and stage appropriate

When adapting activities and resources to support a child with restricted or delayed fine motor skills, it is important to remember that this does not mean giving children resources that are not appropriate for their age.

- Rattles are good to support the development of grasping, but you would not give these to a 3–5-year-old child because these are toys that are aimed at babies, so they would not stimulate an older child.
- Picking up buttons and beads supports children's fine motor skills but you would not give these to 0–18-months-old children as they could be a choking hazard.

Selecting appropriate resources that all children can use

In 'Physical circumstances that may impact on learning and development' you learned how some children may have restricted or delayed fine motor skills. These children will need to be provided with appropriate resources that they can use for grasping, holding, releasing and transferring.

■ Table 3.18: Resources to support children to grasp, hold, release and transfer items

Resources to support grasping	Books with tabs to support the turning of pages. Grippers on pencils and crayons to support children to hold these correctly. Playdough, clay and modelling clay to enable children to practice the movement of grasping.
Resources to support holding	Paintbrushes with knobs at the end of them. Cups or bottles covered in fabric making them easier to hold. Large toys such as soft toys or balls that need to be held with two hands.
Resources to support releasing	Small objects that children aged 3–5 years can hide in their hands and then open their hands to reveal, for example buttons or coins. Hand puppets Toys to push, for example pop-up toys.
Resources to support transferring	Items such as spoons or crayons can be placed in a child's non-preferred hand, so they can transfer it to their preferred hand. Putting in and taking out activities such as shape sorters for 0–18-month-old children or putting coins into a money box slot for 3–5-year-old children.

ACTIVITY

'Sunnyside Nursery' is a new nursery that will be opening soon.

Before the nursery can open, the staff need to ensure that the environment and the activities and resources they are providing will support children with physical needs.

You have been asked to go and talk to the staff about how they can do this.

Prepare a presentation for the staff. Your presentation must include:
- making adjustments to the environment
- choosing resources that are age and stage appropriate
- selecting appropriate resources that all children can use.

LINK IT UP

To remind yourself of health and safety considerations for inside environments, go to 'Health and safety considerations for inside environments' in this component. To remind yourself of health and safety considerations for outside environments, go to 'Health and safety considerations for outside environments' in this component. To remind yourself of choosing age and stage appropriate resources, go to 'Managing risks and hazards of environments and activities' in this component.

CHECK MY LEARNING

1 Give two ways that adults can ensure there is sufficient space for children with physical needs.

2 Name one suitable resource to support each of the following:
- grasping
- holding
- releasing
- transferring.

3 Explain the possible adaptations for children aged 3–5 years with a visual impairment, giving two examples.

Supporting children with physical or sensory needs

If children have a sensory impairment, which means they require support, this is called having **sensory needs**. It is important that adults provide materials and resources for sensory needs.

It is important that materials and resources provided are appropriate to the age group. Children aged 0–18 months put everything in their mouths, therefore it is important that the materials and resources provided are safe. How can adults ensure this?

Children with physical or sensory needs may need movable objects to be secured so they remain still. It may also be appropriate to adjust the level of activities and resources to suit children's needs. You have already learned about the use of equipment at different levels in 'Health and safety considerations for outside environments'.

Securing movable objects

In order to support children who have physical or sensory needs to use equipment and resources, it may be necessary to secure movable objects to keep them still. If an object is moving when a child is trying to use it, this can frustrate the child and have an impact on a child's ability to engage in the activity, and could even be dangerous.

Some examples of securing moveable objects are shown below.

How could the objects in these pictures be 'secured' to stop them moving?

Adjust the level of activities and resources

It may be necessary to adjust the level of activities and resources to support children with physical or sensory needs.

- Some children may prefer to have activities on the floor rather than at a table. For example, mats can be put down so creative activities such as painting, sand or playdough can take place on the floor.
- Different children may need tables of different heights, so it is a good idea to have adjustable tables, so the height can be changed quickly and easily.
- Some children may benefit from tables with a slanting top. This can support children aged 3–5 years to read and write more comfortably as they promote good posture and enable children to see more clearly.
- In the outdoor environment there should be climbing frames of different heights and ramps and slopes to enable children to access various parts of the outdoor area easily.

Provide materials and resources for sensory needs

Sensory needs may mean that a child has a visual or hearing impairment, for example they have difficulty seeing or hearing. This can be permanent or temporary. Adults need to provide materials and resources for sensory needs. When a child has a hearing or visual impairment it is important that adults maximise their other senses to enable children to access activities.

LINK IT UP

To remind yourself of sensory activities, go to Component 2, section A.

To remind yourself of sensory impairment and how this can impact on learning and development, go to 'Physical circumstances that may impact on learning and development' in this component.

To learn about the use of equipment at different levels, go to 'How individual circumstances may impact on physical learning and development' and 'Health and safety considerations for outside environments' in this component.

■ **Table 3.19: Materials and resources for sensory needs**

Sight	• **Contrasting colour schemes,** for example bright colours alongside softer, paler colours or different colours alongside each other • Mirrors • Pictures • Brightly coloured and shiny objects
Sound	• Objects that make sounds • Balls with bells inside • Rattles • Squeaky toys • Toys that play music
Smell	• Scented playdough • Bags containing herbs or dried flowers, for example lavender • Scented toys • Flowers and plants
Taste	• Different foods • Playing with food items such as mashed potato, cooked cold pasta, baked beans
Touch	• Sand • Water • Dough, clay and modelling play • Gloop • Soil • Gravel • Treasure baskets (basket of items that are not plastic, for example wood, metal, shell, fabric, stone, cork and cardboard) • 3D art materials such as sculptures, canvas and wood

When providing materials and resources for sensory needs it is important to ensure that they are appropriate for the age group. For example:

- playing with gravel may be a choking hazard to children aged 0–18 months
- squeaky toys may not be stimulating enough for a child aged 3–5 years.

ACTIVITY

Create three mind maps, one for each of the following:

- securing moveable objects
- adjusting the level of activities and resources
- providing materials and resources for sensory needs.

Ensure you consider the different age groups:

- 0–18 months
- 18 months–3 years
- 3–5 years.

CHECK MY LEARNING

1 Give one example of a movable object that could be secured to make an activity easier for a child with physical or sensory needs.

2 Give one example of how the level of activities and resources could be adjusted.

3 Assess the importance of making adjustments for children with physical needs.

Adapting activities to support a child with cognitive and intellectual or communication and language needs

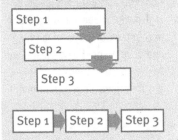
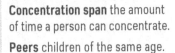

■ How are these children learning from each other?

Children with cognitive/intellectual and communication/language needs may have learning difficulties. This means they may have difficulty acquiring knowledge and skills.

Children with cognitive/intellectual and communication/language needs will benefit from adults providing opportunities for them to learn and play near to other children doing the same activity to encourage the sharing of ideas. Encouraging children to play where there are adults and other children present will create opportunities for the modelling of activities.

Some children with cognitive/intellectual and communication/language needs have a short **concentration span**, which means they cannot focus their attention for a long period of time. It is the adult's role to support these children by shortening activities. Adults may also need to break activities down into short steps. You may have heard the term 'practice makes perfect' – what does this mean?

Providing opportunities to learn and play near to other children

It is important to support children with cognitive and intellectual or communication and language needs by ensuring that the environment is arranged both physically and socially in a way that enables children to play near to other children, so they can see them and learn from them.

For example, in the creative activities, placing painting easels facing each other rather than in a row.

There should be enough space for more than one child to take part in activities at a time. This will encourage sharing of ideas and children who are unsure how to use equipment or engage in an activity will be able to copy children who are doing the same activity.

Shortening activities

There are times when activities will need to be shortened to suit concentration spans because some children cannot concentrate for a long time. This can mean that if activities take a long time, they will lose interest and not learn.

- Rotate toys for 0–18-month-old children so they do not get bored. For example, move the treasure basket elsewhere so they can access something different.
- When counting with a group of 18-month-olds concentrate on counting to five or ten rather than beyond this.
- Choose shorter reading books with less pages and words for children aged 18 months–3 years who find it hard to listen for a long time.
- When baking with children 3–5 years old make something that is quick such as chocolate crispy cakes that do not need to be cooked, rather than something like bread which takes a long time as you need to wait for it to rise.
- During a card matching game with 3–5-year-olds use only half the sets of cards so the game does not take too long.

Using peers or other adults to model activities

Children learn by observing others and copying. This can be their peers or adults. Children or adults may show children how something works.

To ensure 'modelling' can take place, adults need to ensure that children can see adults and other children and that the furniture and equipment is arranged appropriately.

Breaking activities down into short steps

Some children need activities to be broken down into steps to make them more manageable.

Children learn through exploring and through trial and error. This means learning from their mistakes. Breaking activities into steps supports children to practise their skills.

Figure 3.16 shows how putting on a coat for outdoor play can be broken down into steps for a 2-year-old child.

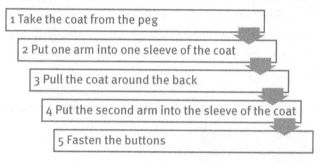

1 Take the coat from the peg

2 Put one arm into one sleeve of the coat

3 Pull the coat around the back

4 Put the second arm into the sleeve of the coat

5 Fasten the buttons

▣ **Figure 3.16: Putting on a coat for outdoor play can be broken down into steps**

Breaking this down into steps enables the child to understand the task of putting on a coat, one step at a time.

The child will be able to process each step separately, which makes the task much more manageable than if the adult said, "Put on your coat" and expected the child to do this in one go.

Some of the steps may need to be repeated in order for the child to grasp what they need to do next.

When breaking activities down into steps it is important that adults give simple, clear instructions to children, so they concentrate and process the different steps.

LINK IT UP

To remind yourself of children's cognitive and intellectual development across the ages of birth to 5 years old, go to Component 1, section A. To remind yourself of cognitive/intellectual play and learning, go to Component 2, section B. To remind yourself of role models, go to 'Social and emotional circumstances that may impact on learning and development' and 'Supporting children's play' in this component.

▣ **How could an adult support this child to put on his coat?**

ACTIVITY

Create a list of 'top tips' on how to adapt activities to support children with cognitive and intellectual or communication and language needs to be displayed in a day nursery staff room.

You should include:

- providing opportunities to learn and play near to other children doing the same activity
- shortening activities
- using peers of other adults to model activities
- breaking down activities into short steps.

CHECK MY LEARNING

1 Give one way that adults can provide opportunities for children to learn and play near to other children doing the same activity.

2 Explain why some children need activities to be shortened.

Adapting activities to support individual needs

It is sometimes necessary for adults to **modify** toys and equipment to support a child with cognitive/intellectual or communication and language needs. During activities, it may also be necessary to **limit** the number of materials available to avoid **overwhelming** the child. Have you heard the term 'less is more'? Sometimes 'less' materials can have more benefit to the child because when there are 'more' this is too much for them to deal with.

Some children can benefit from the use of **technological** or **digital resources**. This term refers to computers and digital equipment that can be adapted through apps and programmes to allow children with particular needs to be more independent.

Modifying toys and equipment to suit individual needs

In order to support the individual needs of children it may be appropriate to modify toys and equipment so that they are able to use them.

Materials for children with individual needs do not have to come from special shops or websites and cost a lot of money. Regular toys and equipment can be modified to make them more suitable:

■ Table 3.20: How regular toys and equipment can be modified to make them more suitable

Reducing the number of parts	Remove some items from a treasure basket leaving just a few items
Removing items that are too small	Remove the small blocks from the building blocks
Using specific colours	Have only two or three colours of paint in the creative area

Not all children with individual needs will need the same changes to be made. Remember the changes that are needed will depend on the age of the child.

■ Why might this area be overwhelming for a child?

Limiting the number of materials available

Some children with cognitive needs are very rigid in their thinking, which means they may have limited ideas. If there are too many resources in an area, this can be overwhelming for a child as they may not know where to start and what to do.

Adults may need to limit the number of materials available in order to meet the child's needs.

For example, in the literacy/reading area, just having a few books for the 18-month-old–3-year-old children to choose from rather than a shelf full of different ones, which may be too much for some of the children. More books can be introduced at a later stage when the children are ready.

The use of technological/digital resources

Some children can benefit from the use of technological or digital resources in order to meet their individual needs.

- Digital devices such as computers and tablets can be adapted. There are apps and programmes that use screen reading technology. These can help children aged between 3–5 years who are struggling to recognise their name. The device will read the name on the screen out to the child, so they can hear it being said.
- There are also apps and programmes that enable children with speech and language needs to be able to communicate more effectively. For example, children click or press on a picture of what they want, and the computer/tablet speaks this out to the adult or other children. This can be used to help children communicate what activity they want to play or what colour they would like to use when painting.
- For younger children (0–18 months) there are battery operated digital toys, for example toys that have animals on them and buttons to press that make the animal sounds.

LINK IT UP

To remind yourself of children's cognitive and intellectual and communication and language development across the age ranges of birth to 5 years, go to Component 1, section A.

ACTIVITY

You are planning a painting activity for children aged 18 months–3 years. In the group there is a child with a visual impairment and a child who has delayed fine motor skills.

Produce a plan to show how you will:
- modify the equipment to suit individual needs
- limit the number of materials available.

Present your plan sheets to each other and make some notes on other people's ideas.

CHECK MY LEARNING

1 Give one example of how technological/digital resources can support children aged 3–5 who have communication and language needs.

2 Explain why adults may need to limit the number of materials available to children aged 18 months–3 years.

Adapting activities to support a child with communication and language needs (1)

Adults may need to adapt activities to support a child with communication and language needs. Adults can use group and/or team activities to promote **social inclusion**, encourage friendships with other children and build bonds and trust with adults.

It is important that where a child has communication and language needs they are supported to build confidence in their own skills. One way this can be achieved is through the use of **alternative communication**. This enables children to 'communicate' alongside speech that is not clear.

Alternative communication methods such as **Picture Exchange Communication System (PECS)** and **Makaton** relieve a child's frustration if they are unable to speak and give them the confidence to initiate their own conversation and be independent. Do you know of any other alternative methods of communication?

Using group and/or team activities to promote social inclusion

Some children who have additional needs are not very interested in other people and can have difficulty making friendships. Using group and/or team activities can promote social inclusion and give children a reason to need to interact with others.

Taking part in an activity in a group or a team:
- extends a child's speech, language and communication development
- can allow some children to overcome the difficulties they have communicating with others
- enables them to build friendships, build bonds and trust with adults and learn to accept other people around them.

It is important to recognise which group and team activities are appropriate for different age ranges. For example a circle time activity would not be suitable for children 0–18 months or 18 months–3 years because they are not at the stage where they are interacting with others. You have already learned about the stages of children's play in Component 2.

Build children's confidence in their own skills

Children with communication and language skills may lack confidence. Adults can build children's confidence in their own skills in the following ways.
- Emphasise key words in a sentence when speaking to children.
- Give clear instructions that children can follow. These may sometimes be non-verbal. For example, when asking a child to put a cup on the table, the adult can give them the cup and point to the table.
- Model correct use of language rather than correcting a child's mistake. For example, if a child said, "I goed to my Grandma's" the adult can say back, "Yes, you went to your Grandma's" rather than telling the child they should have said 'went' instead of 'goed'.
- Use alternative communication, which can enable children who are non-verbal to initiate their own conversations and be independent.

Building up confidence in children's own skills will increase their self-esteem and this will support their language and communication development.

Use alternative communication

Alternative communication refers to different forms of communication that can be used instead of or along with talking.

Picture Exchange Communication System (PECS)

PECS is a system that enables children to initiate their own conversation through the use of picture cards.

The child hands a picture card to an adult to tell them that they want something.

Just like verbal communication PECS will start with children aged 18 months–3 years learning simple words before moving on to building sentence structures with children aged 3–5 years. This is done by using sentence strips.

A sentence strip enables the child to arrange pictures together in a line to make up a sentence.

◘ What do you think these PECS cards are saying?

Makaton

Makaton is a form of communication when children use signs and symbols to support speech or instead of speech. Drawn symbols are used alongside signs made using hands and facial expressions.

LINK IT UP

To remind yourself of children's communication and language development across the ages of birth to 5 years, go to Component 1, section A.

To remind yourself of the stages of children's play, go to Component 2, section A.

To remind yourself of communication and language and social play and learning, go to Component 2, section B.

To remind yourself of how social and emotional development circumstances may impact on learning and development, go to 'How individual circumstances may impact on social and emotional learning and development' in this component.

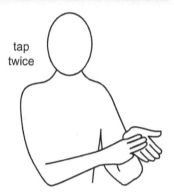

tap twice

◘ Makaton symbol for 'mummy'.

◘ Makaton symbol for 'hello'.

ACTIVITY

Plan a group activity for children aged 3–5 years that will promote social inclusion.

Your plan must include:
- ways to build children's confidence in their own skills
- ways to include children who use alternative communication.

Share your plan in a group and compare your different ideas.

CHECK MY LEARNING

1 Describe how children may benefit from the use of group and/or team activities.
2 Explain the difference between PECS and Makaton.

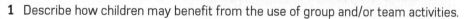

Adapting activities to support a child with communication and language needs (2)

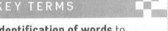

KEY TERMS

Identification of words to establish what words mean.

You learned in Component 2 about communication and language play and learning including nursery rhymes. Nursery rhymes and songs encourage children's listening skills. The use of these, particularly when they have actions and words that are repeated, can support children with the **identification of words**.

Labelling also supports the identification of words. Labelling is a form of communication and, if children see pictures, they begin to associate the written word with the object. Labels also encourage independence and choice as they enable children to understand where things are and where to find them.

Labels can also be used to display routines and activities. Children often need help in learning routines. Why do you think it is important that children understand their routine and what is going to happen next?

Using nursery rhymes with actions to promote the identification of words

Children love to join in with singing led by an adult. Nursery rhymes with actions can be used to promote the identification of words.

For example, in the song 'Head Shoulders, Knees and Toes' children are encouraged to point to their head, shoulders, knees and toes when saying the words. This helps them to identify what the words 'head', 'shoulders', 'knees' and 'toes' mean.

The use of nursery rhymes with actions will vary according to the child's age and stage of development. Table 3.21 shows some examples of rhymes that are appropriate at each age range.

◨ Table 3.21: Nursery rhymes that are appropriate at each age range

0–18 months	Simple finger rhymes where the adult makes actions on a child's hands or feet, for example *'Round and round the garden, like a teddy bear ...'*
18 months–3 years	Action songs can be introduced including songs where actions and words are repeated, for example *'Five little ducks went swimming one day...'* (the rhyme is repeated with the number of ducks reducing in every verse until there are none left). Children begin to anticipate movements whilst hearing and singing the words, for example the action for *'swimming'.*
3–5 years	Children this age begin to notice patterns in songs, for example words that rhyme, for example 'Miss Polly Had a Dolly who was **sick**, so we phoned for the doctor to be **quick**...' Children also notice the repetition of initial sounds. This is called alliteration, for example '**P**eter **P**iper **p**icked a **p**eck of **p**ickled **p**eppers'.

Labelling equipment

It is good practice for adults to label equipment. This encourages independence and choice as children will know where things are. Common items such as the clock, sink and table can be labelled as well as activity areas and boxes/drawers containing equipment.

For younger children, pictures can be used.

The benefits of labelling equipment are that it:
- assists with tidying up
- helps children learn the words for what is on the picture

◨ Which area could this picture be used to label? Which words could you add to the picture?

- supports children with the development of reading
- enables children to know where things are
- keeps things organised for the adults
- helps children learn that words have meaning.

Displaying routines and activities as pictures

You have already learned about the use of labels for equipment. In order to support children with communication and language needs, it is a good idea to display the routine of the setting using pictures and simple words.

This will enable children to understand the order in which the activities happen, so they know what will be coming next.

Pictures can also be used to give children step-by-step instructions for an activity or part of their routine.

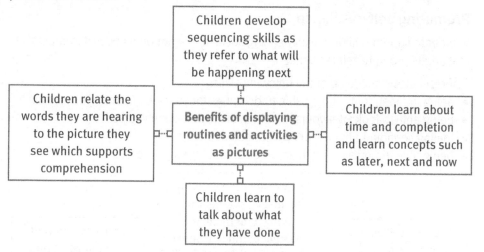

LINK IT UP

To remind yourself of children's communication and language development across the ages of birth to 5 years, go to Component 1, section A.

To remind yourself of communication and language play and learning including nursery rhymes, go to Component 2, section B.

To remind yourself of how resources can be organised to enable children to find things easily, go to 'How resources can be organised and the use of specific areas' in this component.

DID YOU KNOW?

It is common practice in childcare settings for adults to put photographs of children on their coat pegs and drawers.

◻ Figure 3.17: Reasons to display the routine of a setting using pictures and simple words

ACTIVITY

1 Design a set of labels, one for each of the following:
   - physical activities, for example outdoor area
   - creative activities
   - imaginative play activities
   - literacy/reading area
   - mathematics/counting area
   - imaginative play etc.

Your labels will need to include pictures and simple words.

2 Design a set of pictures with words to show step-by-step instructions for one of the following:
   - putting on a coat
   - snack time
   - painting.

CHECK MY LEARNING

1 Explain how the use of nursery rhymes with actions can support children with communication and language needs.

2 Give two benefits of labelling equipment for children.

3 Give two benefits of displaying routines and activities as pictures.

Adapting activities to support a child experiencing social and emotional needs

GETTING STARTED

Discuss in a group at what age you think children can do the following by themselves:
- feeding themselves
- washing hands
- going to the toilet
- dressing themselves
- brushing their teeth.

Write down for each activity what adults could do to support the children with their self-resilience.

KEY TERMS

Self-resilience the ability to be independent and prepare for life's stresses and challenges.

Overwhelmed overcome by emotion.

Structured approach a planned and organised way of dealing with a situation.

Engagement taking part in an activity.

Some children have specific social and emotional needs, which may mean that activities need to be adapted in order to support the development of their **self-resilience**. Self-resilience can be promoted by providing activities that will help the child feel capable and help them feel they 'can do it'.

Self-resilience can also be promoted by giving children choices. However, sometimes it is necessary to limit the choices of activity, so a child does not feel **overwhelmed**.

Can you remember what 'transitions' are and how they can affect children? One way in which adults can support children experiencing transitions is to plan tasks for them to reduce their worry. This is called providing a **structured approach**.

Promoting self-resilience

In order to support children experiencing social and emotional needs it is important that adults promote self-resilience.

Self-resilience is made up of the following skills:
- being independent – being able to do things for yourself and think for yourself
- being able to look after yourself – feed, dress and clean yourself
- feeling confident about your own capabilities
- being able to persevere with activities and not 'giving up easily'.

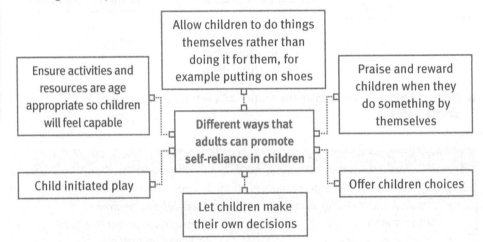

■ Figure 3.18: Adults should promote self-resilience in children

Allowing children to do things by themselves

To promote children's emotional development, adults need to let children do things like getting dressed or brushing their teeth by themselves, even if this takes a long time. However, it is important that activities are age appropriate. For example, we would not expect a 0–18-month-old to pour their own drink, but this would be appropriate for a 3–5-year-old child.

Limiting the choices of activity

Although it is important to offer children choices, sometimes adults may need to limit these to avoid stress.

Providing a structured approach

To support children during transitions adults can provide a structured approach, which means planning and organising specific tasks to be assigned to the child to reduce their worry. Table 3.22 shows some examples.

◼ Table 3.22: Supporting children during transitions

Starting or moving care/ educational providers	Ask children aged 3–5 years starting school or nursery to choose their own items of uniform and pack their own bag or lunchbox.
Birth of a new sibling	Give a child of 18 months–3 years a job to do to support the new baby, for example bring the nappy at changing time.
Moving house	Ask a child aged 3–5 years to be in charge of packing and unpacking their toys.

Giving children a task to do during the transition will give them something to focus on and make them feel helpful, which will increase their self-esteem and reduce their worry, and will support their emotional development.

Maintaining engagement

It is important that adults maintain the **engagement** of children. This means being able to keep children involved. This is important during tidying up periods as some children do want to tidy up and become upset if they find themselves with nothing to do, which can be unsettling and distressing.

Adults can fill tidying up periods with short activities, for example:
- a tidying up game of putting all the animals to bed/putting all the cars in the garage
- counting resources as they are put away into containers
- having child sized sweeping brushes and dustpans and brushes for clearing away materials such as sand
- matching games, for example matching different equipment to different containers – all the red bricks in the red box, all the yellow bricks in the yellow box
- singing a song about tidying up.

Having short activities in tidying up periods enables children to feel important. It allows them to deal with the tidying up but keeps them engaged. This supports the development of their self-resilience.

LINK IT UP

To remind yourself of children's social and emotional development across the ages of birth to 5 years, go to Component 1, section A.
To remind yourself of child initiated play, go to Component 2, 'How play can be organised to promote learning, child-intiated play'.
To remind yourself of a child experiencing a transition, go to 'A Child experiencing a transition' in this component.
To remind yourself of adapting activities to support a child with cognitive and intellectual or communication and language needs go to 'Adapting activities to support individual needs' in this component.

◼ How could adults support this child who is worried about moving house?

ACTIVITY

1 Create a factsheet to explain to a group of child development students what self-resilience is and how to promote it.
2 Create a list of ways that children experiencing transitions can be supported by the provision of a structured approach.
3 Write a paragraph to explain how adults can maintain children's engagement by filling tidying up periods with short activities.

CHECK MY LEARNING

1 Explain why adults may need to limit children's choices of activity.
2 Give one reason why a structured approach supports children experiencing transitions.

Supporting children in activities

GETTING STARTED

Working with a partner, make a list of as many different feelings as you can think of.

Write down how children might express these feelings.

LINK IT UP

To remind yourself of children's social and emotional development across the ages of birth to 5 years, go to Component 1, section A.
To remind yourself of role play, go to Component 2, section B.
To remind yourself of transitions, go to 'A child experiencing a transition' in this component.
To remind yourself of giving children a choice when planning and choosing activities, go to 'Supporting children in activities' in this component.
To remind yourself of using group/team activities, go to 'Adapting activities to support a child with communication and language needs' in this component.

In order to support a child experiencing social and emotional needs it is important that adults set out activities that focus on a child's areas of interest.

It is important that children are given opportunities to express themselves. They need to feel confident that it is ok to have different feelings, which will make them more likely to talk about how they feel. Children use play to work out their emotions and adults can encourage expression of thoughts, feelings and ideas by providing appropriate resources.

Adults should encourage group activities because these build confidence in participating with other children and encourage sharing and turn taking. However, it is important that the group activities planned are different for the different age groups. How do you think group activities differ across the age ranges?

Setting out activities that focus on a child's areas of interest

Setting out activities that focus on a child's areas of interest can support children who are experiencing social and emotional needs as their confidence and self-esteem will be raised because they will feel valued.

There are times when activities can support a child who is experiencing a particular issue. Adults can choose books and games to support a child to help them come to terms with the issue that is worrying them. They could set up different role play areas such as:

- a dentist surgery for a child who is going to the dentist for the first time
- an airport/pretend plane for a child who is anxious about flying.

This kind of play gives the child an idea of what is going to happen, which can reduce their anxiety and give them confidence when the time comes.

There are also a number of books and stories available that can support children going through transitions, for example stories about families who have separated, books about the first day at school, stories where a child experiences the death of a significant adult. These books help to reassure children, show them that other people have experienced the same thing and can support them in expressing their feelings.

Promoting choice and control over the environment

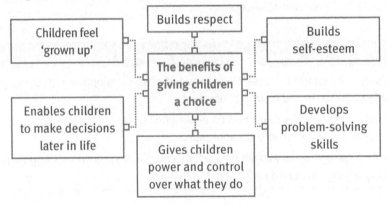

Figure 3.19: Reasons to allow children to have choices

To support their emotional and social needs children need to be provided with choice and control over their environment.

This can be achieved by providing a range of materials and resources that can be used to complete an activity. For example, in the creative play area having different coloured paper and card, glue, paint and collage materials so that children can choose what they would like to use.

Encouraging expression of thoughts, feelings and ideas

It is important that children are given plenty of opportunities to express their thoughts, feelings and ideas. Pretend play gives these opportunities to children.

Pretend play enables children to develop their imaginations. They can be things that are not possible in real life and can imagine what it feels like to become someone else.

◻ **Table 3.23: How pretend play can enable children to develop their imaginations**

Dressing up clothes	Children may dress up as a superhero to experience what it is like to be 'good' or a pirate to pretend to be 'bad'.
Role play	Whilst in 'character' children can pretend to be angry, sad or to cry. They can comfort distressed peers who are also in character.
Cooking materials	Banging a spoon on a bowl or banging pan lids together can support children to express their anger.
Puppets and dolls	Puppets and dolls can be put into character by both adults and children. A child may be more likely to talk to a puppet or a doll than an adult.

Encouraging group activities

Group activities build children's confidence in participating with other children and encourage sharing and turn taking. They enable children to form relationships, which is an important aspect of social development. When encouraging group activities, it is important to ensure that these are appropriate for the ages and stages of development.

◻ **Table 3.24: Examples of suitable group activities for different age ranges**

0–18 months old	Provide opportunities for children to sit together. Put them facing each other so they can see and touch each other.
18 months–3 years	Provide opportunities for children to play alongside each other, for example dancing to action songs together.
3–5 years	Plan circle time activities that enable children to talk in a group and also develop their listening skills.

◻ How can using puppets support children?

Learning aim C: assessment practice

How you will be assessed

Section C of the external assessment will test your knowledge of C: Adapt play to promote inclusive learning and development.

In section C you have learned how to adapt activities for children with individual circumstances to promote their learning and development. You have learned about adapting:

- physical activities
- creative activities
- imaginative play activities
- literacy (reading)
- mathematics (counting)

for each of the age groups:

- 0–18 months
- 18 months–3 years
- 3–5 years.

In section C of your external assessment, you will be presented with some case studies and will be asked to give ways adults can support children, give explanations and assess the benefits for children's learning and development.

CHECKPOINT

Strengthen

- Ensure you understand what is meant by 'inclusive' learning and development.
- Check your understanding of adapting activities for children with individual circumstances to promote their learning and development.
- Check your understanding of adapting activities for the following age ranges: 0–18 months, 18 months–3 years and 3–5 years.

Challenge

- Make your explanation of the benefits of adapting activities for all children in play, learning and development clear.
- Ensure you understand how to assess the benefits of adapting activities for all children in play, learning and development.
- Check you understand how to adapt activities and resources to support a child with different needs as appropriate to the age group.

ASSESSMENT ACTIVITY — LEARNING AIM C

1 Stuart works at a nursery with children aged 18 months–2 years. One of the children, Tabitha, has delayed gross motor skills.

a) Give two ways that Stuart can adjust the level of activities and resources to support Tabitha. (2 marks)

b) Explain two activities that Stuart can use to support Tabitha's physical needs. (4 marks)

2 Mrs Mayat is a teacher for 4–5-year-old children. Megan is in her class. She has had limited experience of play before coming into reception class. There are two children in the class who have additional needs.

a) Explain one way Mrs Mayat can provide opportunities for Megan to learn and play near to other children doing the same activity. (2 marks)

b) Explain two ways Mrs Mayat could support Megan with her social and emotional development. (4 marks)

Mrs Mayat has arranged a meeting with Megan's father to find out about her interests.

c) Assess the potential benefits to Megan of setting out activities that focus on her areas of interest. (6 marks)

TIPS

Read the questions carefully.

Think about what the scenario tells you to help focus your answer. Underline key words such as the age group of the children or any information about their needs.

Focus on the case study, including the age of the children.

Make sure you cover the number of points you have been asked to. For example, if you have been asked to explain two ways, make sure your answer includes two ways not just one.

Check you are writing 'concisely'. This means focusing on the question without adding unnecessary information.

TAKE IT FURTHER

- Check your understanding of the term 'assess'. What is the difference between 'assess' and 'explain'?
- Remember 'assess' means you need to consider the factors or events that apply to a specific situation or to identify those that are the most important or relevant and arrive at a conclusion.
- Check your understanding of what a 'conclusion' is – a summary of main points.

Glossary

Abuse deliberate harm.

Accessibility how easy it is for an area to be reached or entered.

Accurate free from mistakes.

Acute condition a condition that starts suddenly and, usually, is not long-lasting.

Adapt make something suitable for all children.

Additional needs a term used to indicate that a child requires extra support or services to enable them to participate fully in activities.

Adjustments alterations or movements made to achieve a desired fit, appearance or result.

Adult to child ratio the number of adults to the number of children.

Adult-initiated adults provide resources for an activity but let children play with them in a way they choose.

Adult-led adults make and lead an activity for children to complete.

All areas of development physical, cognitive/ intellectual, communication and language, social and emotional.

Alternative communication forms of communication used instead of or along with talking.

Appropriate clothing suitable for the weather.

Areas of deprivation can be areas where there are potential health risks due to poverty, unemployment and lack of financial investment.

Associative play sharing resources but playing alone.

Attention skills noticing and concentrating on something.

Available being there to supervise.

Average a number showing the typical value in a set of data, in particular the mode, median or most commonly the mean.

Babbling a stream of sounds babies make before they can say actual words.

Bodily coordination movement of different areas of the body.

Body management skills used to control the body.

Bond an emotional tie between two people.

Care or educational providers settings that provide formal care or education for children.

Child-initiated play children organise their own play activities without the support of adults.

Chromosome part of a cell that carries the information that determines traits a person will inherit.

Chronic condition a condition that is long-lasting.

Circle time a time when children sit together with an adult to take part in an activity or a discussion.

Circumference the distance around something, in this case, the baby's head.

Cognitive development information processing, memory and problem solving.

Communication methods the different ways in which we can communicate with each other.

Concentration span the amount of time a person can concentrate.

Conflict a serious argument.

Congenital disorder a condition that a child is born with.

Connective words connect other words or phrases.

Consistent something that remains the same over time.

Constructive intending to have a use or purpose.

Contrasting colour schemes the change in the appearance of a colour surrounded by another colour.

Cooperative play when children are playing with each other.

Delayed fine motor skills the small movements of a child's hands and fingers are not progressing as quickly as other children of the same age.

Delayed gross motor skills the large movements of a child's body are not progressing as quickly as other children of the same age.

Delayed literacy skills when a child's reading and writing skills are not progressing as quickly as other children of the same age.

Desired behaviours the way in which we want children to behave.

Development skills and knowledge gained over time.

Disruptive behaviour unwanted behaviour that disturbs and interrupts activities.

Emotion face showing different emotions on your face. This can be done by a child or adult, or shown through images or video.

Emotional bonds having a connection with a person.

Emotional resilience a person's ability to adapt to stressful situations.

Engagement taking part in an activity.

English as an additional language when English is not the first language of a child and the first language is the language to which the child has been exposed to from birth.

Enhance increase or improve something.

Expected milestones development that is expected at a particular age.

Exploitation issuing threats or violence to benefit from someone's actions.

Expression the action of making known one's thoughts or feelings.

Family structure the way in which a family is organised.

Foetus unborn baby growing in the womb.

Friendships relationships between friends.

Full-term a baby that is born on or around 40 weeks of pregnancy.

Genes are inherited from both parents and are made up from DNA that give instructions for making up a human, animal or plant.

Grasping the movement of grabbing something by closing the fingers around it.

Growth an increase in size and mass.

Hand–eye coordination coordinated control of eye movements with hand movements.

Hazard potential for an environment, activity and/or resource to cause harm.

Holding to have a grip of something.

Holistic parts that are interconnected.

Housing needs when families do not have suitable housing, for example living in temporary accommodation or overcrowded housing.

Identification of words to establish what words mean.

Illegal drugs drugs that are not prescribed and have no benefit for health.

Imagination using your mind to be creative.

Immovable fixed and impossible to move.

In app purchases buying something using an app.

Inappropriate content information or pictures online that could upset a child, material that is directed at adults, that might lead a child into unlawful or dangerous behaviour. This could be pornographic or violent material, or inappropriate language.

Inclusive including everyone.

Independent learning skills being able to think, problem solve and act without an adult helping.

Initiate play to start play.

Interaction involvement with others.

Internet enabled the term used for devices that are able to connect to the internet.

Intrusive causing disruption or annoyance through being unwelcome or uninvited.

Isolate cause a person to be alone/apart from others.

Key person the named practitioner in an early years setting with responsibility for a child.

Lack of responsiveness not responding to people.

Levels surfaces at different heights.

Lift-the-flap books have flaps on pages which show images or text underneath.

Limit to restrict the amount.

Limited interaction with adults not much communication and contact with adults.

Listening walk being silent whilst walking in order to hear what is going on around you.

Makaton a language programme using signs and symbols to help children to communicate.

Manipulate handling or control over objects.

Mean an average worked out by adding all the numbers up and dividing by the number of numbers.

Milestone a stage or event in a process.

Modify to make changes to something.

Motivating a reason to do something.

Movable capable of being moved.

Mutilation to disfigure or cause serious damage.

Navigate move with planned direction.

Negative role model someone who does not set a good example.

Neglect failing to meet basic needs.

Organised when things are arranged systematically and in order.

Overwhelmed overcome by emotion.

Overwhelming very intense and hard to deal with.

Parallel play playing at the side of others but not playing with them.

Parental controls software and tools that can be installed on internet enabled devices to keep children safe online.

Peers children of the same age.

Perceived interpreting something in a particular way.

Perseverance continued effort and determination, despite difficulty.

Personal information private details about someone, for example full name, address, phone number, email address and date of birth.

Personal interests topics that children are interested in or things they like to do.

Picture Exchange Communication System (PECS) a form of alternative communication which allows children with little or no communication abilities to communicate using pictures.

Placenta a circular organ in the uterus of a pregnant woman that nourishes and maintains the foetus through the umbilical cord.

Poor concentration levels when children find it difficult to focus on what they are doing and/or focus for long.

Positive behaviours behaviours that are good and desired.

Positive relationships a relationship between two people that makes them happy.

Positive risk taking balancing the potential risk of harm against the benefit of children participating in activities.

Praise express approval.

Preferences things that children prefer to do.

Premature a baby born before their expected date of arrival. Medically, this is before 37 weeks of pregnancy.

Prescription drugs medication that is prescribed for a person by a medical professional.

Primitive the historical development of something. Primitive reflexes are possibly left-over skills needed before humans evolved.

Proportion considered in comparison to something else.

Psychiatrist a medical professional who specialises in mental health.

Psychologist a professional who studies the human mind and why people do things.

Ramp a sloping surface joining two different levels.

Refining making changes to improve.

Releasing the movement of letting go of an object that has been grasped.

Repetition repeating something.

Restricted fine motor skills a child is unable to control the small muscles in their hands and fingers as well as other children of the same age.

Restricted gross motor skills a child is unable to control the large muscles in their bodies as well as other children of the same age.

Reward something given to someone to recognise their efforts or achievements.

Right to learn a moral or legal entitlement to have an education and learn.

Risk likelihood of an environment, activity and/or resource causing harm.

Risk assessment a process of evaluating what might cause harm to people (the potential risks) and making sure things are in place to manage the risk and prevent harm.

Role model a person looked to by others as an example to be imitated.

Routine a sequence of actions that is regularly followed.

Self-esteem confidence in own abilities and worth.

Self-resilience the ability to be independent and prepare for life's stresses and challenges.

Sensory needs difficulty seeing or hearing.

Sibling a brother or sister.

Significant family member a close family member such as a parent, sibling or grandparent.

Smart devices allow us to connect different devices or networks.

Social bonds attachment to other people.

Social inclusion the process of joining in with others.

Social norms and values attitudes and behaviours that are considered normal in society.

Social skills used when interacting with each other.

Socio-economic the relationship between social and financial factors.

Solitary play playing alone.

Spatial awareness understanding where you are in relation to the objects in your environment.

Specific areas different areas in a setting that organise the play activities and resources.

Spectator/onlooker play watching others play but not playing with them.

Spina bifida a birth defect where bones in the spine do not form properly around the spinal cord.

Stimulation giving something interest, enthusiasm or excitement.

Story sacks a sack or box that has a storybook and other resources that are linked to the story.

Structured approach a planned and organised way of dealing with a situation.

Sufficient space enough/adequate space.

Sustain involvement being involved for an extended period without interruption.

Technological/digital resources computerised resources.

Textured stories use materials to suggest what something feels like, e.g. fur to represent animals.

Textures the feel, appearance or consistency of surfaces or substances.

Toileting needs the need to use the toilet.

Transferring moving something from one hand to another.

Transition changes in children's lives.

Trip hazard object(s) on the floor that could cause someone to trip and possibly fall.

The United Nations Convention on the Rights of the Child a statement of children's rights that must be followed.

Unoccupied play a child does not interact with others and makes movements with their body.

Varying levels surfaces at different heights.

Visibility the state of being able to see or be seen.

Wipe board plastic backed board that can be wiped clean. Specially designed pens are used.

Index